Fly-Fishing the Flats

Fly-Fishing the Flats

Barry and Cathy Beck

STACKPOLE
BOOKS

Published by
STACKPOLE BOOKS
5067 Ritter Road
Mechanicsburg, PA 17055
www.stackpolebooks.com

Printed in China

First edition

10 9 8 7 6 5 4 3 2 1

Cover design by Wendy Reynolds

Library of Congress Cataloging-in-Publication Data
Beck, Barry.
Fly-fishing the flats / Barry and Cathy Beck.
p. cm.
Includes bibliographical references (p.) and index.
ISBN 0-8117-2764-5
1. Saltwater fly fishing. I. Beck, Cathy. II. Title.
SH456.2.B435 1999
799.1'6—dc21 98-30317
CIP

To Lefty Kreh and Jack Gartside,
for introducing us to the salt;

to Frontiers International, travel consultants,
for getting us there;

and to all the guides who helped
make this book possible.

CONTENTS

The Transition From Fresh to Salt Water

THE SALT IS DEFINITELY THE NEW FRONTIER IN FLY fishing. This is not to say that fly fishing in saltwater is new; fishermen have been casting flies into the salt almost as long as they have in fresh water. What is new is that countless numbers of freshwater anglers are venturing into the saltwater world. The majority are trout fishermen looking to expand their horizons, and, like us, they will probably also continue to fish for trout or other freshwater species. But the salt offers new adventure, and with the success of the east-coast striper and bluefish fishery, more and more anglers are finding their way onto the flats.

Sporting travel businesses are reporting record bookings to tropical saltwater fly-fishing destinations, from the Florida Keys, the Bahamas, Venezuela, and the coast of Mexico to the far distant flats of Christmas Island.

Rod and reel manufacturers are selling more saltwater models than ever before, and fly-line companies are developing innovative ideas in fly-line technology for the saltwater market. These companies know the beating that tackle takes in the salt and are constantly working on designing superior technical gear intended to handle the problems that come with fishing in salt water.

To the entry-level saltwater fly fisherman, this is a brand new world that comes with a brand new set of rules. To be successful, you need to know how to cast—really cast. We're not talking about casting a size 14 Adams dry fly 30 feet on a 5-weight line. We're talking about 8- and 9-weight lines, or heavier, and flies that can sometimes be as long as the 5-inch brook trout we carefully release in a headwater mountain stream. Fifty-, 60-, or even 70-foot casts are sometimes necessary, and they may have to be made into an unforgiving headwind.

In the trout world, you generally have time to make a few false casts before presenting the fly to the fish. Trout are often stationary targets. If the fish refuses, you almost always have time to try another pattern. In the salt, it's more often than not a one-shot deal, and it had better be on the money. There is little room for error. Flats fish are almost always on the move, and you need to react quickly. Casting is the name of the game, and one of the most important assets a caster has is the double haul. The casting chapter addresses the correct techniques and steps for learning the double haul, which will increase line speed and make longer casts possible, provided you have first mastered the basic mechanics of casting.

Saltwater fish are stronger than their freshwater counterparts, and hooking, playing, and landing a saltwater fish will be a new experience. These

are wild fish, not hatchery-bred trout. They are strong and fast, and whereas a freshwater fly fisherman may need only 50 yards of backing that rarely gets used, a saltwater fly fisherman may see his backing go through the guides on almost every hook-up. The average flats saltwater reel will carry at least 150 yards of backing and have a superior drag system to fight the fish. Tippets may need to be wire instead of monofilament, and you will have to learn some new knots. Whereas the butt section on a trout leader may test out at 25 pounds, the saltwater shock tippet may test out at 70 pounds or more.

In fresh water, the angler is generally casting to one target; in saltwater, your target can be a single fish or a school of fifty or more. Reading water is as important in saltwater fishing as it is in fresh, but in saltwater it can be much more difficult. On a trout stream, a flat may be 20 to 50 yards long and the cover may be undercut banks or overhanging trees. In saltwater, a flat may appear to go on forever and there may be little or no apparent structure visible to the angler. Tides play a major role in the world of saltwater fly fishing, and anglers need to understand their effects on the fishing. There is much to learn, but that's what makes it fun.

Saltwater fly fishing can be a game of hunting. You need to be constantly on the alert, as this is often a visual game where you look for the fish. It's the thrill of the hunt that makes this kind of fishing so appealing. Like trout fishermen who quietly wade and cast to rising fish, the saltwater angler too can wade and cast to tailing or cruising fish. To be alone wading on a tropical flat with tailing bonefish within casting range is an unforgettable experience and one that, like trout fishing, will captivate you and entice you to return.

Pay close attention to the casting chapter—it's your first step to success. A saltwater guide once commented that most trout fishermen can't get the fly out of the boat. Don't get caught in this situation—learn to double haul. Buy the best tackle you can afford; you'll never regret it. Hire a guide for your first few times out; you'll save yourself a lot of wasted time and frustration. Enjoy what has become the new frontier in fly fishing.

Left: Sunset in the Bahamas, angler and guide. Productive times relate to tides, and you have to be able to see the fish. But sunset is a very pretty time to be on the flats.

NOTICE!

CHAPTER 1

The Basic Outfit

ALWAYS USE THE RIGHT TOOLS FOR THE JOB. THIS IS good advice when it comes to selecting the proper outfit for saltwater fly fishing. On the average, you'll be casting flies that are heavier and more wind resistant than your favorite trout flies. Your casts may have to be longer, and the fish you catch will be stronger.

In most cases, buying your first saltwater outfit can be quite an investment. When purchasing a fly rod, reel, and line, buy the best you can afford. Most of today's better graphite fly rods have lifetime warranties and will be replaced at no charge if you break the rod.

Before choosing an outfit, consider the fish species you'll be fishing for, the fly sizes, and the line weight needed to do the job. (See Chapter 5 for specific recommendations.) No one outfit will cover all freshwater needs, and the same holds true for saltwater.

Fly Rods

The most popular material for saltwater fly rods is graphite. Graphite rods are lighter than fiberglass or bamboo and are strong enough in fighting and lifting power to handle the strength and endurance of a saltwater game fish.

Left: Basic 8- and 9-weight saltwater outfits, with rods by Sage, reels by Pate, along with pliers, hook hone, and fly box with bonefish and permit flies.

When selecting a fly rod, saltwater anglers need to consider length, action, line weight, handle design, number of sections, and guide size. A rod length of 9 feet is by far the most popular choice; it offers good leverage and casting advantages, especially when wading. Other fishermen favor a rod length of $8^{1}/_{2}$ feet. In the end, like everything else, it comes down to personal preference.

Most saltwater fly rods have medium to fast action. Saltwater fly rods need to load quickly, even on short casts. High line speed is essential and is accomplished best by the higher modulus of graphite found in most saltwater fly rods.

Your first cast is usually your most important one. It may need to happen fast, and it must be accurate. The right fly-rod action can help you make that happen. It's very important that the rod have enough strength and muscle, especially in the butt section, to lift off the bottom a fish that has gone deep. Most fly fishermen think that the longer the rod, the more leverage there is for lifting. Interestingly enough, a shorter rod can have more lifting power than a longer rod, although it is not as good at casting. Many charter boats go offshore equipped with super-stiff 6-foot trolling rods that offer tremendous lifting power.

Fly rods with full wells handles and fighting extensions. This handle design makes gripping the rod easier and more comfortable when fighting big, strong fish.

Handle designs are important, and a full wells grip, offered by most top fly-rod manufacturers, is by far the most popular for saltwater fly rods. It's a comfortable grip that puts less stress on the angler's hand and wrist.

Reel seats should be anodized to resist corrosion from salt water. Your fly reel needs to be firmly locked in place on the rod, and an uplocking reel seat is the most popular, efficient, and preferred.

Most saltwater fly rods come with a fighting butt. This is a short extension behind the reel seat used to create a pivot point for pumping and fighting fish. Some manufacturers offer fighting butts that can be removed. Beware—the fly line can easily get wrapped or fouled around a fighting butt that's more than a couple inches long. Most fighting butts have a large, rounded end of soft rubber or neoprene for added comfort.

Larger, oversize ceramic stripping guides, snake guides, and tip-tops will allow the fly line to travel faster and shoot farther. Another advantage is that knots seldom foul or get caught in the larger guides.

If you see a knot in the fly line headed for the guides, simply turn the rod upside down so that the knot rides against the rod instead of hanging down in the guides. It will often slide right through all the guides and out through the tip-top when the rod is turned upside down. Otherwise, it will get hung up and can rip the guide off the rod.

Selecting your first saltwater fly rod is much easier if you can try casting it first. It's a real advantage if the fly shop carries rods by a number of different manufacturers. This will give you the opportunity to compare action, handle design, guide size, and the general aesthetics of the rods.

Fly Reels

Saltwater fly reels differ greatly from their freshwater counterparts. A major fly-reel manufacturer once stated that a trout reel does nothing more than store the fly line. This may be true when you're after small fish, and although trout worldwide do grow large and strong enough to

require backing and a sturdy drag, most you encounter will not run line off the reel. In salt water, however, it can happen with almost every fish you hook. Whenever any fish is strong enough to run line off the reel, the angler needs to get it under control. Control is usually accomplished by getting the fish on the reel and letting the drag system tire it out.

Another aspect of saltwater fishing is corrosion of reel parts. Few freshwater anglers think about cleaning their favorite trout reels after every outing, but saltwater reels should be maintained daily.

A good-quality saltwater reel often costs at least as much as a fly rod. Many high-priced saltwater fly reels are made from expensive bar-stock aluminum and designed by highly skilled machinists. The performance, fittings, and finishes are top shelf, and the drag systems are state-of-the-art.

The drag system on any saltwater fly reel should be adjustable. The external adjustment knob should be easy to reach and the adjustment clicks clearly defined. A wonderful feature is an external rim for palming, pretty much standard on most saltwater models. We prefer an audible click on the outgoing fly line but a silent retrieve.

When storing your saltwater reel at the end of the trip, always back off the drag. Most reel manufacturers recommend this. Allowing the drag to stay on may compress the cork drag washers used on many saltwater fly reels. If this happens, they won't function properly and will eventually deteriorate.

The size of the reel spool is important. Wide spools allow for additional line capacity, but rewinding the fly line evenly on the spool can be difficult when fighting a fish. If the fly line comes back on the reel unevenly, it will bulk up on one side or the other, and the fly line or backing can collapse into a tangled mess. Large arbor narrow spool reels are becoming more and more popular with a lot of anglers. The reel may at first appear too large for the intended fly rod, but in reality, the larger arbor will recover the fly line and backing at a much faster rate, and the narrow spool keeps the fly line in place.

Right- or left-hand retrieve is a matter of personal preference. We both cast with our right hands and reel with our left. Neither of us likes to switch hands after the fish is hooked, and we like having control of the rod in the stronger hand.

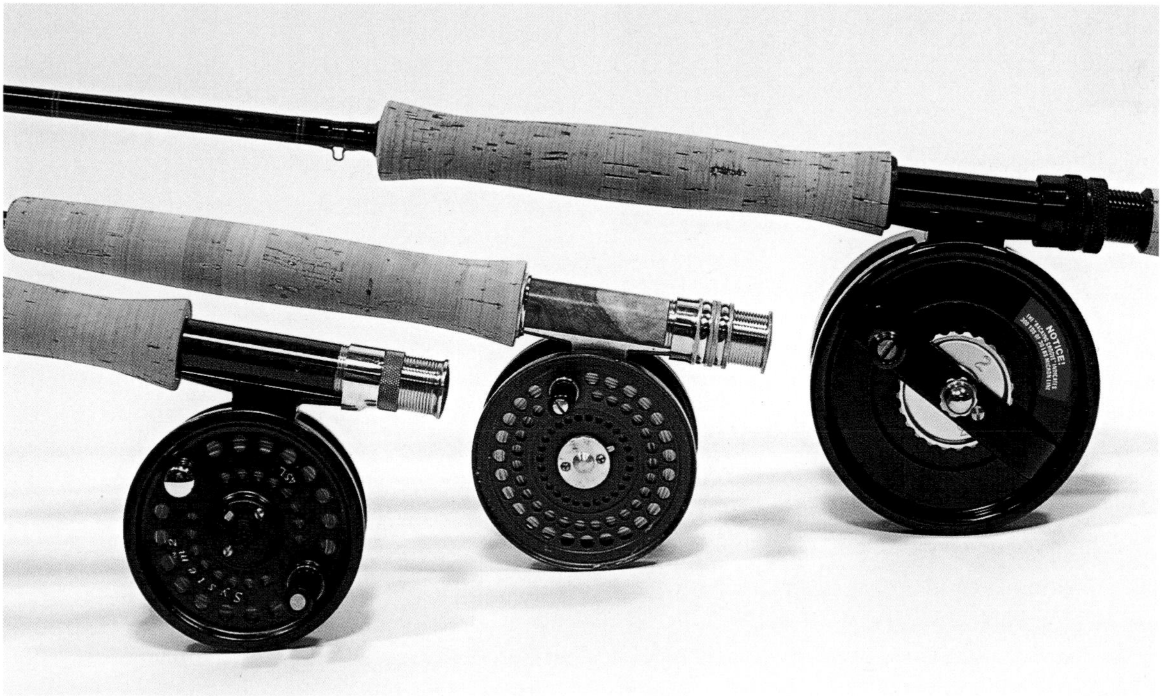

A typical saltwater fly reel (right) is much larger than the average trout reel, like the two on the left. The typical freshwater reel may hold 50–75 yards of backing, whereas the average saltwater model holds 200–300 yards.

Most saltwater fly reels have external rims so that the angler can apply additional drag pressure by palming the reel.

Many skilled anglers, on the other hand, prefer to cast and reel with the same hand. They feel that the dominant hand can reel faster and for longer periods of time because it is the stronger hand. Our suggestion is to reel your saltwater reels with the same hand that you use to reel your freshwater reels.

The reel handle can spin very quickly on a direct-drive fly reel as the fish runs and takes line off the reel spool. In a fight with a saltwater fish that is running line, it becomes a game of give and take. He takes some line, and you work to get some back. In this process of fighting the fish, it's easy to get banged-up knuckles from a poorly designed reel handle. The handle should taper out from the side of the reel spool to a smaller end. This taper will allow your fingers to easily slip off and clear the spinning handle when the fish runs. Reel handles that are large and flat can give you a nasty whack on the knuckles.

The line capacity of the reel is extremely important in saltwater fly fishing. It's not uncommon to see a bonefish run 70 to 80 yards in a blink of an eye, and most of the inshore species can run that and more. Your saltwater reel for flats fishing should carry at least 100 yards of 20-pound backing. If you're after larger fish like big tarpon or other offshore species, carry a minimum of 250 yards of 30-pound backing.

Backing

We like a round Dacron backing that resists rot and mildew and a highly visible color that differs from the color of the fly line. The color difference makes it easy to see when all the fly line is out through the rod tip and you're into the backing. It's also helpful as the backing and line are reeled back on the spool.

Gel-Spun Poly is a relatively new backing material that is thinner in diameter than other backings, yet it is ten times stronger than steel of the same diameter. Manufacturers claim that the new material is extremely abrasion resistant and offers a low coefficient of friction, which creates less wear and tear on the fly-rod guides. The smaller diameter of the Gel-Spun Poly will allow for significantly more backing on your fly reel.

The best way to install backing on your fly reel is to take it to a fly shop with a line winder and let the shop install it for you. The backing must go evenly and firmly on the spool. A line winder can do the job correctly in just a few minutes. You'll have trouble if you allow the backing to bulk up on one side or the other of the reel spool or if the tension varies as the backing is reeled on the spool. Improperly installed fly-line backing will quickly slice down and get underneath itself, creating a tangle that can mean losing a good fish.

Fly Lines

There is a lot to consider when it comes to choosing the right fly line, or lines, for your saltwater fly fishing. In the end, it's the fly line that carries the fly to your intended target. How quickly and how well it performs often depends on the type and taper of the fly line.

Fly-line sizes start at 0, which is the extreme light end of the scale, and run as heavy as 15. In freshwater fishing, 3- and 4-weight lines are considered light lines and are used for gentle presentations. The 5- and 6-weights are more middle-of-the-road, all-purpose trout types, and 7- and 8-weights are on the heavy side for casting larger and more wind-resistant flies.

In salt water, however, 6- and 7-weights are on the light side. They are used, in some situations, for casting smaller flies for bonefish and striped bass. The lighter lines are useful whenever delicate presentations are needed, for instance on thin or skinny water flats. Eight- and 9-weights are often thought of as the general-purpose line sizes for flats fishing. They cover bonefish, redfish, snook, baby tarpon, and many other saltwater fish species in this size category.

The 10-weight feels like a giant step from the easy-handling 8- and 9-weight lines. The 10 is a popular line weight with anglers pursuing larger permit, larger striped bass, medium-sized tarpon, and bluefish. The emphasis now is on casting larger wind-resistant flies and on the fighting advantages of the rod more than on delicate presentation.

We are really talking about serious fly lines and big fish when we look at the 11- and 12-weights and the even heavier 13- to 15-weights. Large to giant tarpon and offshore big-game species of saltwater fish are in a class by themselves and require maximum effort when it comes to casting larger flies and fish-fighting capabilities.

Saltwater fly-line tapers often differ from their freshwater counterparts. Most freshwater fly fishermen are familiar with both double-tapered and weight-forward tapered fly lines. Double-tapered fly lines have always been popular for delicate presentations in freshwater environments when longer casts are not called for. Double tapers also offer economic value to the angler, as the line can be reversed to take advantage of the unused rear taper. Nevertheless, double-tapered fly lines have never found much use in saltwater fly fishing.

Weight-forward tapers, for the most part, dominate the saltwater market. These lines have the weight concentrated in the forward section. Behind the front taper is a thinner running line. The shootability of the smaller diameter of the running line is a real advantage when distance is a priority. With a floating weight-forward tapered fly line, you can quickly and efficiently get the fly line off the water and back out to the target with a minimum number of false casts.

Fly-line manufacturers have modified the basic weight-forward design, creating new ideas for saltwater applications. Scientific Anglers, for example, offers four modified weight-forward tapers for saltwater use. The Bonefish Taper has a longer-than-average belly and a longer rear taper, an overall reduced line diameter, and a stiffer line core. With these improvements, more fly line is carried with less wind resistance and with the distance and accuracy needed for most bonefish situations.

The basic Saltwater Taper is one of our favorites. It has a smaller line diameter, resulting in less wind resistance and increased distance. The Saltwater Taper is a very user-friendly fly line, with a less modified head and rear taper. It's not quite as stiff as the Bonefish Taper and has very little line memory.

The Tarpon Taper has a special braided monofilament core that is ideal for fast and accurate presentation of larger tarpon flies. The Wind Master taper has a very radical head design that assists in powerful turnovers in the worst of wind.

Shooting heads are favored by many saltwater anglers whenever greater distances are needed. Heads, as they're commonly called, are basically weight-forward fly lines without the running line. They are usually 30 feet long and have a loop at the rear for attaching specifically designed shooting line or monofilament. This line has a much thinner diameter than the normal rear taper of the weight-forward fly line. Longer casts can be made because the thinner shooting line offers less resistance when traveling through the rod guides and less resistance in the wind.

Saltwater fly lines designed for tropical use are usually stiffer or harder than fly lines used

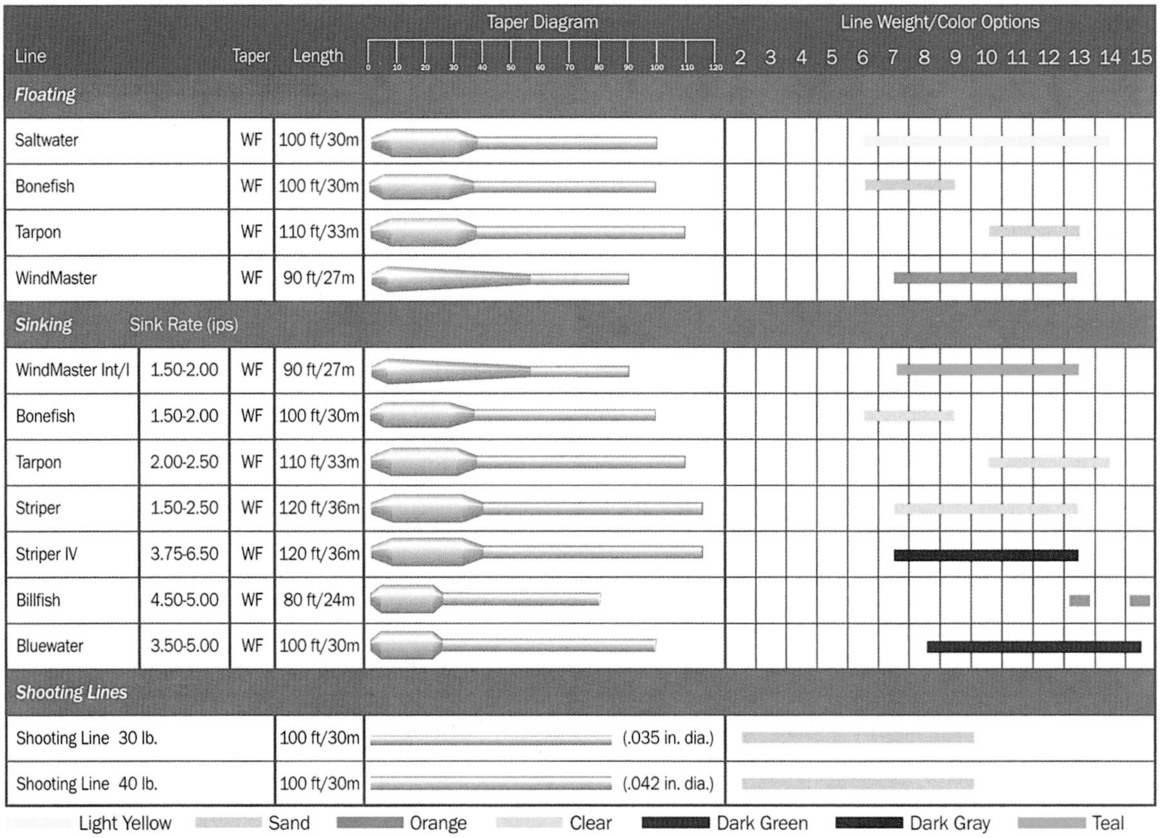
Taper Diagram
Line Weight/Color Options
Line
Taper
Length
0 10 20 30 40 50 60 70 80 90 100 110 120
2 3 4 5 6 7 8 9 10 11 12 13 14 15
Floating
Saltwater WF 100 ft/30m
Bonefish WF 100 ft/30m
Tarpon WF 110 ft/33m
WindMaster WF 90 ft/27m
Sinking Sink Rate (ips)
WindMaster Int/I 1.50-2.00 WF 90 ft/27m
Bonefish 1.50-2.00 WF 100 ft/30m
Tarpon 2.00-2.50 WF 110 ft/33m
Striper 1.50-2.50 WF 120 ft/36m
Striper IV 3.75-6.50 WF 120 ft/36m
Billfish 4.50-5.00 WF 80 ft/24m
Bluewater 3.50-5.00 WF 100 ft/30m
Shooting Lines
Shooting Line 30 lb. 100 ft/30m (.035 in. dia.)
Shooting Line 40 lb. 100 ft/30m (.042 in. dia.)
Light Yellow
Sand
Orange
Clear
Dark Green
Dark Gray
Teal

Saltwater line specifications chart. *Courtesy of 3M Scientific Anglers.*

in fresh water. The heat in tropical environments can soften the finish on a line, affecting the shootability.

Saltwater anglers who fish the east-coast bluefish and striper fishery will find that fly lines designed for tropical conditions will not perform well in cold weather. In cold temperatures, the stiff fly-line finishes will retain memory coils, and the lines become very difficult to cast.

Many saltwater fly lines are denser than freshwater fly lines because salt water is less dense and more buoyant than fresh. Higher-density fly lines are smaller in diameter, which makes them easier to cast in windy conditions.

Functions of saltwater fly lines are comparable to those of freshwater lines. There are lines that float, lines that float and sink, and lines that sink. The floating line is by far the most useful to the saltwater angler. Most flats fishing is done in less than 6 feet of water, so a floating fly line works just fine. It is also the line to use when fishing surface poppers, and it is easier to lift off the water than any of the sinking fly lines.

Sinking-tip lines are useful whenever you need to get your fly deeper than a floating fly line will allow. How much of the tip section sinks and how fast it sinks are determined by the manufacturer's design and by the density of the sinking portion of the fly line.

Full-sinking fly lines are used whenever you need to get down deep, for instance in a deep channel or if you are fishing the deep water off the edge of a flat. Full-sinking lines are harder to cast, because you need to get almost all of the fly line out of the water before you can make a backcast, but there are times when conditions dictate their necessity. Scientific Anglers' Deep Water Express fly line has a coating mixed with tungsten dust that will dive your fly deeper than any other fly line.

Intermediate fly lines are basically slower-sinking lines, extremely popular with many saltwater fly fishermen. These lines sink slowly and stay just below the surface, a real advantage when fishing and retrieving flies in an area that has a lot of weeds or debris on the surface.

There are still other options when it comes to sinking fly lines designed for special purposes in salt water. Sinking Bonefish Tapers sink slowly and have a clear coating that makes the fly line almost invisible to the fish. The Sinking Tarpon Taper sinks to depths of 3 to 8 feet and has a very stiff, hard finish that helps this line shoot. Striped bass fishermen now can buy a Striper Taper with a powerful midlength head and fused braided monofilament running line that performs exceptionally well in colder climates. For offshore fly fishing, a Billfish Taper and a Bluewater Line are designed for quick casts that will deliver large fly patterns.

Good saltwater fly lines can be expensive, but they are worth the investment. These lines have the important job of transporting the fly to the fish and are often the reason for success or failure. The proper fly line for the job will make the experience more fun and the fisherman more effective.

Caring for Your Gear

The most important thing you can do after a saltwater fishing trip is to properly care for your fishing tackle. The trip is not over until all of your tackle has been inspected, cleaned, and properly stored. Preventive measures are needed to ensure that your tackle continues to remain in good working order. Use in salt water can lead to corrosion that, in time, can freeze up the best of fly reels, pit and destroy line guides on your favorite fly rod, and even ruin your fly line. Next to an abusive baggage handler, nothing is harder on your gear.

Fly rods are easy to care for. Wash your rod in warm, soapy water. Use a sponge for the blank and the cork handle areas and a soft toothbrush to clean around the feet of the guides and the threads and rings on the reel seat. After the rod is dry, apply a light coating of WD-40 to the threads on your reel seat. The key word here is *dry*. Never put your fly rod away wet; mildew can quickly form on both the blank and the cork handle if the rod is damp when sealed inside the aluminum tube. Let it sit out overnight to dry completely before storing.

Fly reels take a little more work. Again, use a toothbrush and warm soapy water. Do not submerge the entire reel; many of the more sophisticated drag systems could be adversely affected. Instead, remove the reel spool and carefully scrub the frame, paying close attention to the areas around the foot. If your reel has a palming rim, scrub the areas where the frame and spool overlap. Rinse the entire reel with warm, fresh water, and allow it to air dry. Before storing, lubricate the drag system with the manufacturer's suggested lubricant, usually a Teflon or graphite product. We like to put a protective coating of car polish on the exterior of our reels as an added precaution. And, don't forget to back off the drag adjustment.

Fly lines should be removed and washed in warm, soapy water and then rinsed in fresh water. Dry the fly line with a soft, clean cloth and lubricate it with a good line cleaner before reinstalling it on the fly reel.

With proper maintenance, your gear will give you many years of superior service.

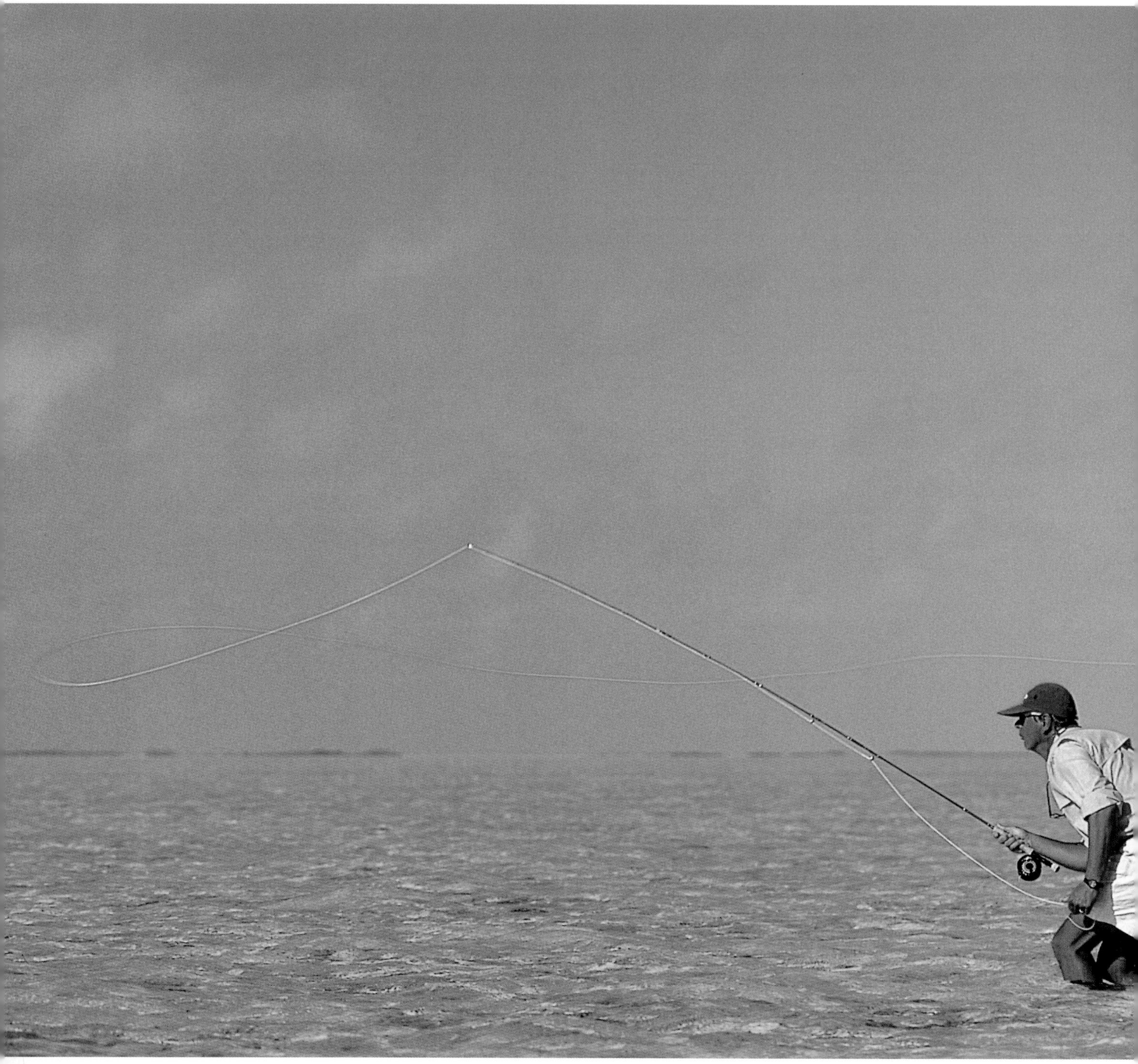

CHAPTER 2

Saltwater Fly Casting

Extending Your Cast

Fly casting may be the heart and soul of fly fishing. Think about it: A fisherman can be in the perfect environment with feeding fish and plenty of casting room, he may have the very best equipment that money can buy, and he may even have the right fly pattern tied to the end of his leader, but if he can't cast and present the fly to the feeding fish, he'll be completely frustrated.

Fly casting in salt water will present the freshwater angler with a new set of elements with which to contend. Heavier tackle will be required; basic 3-, 4-, 5-, and 6-weight trout outfits will be replaced with 7-, 8-, 9-, 10-, or heavier weights. Hook sizes will be larger, as will leader and tippet diameters.

Wind will have a new meaning to the entry-level saltwater angler; it's almost always present, and at times it can be devastating. There will be times when you will be required to cast a long, accurate line into an unforgiving headwind only to have to turn around and make the next cast into a racing tailwind.

Left: Barry keeps a low profile while casting for bonefish in the Bahamas. Tight (or narrow) loops and good line speed produce distance and accuracy.

In salt water you need to be able to make long and accurate casts, and you often need to do it quickly. Certainly there will be times when shorter casts of 20 or 30 feet may do the job. But average casts, especially on a saltwater flat, will go beyond the 50-foot mark.

There are lots of things that will make you a better saltwater fly fisherman. Comfortably handling long casts is one. Learning to effectively double haul is another. The double haul is going to come to your aid in the wind and when you have to quickly reposition the cast. If you use it often enough, you'll get so that you automatically employ it on every cast. If you're already shooting line and making accurate casts, extending the cast and learning the double haul will greatly increase your odds out on the flats.

Casting Fundamentals

Good fly casting comes with knowing what to practice and then practicing it. There are a few basic rules for good fly casting and for extending your cast that with a little patience and practice you will easily master. If you're a freshwater fly fisherman, you already know some casting fundamentals:

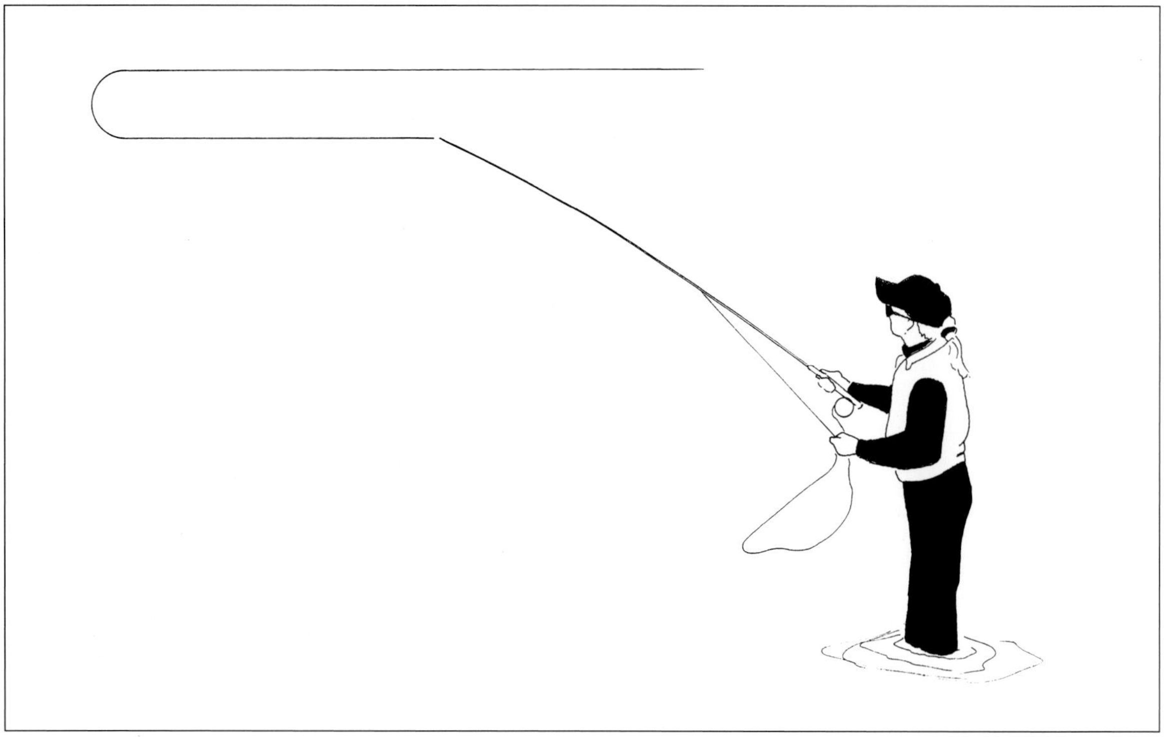

A short, quick speed-up and stop produces a narrow casting loop.

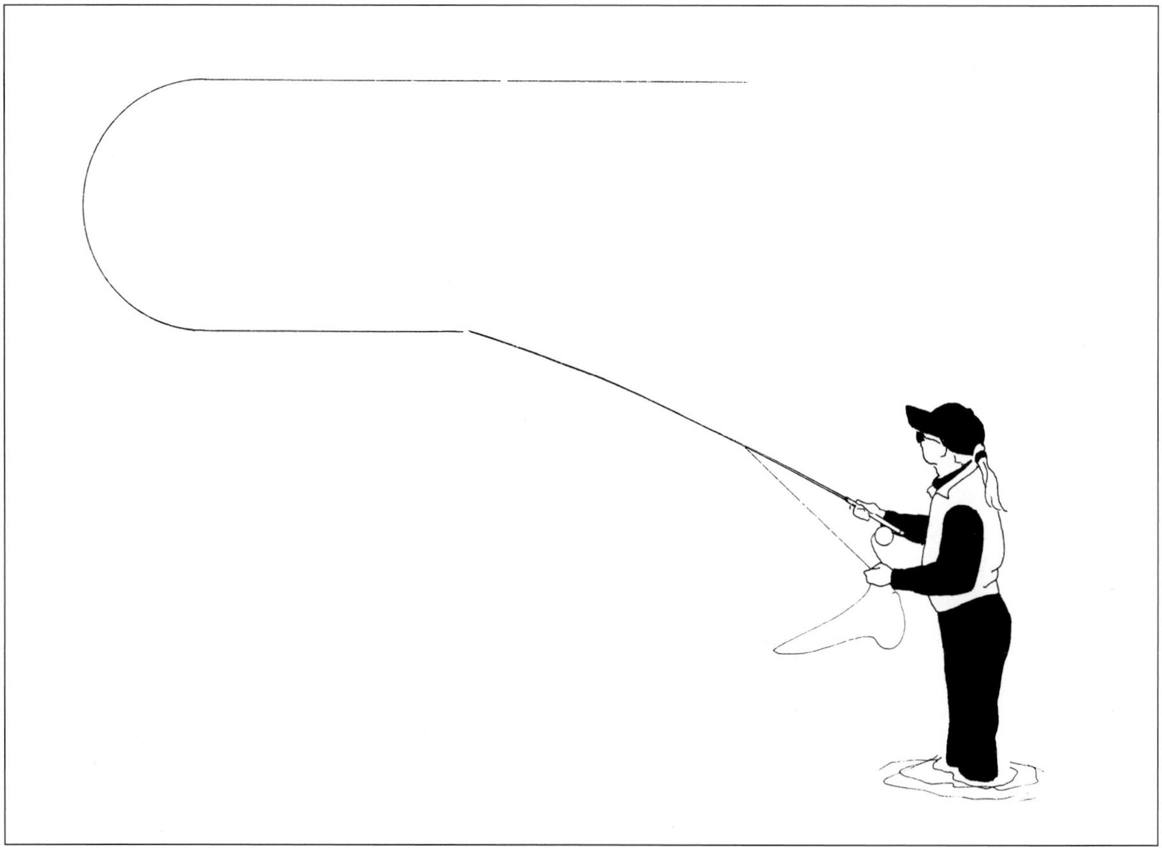

A longer, slower speed-up and stop produces a wider casting loop.

- To make any cast, you need to get the end of the fly line moving and you need to develop line speed to make the cast.
- The fly line goes in the direction that the rod tip leads it.
- The size of the fly-line loop can be controlled by how fast you speed up and stop the rod tip at the end of the cast. Tighter casting loops penetrate the wind better and produce longer, more efficient casts.
- The wrist on your casting arm should stay stiff through the casting stroke, tilting only slightly at the very end of the cast to energize the speed-up and stop.
- The elbow on your casting arm should never be above the shoulder.

Timing the Casting Stroke: Lefty Kreh's Method

Early casting instructors taught us to use the numbers on a clock in reference to rod tip positions on both the forward cast and the backcast. The general rule of thumb was to start at 9 o'clock and continue back to 1 o'clock. Keep the rod tip traveling in a straight line on an even plane and you can make a good cast. This outdated advice will still work, but it severely restricts the caster, especially when making longer casts.

The fly rod is basically a long, flexible lever, so it makes sense that the further the lever is moved through the casting stroke, the more efficient it becomes. For shorter casts, it may only be necessary to move the rod through a short casting stroke, but as the length of fly line increases, the stroke or path of the rod should also increase, or lengthen. The more fly line you have to move, the longer the distance will be that you have to move it through. As with any basic cast, the rod tip needs to stay in the same plane throughout the casting stroke regardless of how long that stroke is.

To be able to take full advantage of this technique, start by holding the rod with the basic grip (thumb on top of the rod handle), and then cant the forearm outward at a 45-degree angle away from your body. The forearm leads the rod tip back behind your body on the backcast. The most efficient backcast will travel directly away from the intended target.

The forward cast should not be started until the fly line and leader have started to unroll at the end of the backcast. The timing here is critical. If you wait until all of the fly line and leader have completely unrolled and turned over, or until you feel a tug on the fly rod, the fly line, leader, and fly will already have started to drop, and you will lose an important amount of casting energy needed to complete the long forward cast.

Moving the forearm, lead the rod forward through a long, sweeping stroke that ends with a quick accelerated stop of the rod tip, which should now be pointing at about eye level in the direction of your intended target. At the very end of the forward cast, slightly drop the rod tip to avoid a tailing loop. The distance that the rod tip drops is minuscule (a couple inches), just enough to allow the fly line and leader to turn over without running into itself. Keep the upper casting arm at shoulder level, and remember that at no time should the elbow rise above the shoulder.

This method of taking full advantage of the fly rod through the casting stroke was developed by

Wrist and elbow position throughout the casting stroke. Note that the elbow stays well below the shoulder.

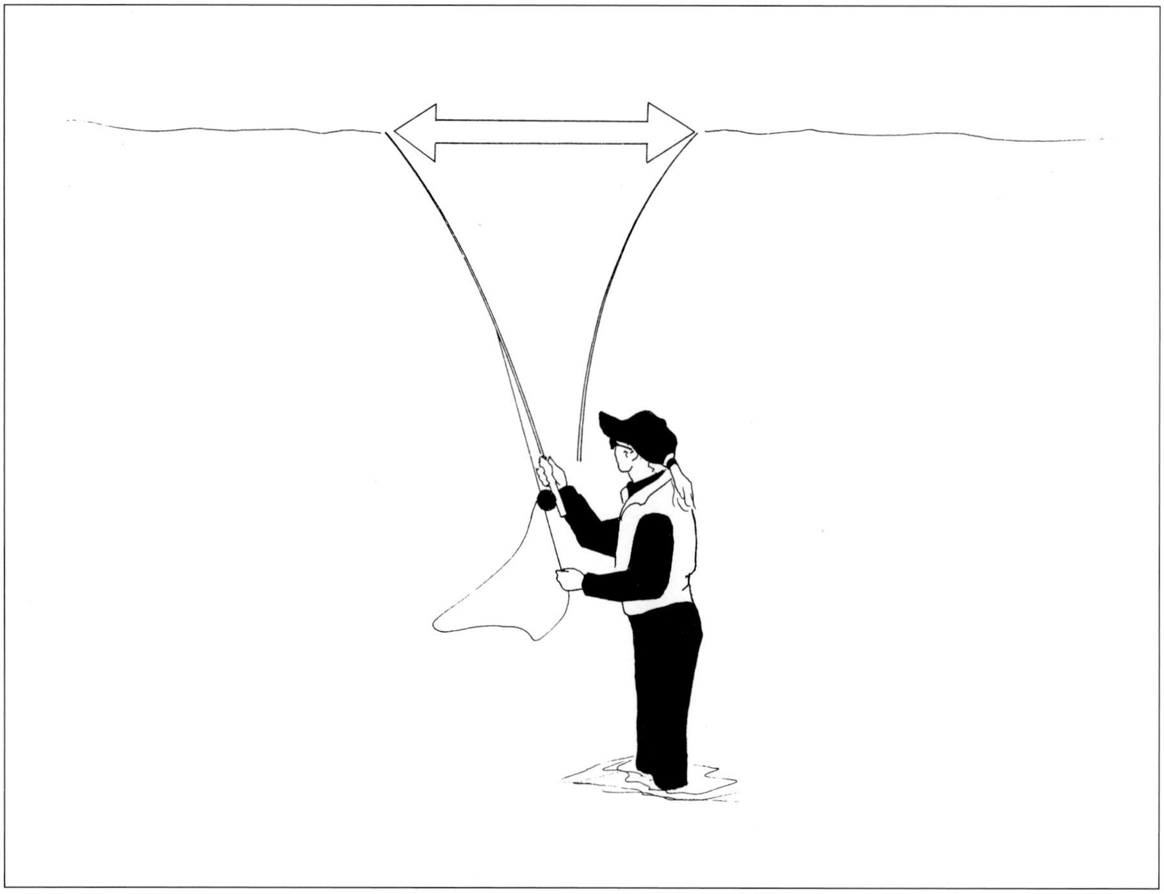

Rod tip travel through a short stroke.

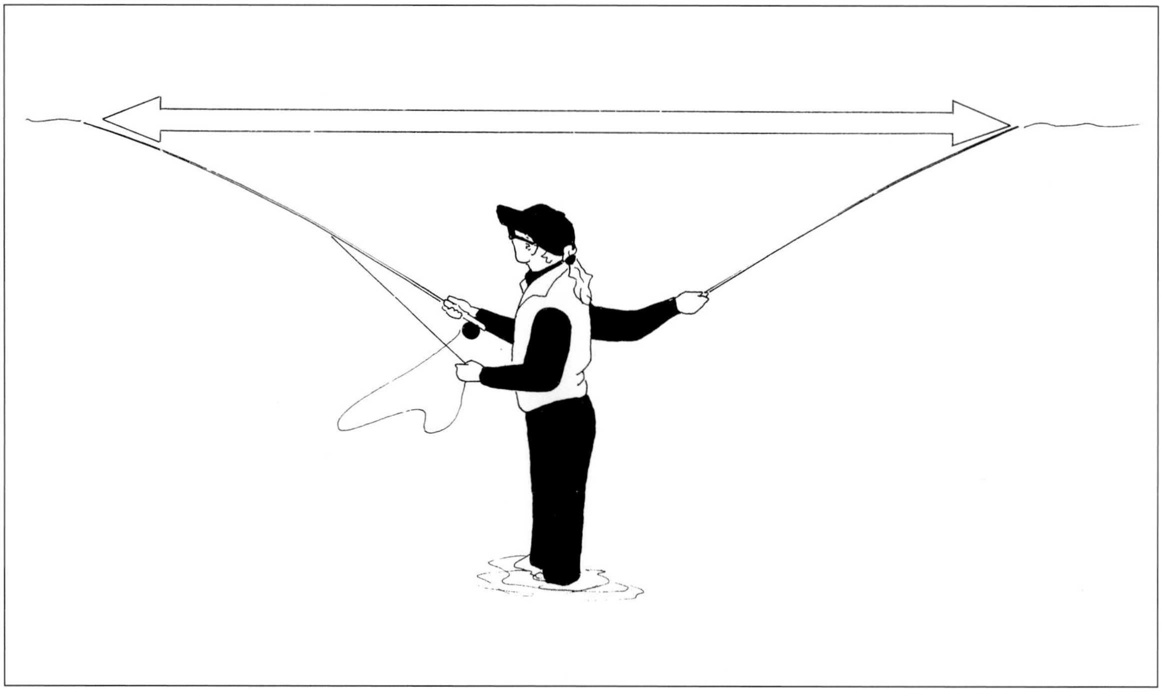

Rod tip travel through a long stroke.

Lefty Kreh, and he'd be the first to tell you that you can cast a long fly line by using the traditional 9-to-1 technique, but you will be required to put a lot more effort and energy into the cast, and it will be very difficult to obtain long distances. Lefty's style of casting is much more efficient and makes throwing a long line a lot easier.

Shooting Line

Shooting line is a technique that quickly and easily extends your cast, and most freshwater anglers are familiar with it. On a trout stream, trees or brush in the background often restrict the backcast. Shooting, or allowing extra fly line to travel through the rod guides at the very end of the cast, will give you the extra distance often needed to reach your intended target.

Total line control is essential to good casting, and with shooting line it's mandatory. To efficiently shoot line requires the use of both your rod hand and your line hand. To practice, start with an amount of line that you can comfortably handle in the air. Make a few false casts, and on a forward cast, present the line to the grass. Now pull off a few extra coils of fly line from your reel and arrange them loosely at your feet. Put the rod tip in the starting position (rod tip pointed straight out at waist level), and hold the fly line firmly in your line hand. Start with a few false casts, increasing your line speed. Once you've got good line speed, on the front end of your forward cast, when the rod tip is pointed ahead during the speed-up and stop, let the fly line slide through your line hand.

Timing is critical; it's easy to let go of the line too soon. If you prematurely let go of the line, no fly line will leave through your line hand, the forward cast will collapse and pile up at the end of the fly line and leader, or both. The line that's out beyond the rod tip must be traveling or pulling *away* from you before it can pick up and carry the additional line that you're trying to feed the cast.

Once you get used to shooting line at the front end of the forward cast, try shooting it at the back end of the backcast as well. On a very long cast, if you have sufficient line speed and can adjust the timing of the cast as the amount of line increases, you can shoot line at either or both ends of the casting stroke.

When shooting line, don't release it abruptly with your line hand when the rod reaches the forward stopping position; the line will not go out smoothly and may even tangle around your rod.

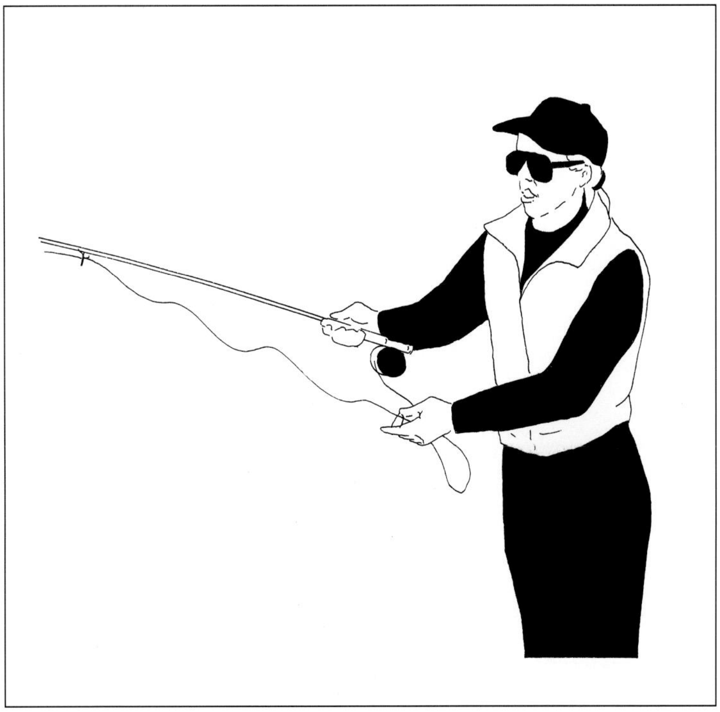

Release line through a circle made with the tips of the thumb and forefinger.

Don't completely let go of the fly line as it's leaving your line hand. If this happens, a number of things can go wrong. The line is no longer under control, it can and often will tangle or wrap around the rod shaft and guides, or it may foul around the handle of the reel. In this situation, if the fly hits the water and a fish takes, you have little chance of hooking it because the line is all tangled around the reel and rod.

If you form a circle between the tips of your thumb and forefinger of your line hand for the line to flow through, this will prevent it from getting tangled, you stay in control of the line, and you can immediately strike to hook a fish should you need to. You can easily stop the line in flight, if necessary, and once the cast is completed, you can quickly hand the line over to the rod hand to start the retrieves.

The Double Haul

Learning to double haul will quickly increase line speed, making longer casts possible with a minimum of false casting. The double haul takes some patience and practice to master, but it will make anyone a better caster.

Like shooting line, the double haul requires the use of both the casting hand and the line hand. The line hand performs a haul, or down-up tug, on the fly line while the rod hand is leading the rod tip to a quick speed-up and stop. At the end of the haul (which is simultaneous with the speed-up and stop from the other hand), the line hand must quickly come back up to meet the rod hand in preparation for the next haul. This marriage of hauling with the line hand and accelerating with the rod hand must happen at exactly the same time. To complete a double haul, this down-up action from the line hand is performed at the end of both the backcast and the forward cast. The haul loads the tip of the fly rod, thereby increasing line speed, which in turn enables the caster to shoot a greater amount of line.

Many casters make the common mistake of pulling or hauling too much line, which results in the line hand and the rod hand getting so far apart that slack fly line tangles around the rod butt and the reel. The longer the haul, the harder it is for the line hand to get back to the rod hand before the next haul can be started. Any slack in the fly line will quickly undermine any benefit from the haul.

Your hands should not separate more than 20 inches at any one time during the haul. Short, quick hauls are much more efficient than long hauls and much easier to complete. The best place to practice is on a lawn with plenty of room to cast. Try learning the double haul by starting with a single haul. Make a comfortable forward cast of 30 feet or so, and let the fly line fall to the grass. With the rod tip pointing low and forward in a starting position, make sure that any slack is out of the cast. Place the line hand next to the rod hand, and as you start your backcast, follow with your line hand, keeping the hands separated by about 6 inches. Remember to keep the rod arm turned outward at about 45 degrees from your body, and as this hand accelerates to a speed-up and stop, quickly pull down and instantly come back up with the line hand. This quick down-up haul should be no more than 12 inches. Complete the backcast and stop. Let the fly line fall behind you on the grass. Pause and think about what you just did. If everything went right, the fly line should have shot back behind you and landed in a straight line on the grass.

With the first haul completed, you are now ready for the forward cast and the second haul. Set up with the rod hand and the line hand close together. The rod hand moves forward, and the line hand follows at the same speed. As the rod tip accelerates to its speed-up and stop, give a quick, short haul, down-up tug, getting the line hand back up to meet the rod hand at the end of the cast. Let the line come down on the grass, and get your hands in position for the back cast. Repeat this process until you are comfortable enough to keep the fly line in the air on both the forward cast and the backcast while completing the hauls.

In distance casting, slack in the fly line is your enemy. It slows down line speed, restricting any chance you have of completing a long cast. A double haul, correctly done, will eliminate unwanted slack and at the same time increase line speed to help achieve long-distance casts. Learning to double haul takes perseverance, but the rewards are well worth the effort.

THE DOUBLE HAUL

The double haul cast will enable you to increase line speed, which in turn will enable you to take less time for the cast and to handle more line with less effort. It will also help you cast in wind, shoot more line when you need to, and conserve your energy—all key elements in flats fishing.

To learn the double haul, start with your hands. Practice position, action, and rhythm of the hands first, even without a rod or line. Start the cast with the hands together. On the backcast, the hands stay together at first. The double haul is just like the basic cast except that as the rod nears the speed-up-and-stop position on the backcast, the line hand makes a downward tug—or haul— and immediately lifts again, letting the line continue out, so that at the finish of the backcast the hands are together again.

The photo sequences that follow were shot with a motor-drive to break down an actual double haul cast into its key movements and to illustrate what the hands are doing in relation to the rod and line. The sequences are intended to help you picture the whole cast and to sense its rhythm.

Practice without a rod. Then try it again with a short amount of line. Rhythm and tempo, important to any cast, are absolutely key here. Learn to count the rhythm as you move your hands through the entire casting motion. Watch an expert do it, and mimic not just the hands' movement but also the rhythm.

Remember, on the flats you're not a trout fisherman anymore. There's no time for false casting and trying a second, third, and fourth cast if the first one isn't right. You have to handle a long line with agility and speed. When the guide sees fish and tells you where to cast, you must react right away. Getting comfortable with the double haul is a must before you get on the plane for your first flats adventure.

1. START: Hands together.

2. Rod lifts, beginning the backcast; hands still together.

5. line straightens . . .

6. behind you . . .

3. Near the speed-up-stop, *haul* . . .

4. speed-up-*stop* and . . .

7. hands come back . . .

8. together.

9. START THE FORECAST: Hands together.

10. Rod leads the cast . . .

13. hands come . . .

14. back . . .

11. approaching speed-up-stop, *haul* . . .

12. speed-up-*stop* and . . .

15. together.

16. Cast is complete as line travels out to target.

1. Hands . . .

2. together . . .

5. hands . . .

6. come . . .

9. hands . . .

10. together . . .

13. hands . . .

14. come . . .

3. back . . .

4. *haul* . . .

7. back . . .

8. together . . .

11. forward . . .

12. *haul* . . .

15. back . . .

16. together.

The Water Haul

A haul during the pick-up of a long cast off the water is called a water haul. It simply means that the tension from the water pulling on the line will help load, or flex, the rod tip. Then with the sharp haul, or tug, from your line hand, you will achieve instant line speed, resulting in a cleaner, smoother lift off the water. Remember to start with your rod tip low to the water, and wait until you have the end of the line moving before lifting and hauling.

When you're shooting a lot of line, keep the rod tip above eye level while the line is shooting out, then lower the tip. This will give the line time to reach the desired distance before collapsing onto the water. If you cast right-handed, drop the right foot behind the left, or vice versa, so that you can balance your weight as you lean back into the cast.

With the immediate faster line speed, you will also be able to quickly get the cast back out, often with no false casts, by using another quick, sharp haul on the forward cast. Saltwater fish are often moving fast, and the quicker you can pick up a long cast and get it back to the fish, the better your chances of it seeing your fly before spooking. Often there is no time for false casts, and the water haul becomes invaluable.

When you fish in salt water, you have to make every second count. These fish are not like a big old brown trout that has positioned himself in a feeding station and waits there for insects to come along. These fish are moving constantly, and you have to get as many good casts to them as possible in the amount of time they are within range and before they see you. This is usually a matter of seconds.

Coping with Wind

Wind is a problem anglers everywhere would gladly do without; unfortunately, it's almost always present on salt water, so the best thing you can do is learn to cope with it. A straight-on headwind usually results in a collapsed mess at the end of the cast, with the line, leader, and fly tangled together.

One February day in the Bahamas, the wind was fighting us on every cast. We could hardly stand upright on the casting deck of the skiff, and whitecaps were forming in the channel. Any angler in his or her right mind would have headed in, but inside the protection of a small key, we found a number of big bonefish cruising and tailing. These were some of the nicest bonefish we'd seen. It was hard to think of leaving.

Simon, our guide, would see a fish and shout to be heard over the sound of the howling wind. Our feeble attempts ended in frustration, and we were ready to call it a day, when he suggested a lower-profile cast staying under the wind. The wind was coming in over the key and racing across the flat toward us. The low mangroves broke up the wind close to the water, so by casting low to the water and underneath the wind, we were able to stay in the game. It certainly was not what you'd call easy or pretty casting, but with some effort, we finally managed to get a few casts to the fish and even ended the day with one 10-pound bonefish. We will never forget that wind, the fish, or the terrible ride home.

Supertight casting loops penetrate wind far better than wide loops. In difficult headwind situations, accelerate your speed-up and stop, and punch the rod tip into the wind and directly at your target area. Try a low-profile cast, incorporate a double haul so that you get as much line speed as possible, and minimize any false casting, which will only get you into more trouble.

A tailwind can be a blessing if you learn how to use it to your advantage. As with the headwind, you need a low-profile backcast, but now tilt it *slightly* downward. With a supertight loop (a fast speed-up and stop in the back), you'll penetrate the wind. As you bring the rod tip forward, *slightly* elevate your cast, and let the wind help you carry the fly line forward. Make sure the line is clear and ready to go off the deck, because if you do this right, you may make the longest cast of your life.

Wind coming at you from the side presents other problems. The worst-case scenario is when the wind is blowing at your rod side and you're trying to throw a big saltwater fly. You end up ducking

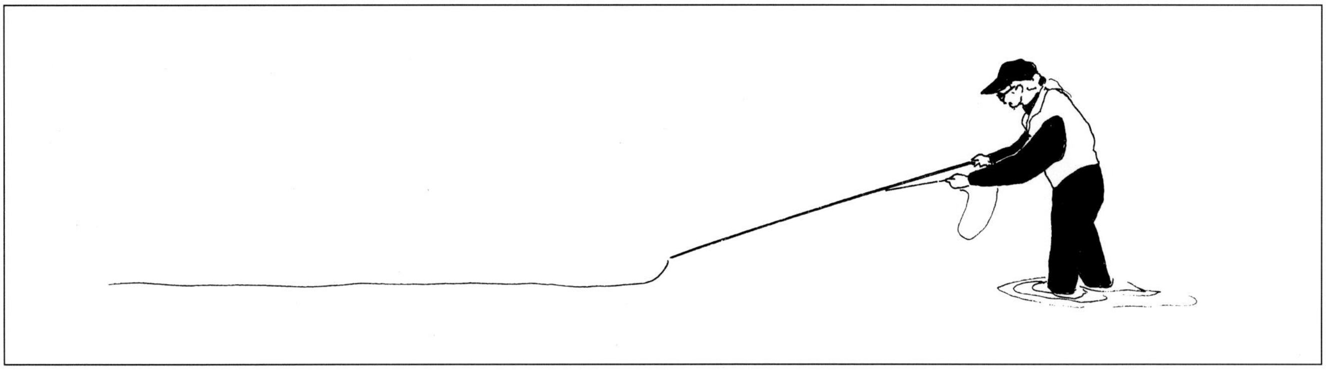

An angler picking up a water haul: lots of line out, no slack, rod tip low, right foot back, left hand reaching toward the stripping guide.

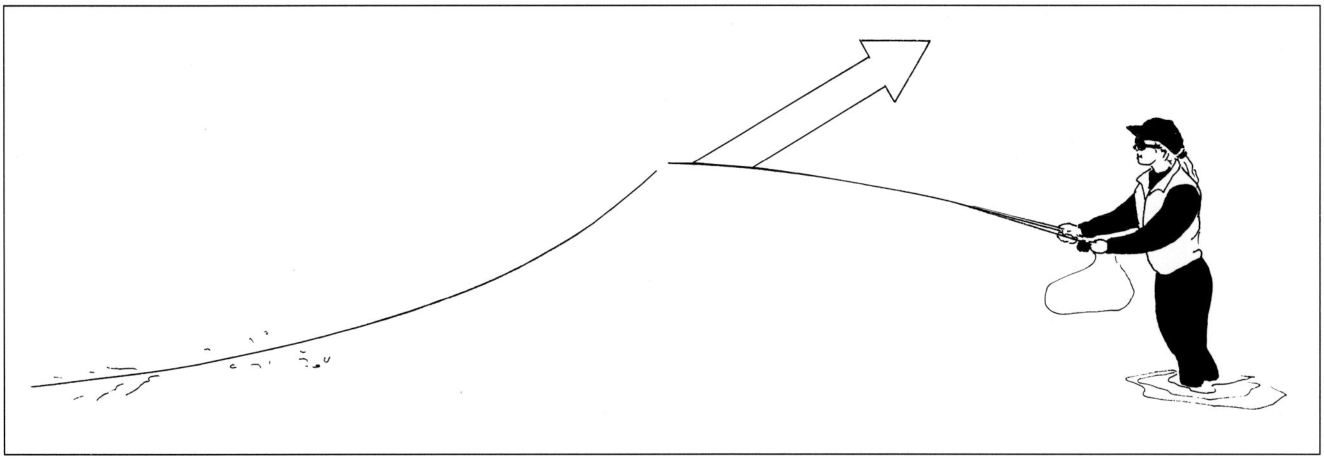

Line comes off the water as the rod starts the backcast of the water haul.

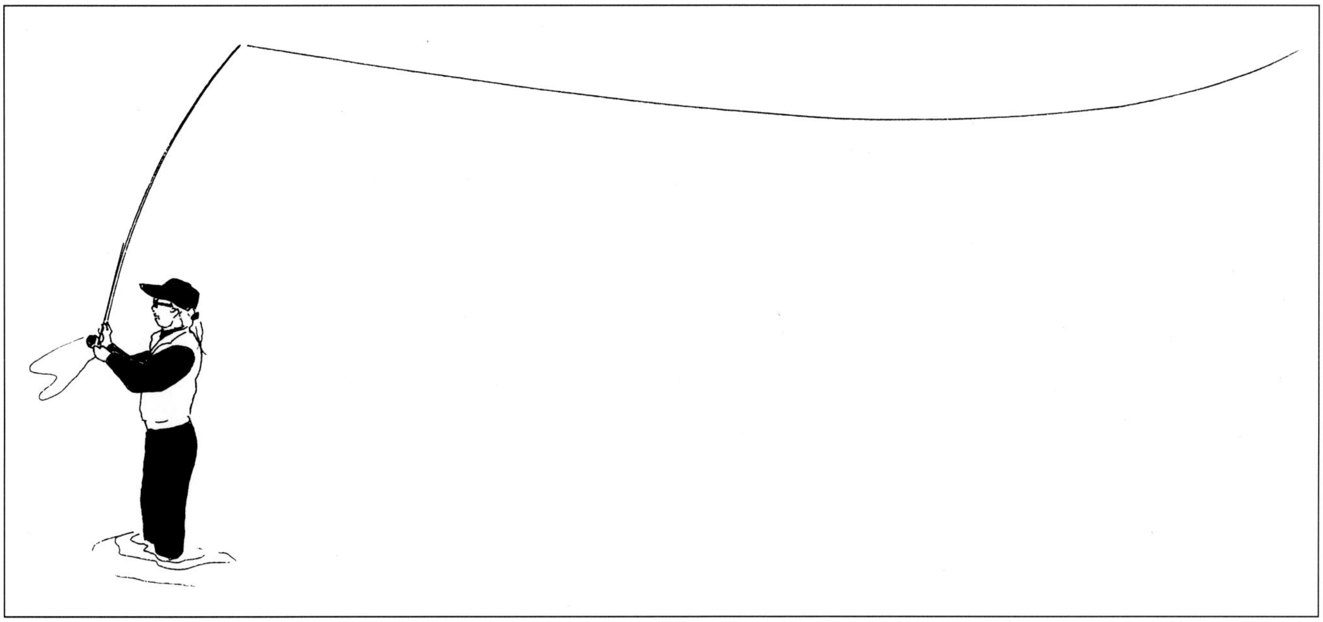

Rod tip at the end of the backcast. The angler's weight is shifted back on the right foot.

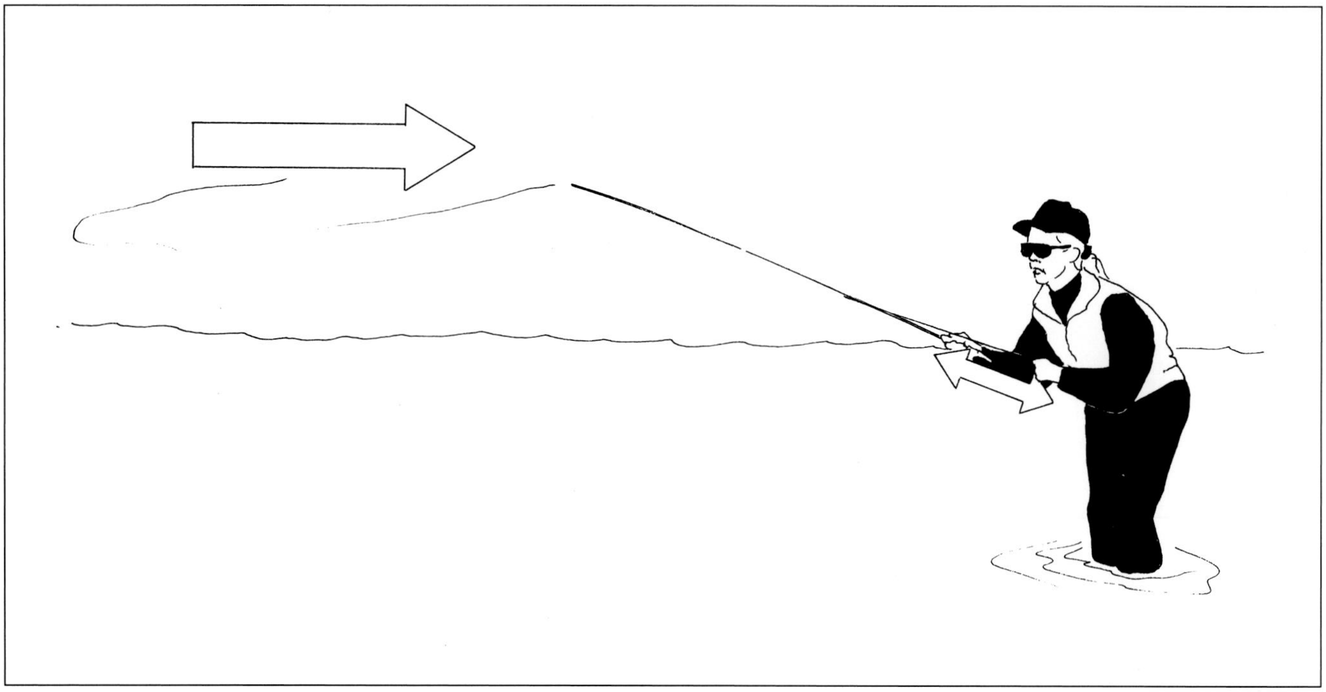

A low-profile cast staying just above the water, under the wind. Angler is double hauling to make the cast.

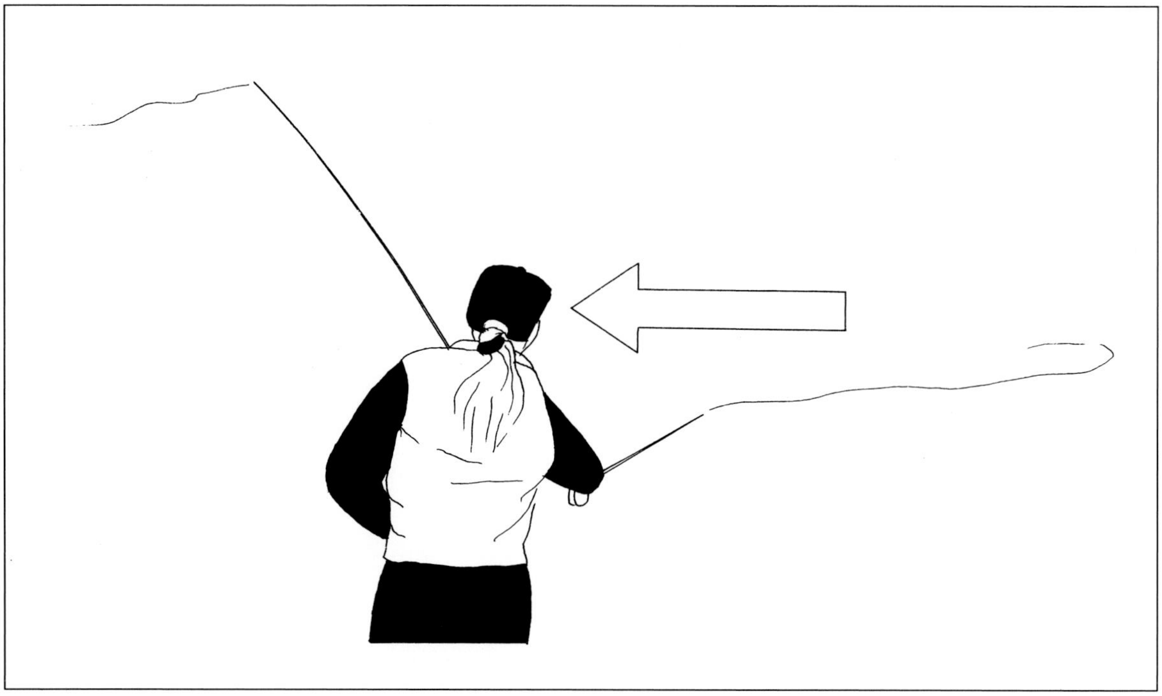

Cast over the left shoulder to fight wind coming from the right side.

the fly on both the backcast and the forward cast. Try a side-arm low-profile cast across the water surface so that instead of the fly traveling close to your head, it's now out to the side over the water.

Casting over your left shoulder also will help when the wind is coming at your right side. Unless you use this side often, it will feel awkward and it will be hard to get the line speed that you're used to from the right side, but with a little practice it can become a very useful cast. Practice this cast when you don't need it to stay comfortable with it.

Side wind that comes from the opposite direction carries the line, leader, and fly away from you, so there is little or no danger of getting hooked, but in any side wind your accuracy can be drastically affected. Again, resort to a low-profile tight-loop cast and, if necessary, try to compensate for the direction of the wind: If it's blowing from left to right, aim more to the left because the wind will blow the fly more to the right.

Learning to handle wind and cast long distances are the major challenges for most freshwater fishermen making the transition to salt, but with the right tackle and practice, anyone can learn and accomplish the mechanics needed to reach distances of 70 or 80 feet or longer.

CHAPTER 3

Tapered Leaders and Knots

Tapered Leaders

The basic requirements of a saltwater tapered leader are similar to those of a freshwater design. First, the leader through its taper needs to transfer enough energy to properly turn over the fly at the end of the cast. The leader also serves as the invisible connection between the fly and the fly line. In fresh water, most of us prefer tapered leaders that are soft and supple and designed for quiet presentations, especially when trout are our intended quarry. Tippet sizes of 4X, 5X, and 6X are quite common and relate to smaller hook sizes often necessary for trout fishing.

Saltwater flies and their related tippet sizes are another story. A size 6 hook is a small size in salt water, and larger 2/0 and 3/0 saltwater fly patterns are often dressed with heavy wind-resistant materials. Consequently, saltwater leaders generally have longer, stiffer butt sections to handle the larger, more wind-resistant flies. The butt diameter of a standard 9-foot Scientific Anglers trout leader is .020 to .022. An average 9-foot saltwater tapered leader will have a considerably heavier butt diameter of .026.

Left: Lefty Kreh uses a Nonslip Mono Loop on one of his favorite snook and tarpon patterns.

The length of a saltwater tapered leader will vary, just as with trout leaders, and should relate to the fishing situation at hand. As a general rule of thumb, we rely on 9- to 10-foot tapered leaders for most of our saltwater and freshwater fishing. This average-length leader provides easy turnover and puts the fly far enough away from the end of the thick fly line that the fish is not frightened.

Shorter leader lengths of 4 to 7$^1/_2$ feet work well under windy conditions as well as with sinking-tip or full-sinking fly lines. They also provide easier turnovers for using larger wind-resistant surface poppers. Longer tapered leaders of 12 to 16 feet are often necessary on thin-water flats when fishing to spooky bonefish or sometimes for tarpon that are cruising over a light sand-colored bottom. These fish can be easily spooked by a noisy presentation or a shadow from the fly line.

As with trout anglers, saltwater anglers have a choice of knotted or knotless tapered leaders. This is a matter of personal preference. We are very happy with either Scientific Anglers or Orvis saltwater knotless tapered designs. For anglers who prefer a knotted tapered leader, Orvis offers a variety of choices, including fluorocarbon leaders in both knotless and knotted tapers. Fluorocarbon is a relatively new leader material that is almost invisible underwater. Manufacturers claim that fluorocarbon offers superior abrasion resistance, stiffness, and a higher degree of wet knot strength.

The tippet on a tapered leader (knotless or knotted) is the last level section of leader material to which the fly is attached. A "class tippet" is one recognized by the International Game Fish Association (IGFA) and is required for certification of world-record fish. The size or diameter of the tippet must be compatible with the intended hook size to maximize the strength of the connection between the two. Also, the kinds of leader materials being attached to one another need to be compatible. Whenever possible, use different diameters of the same brand of material. Some brands will be stiffer or limper than others, so by staying with the same brand throughout, you're keeping the sections compatible with each other—in other words, limp to limp or stiff to stiff.

Use shock or wire tippets whenever you are fishing for fish such as tarpon and snook that can bite or have abrasive mouths that can saw through thinner diameters of monofilament. Tarpon have a sandpaper mouth that can quickly go through monofilament. Snook have a razor-sharp cutter blade on the side of the gill plates. Monofilament shock tippets can be anywhere from 40 to 100 pounds in test and range from 12 to 16 inches in length. Wire is used for really toothy critters like the barracuda, which will easily cut through the heaviest monofilament.

Knots

It's impossible to get by in fly fishing without knowing how to tie knots. They connect the reel to the backing, the backing to the fly line, the fly line to the leader, the leader to the tippet, and the tippet to the fly.

Many kinds of knots are used in saltwater fly fishing. An excellent book by Lefty Kreh and Mark Sosin, *Practical Fishing Knots II*, has 135 pages of illustrations and instructions on tying useful fishing knots. Fortunately, you don't need to know that many knots to get started fishing in salt water. In fact, you can get by with six or seven simple knots, and if you are a freshwater angler, you probably already know some of them. You should learn to comfortably and quickly tie these knots before you go fishing. Standing knee-deep on a saltwater flat is not the place to master an unfamiliar knot.

Everything happens fast in saltwater fishing, and it holds true with tying knots. There will be times when you need to change flies as quickly as possible, such as when a tarpon has refused your fly twice but is still in the area and the guide suggests another color fly. Your fingers need to move quickly; the fish won't stay for long. Being able to quickly complete the fly-to-tippet knot is essential to success.

How strong a knot is will be determined by how well the knot is seated, or drawn tight. Lubricating the sections of monofilament with saliva before drawing the knot tight will reduce friction and allow the knot to seat properly. Knots need to be drawn as tight as possible. When you are working with heavy diameters of monofilament, you may have to use pliers to pull the knot tight.

Once the knot is tied, the tag end needs to be trimmed as closely as possible. Any extension of monofilament could get caught in the fly-rod guides. You may even want to coat your knots with a flexible rubber cement so that they can pass easily and smoothly through the guides.

Because saltwater fish in general are stronger than their freshwater counterparts, you'll want to do everything possible to ensure that your entire system is correctly connected. When you tie your knots, pay close attention to the number of turns needed to complete each knot. Too few will result in a knot that prematurely slips; too many will not allow the knot to seat, and this, too, will cause it to easily slip. The following instructions will take you through the fundamental mechanics of tying the basic saltwater knots.

Uni-Knot

The Uni-Knot is perhaps the most popular knot used by saltwater anglers for attaching the backing to the arbor of the reel spool. It's basically very similar to a Clinch Knot and is easily performed.

Start by passing the end of the backing around the arbor of the spool, going over the top and out underneath the bottom. Bring the end of the backing (allow about 8 inches in length) up and alongside the standing section of backing. Take the tag end, and bend it back to the left toward the reel spool, forming a loop beneath the two strands of backing.

Wrap the tag end going right five times around the two strands and staying inside the loop. The tag end exits out through the loop. You can now draw the wraps together by pulling on the tag end.

Now moisten the knot with saliva and pull on the backing, drawing the knot tight against the reel arbor. Once the knot is seated, trim off the remaining tag end. You are now ready to reel the backing on to your fly reel.

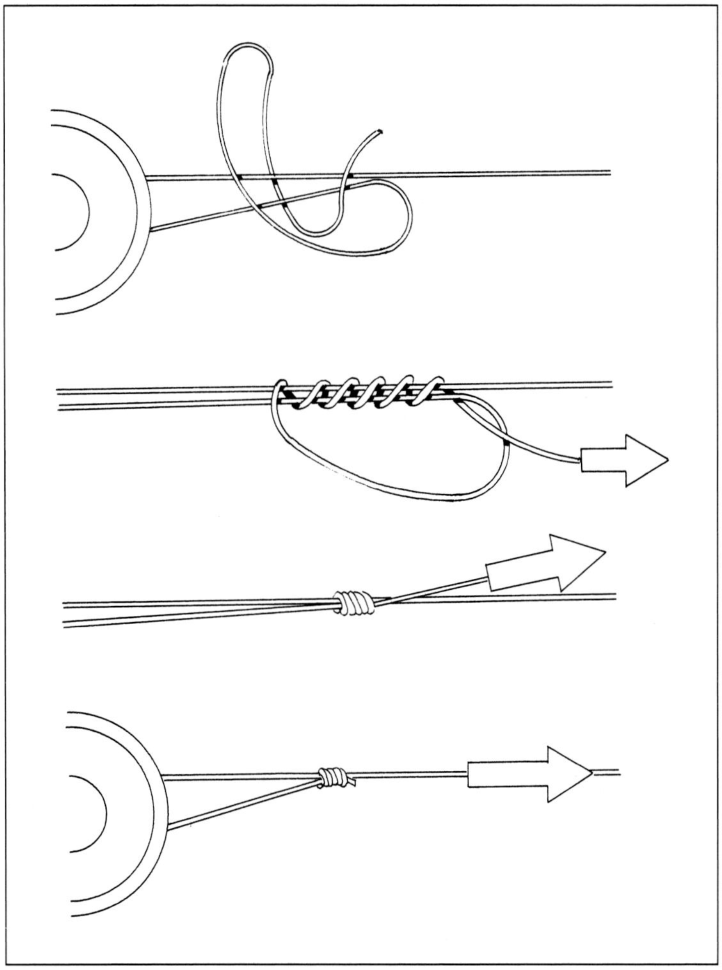

Uni-Knot

Tie Fast Nail Knot

Unless you are going for very big fish, the basic Nail Knot works fine for joining the backing to the fly line. It is best accomplished with a simple tool called the Tie Fast Knot Tyer. With this tool, the knot can be completed in twenty seconds or less.

Start by laying the tag end of the backing on top of the thumb plate, allowing the tag end to hang out the front of the tool about 6 inches. Pull the tag down and out of the bottom of the tool, and wrap away from you around the tool, working toward the thumb plate, five times. Make sure the wraps are tight and close together. Anchor the tag end by moving the index finger of the tool hand up on the wraps on the back of the trough of the tool. Now slide the tag end under the wraps and out the front of the tool.

Insert the end of the fly line, starting at the front of the tool, and push the end of the fly line underneath the five wraps and up on top of the thumb plate. Tuck the protruding end of the fly line under your thumb so it, too, is lying on the thumb plate with your thumb. Be careful here; the fly line will often want to go under the thumb plate, and you may have to use a scissors point or fingernail to get it up on top of the thumb plate with the backing. Your thumb will now be holding both the backing and the fly line on the thumb plate.

Keeping pressure with your thumb on the thumb plate, pull the end of the backing, allowing the knot to slide off the end of the tool. Pulling the tag end will draw the backing wraps tightly against the fly line. At this point, you can use your thumbnails to push the wraps together if they separated coming off the tool. Tug firmly on both ends of the backing, then on the long ends of the backing and the fly line, making sure the knot is tight. Trim both the tag ends of the backing and the fly line.

We coat our Nail Knots with a flexible rubber-based cement or with Pliobond to form a catch-free knot. Though in fresh water the fly-line backing seldom travels through the rod guides, it commonly does in salt water, and you don't want a knot to get caught in a rod guide. All knot connections need to pass through your rod guides as easily as possible. Once the cement coating is dry, you are ready to reel the fly line onto your reel.

The Nail Knot using the Tie Fast Knot Tyer will also quickly attach the butt section of a tapered leader to your fly line. Use the same number of wraps recommended for the backing, and remember to coat the connection.

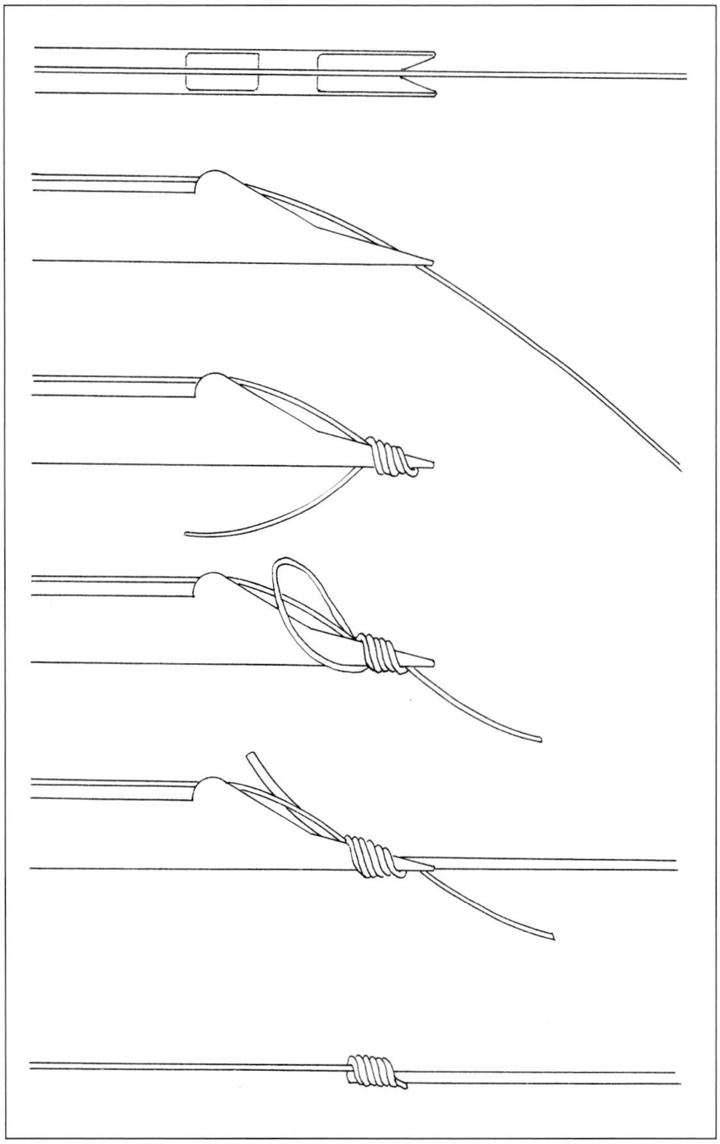

Tie Fast Nail Knot

The monofilament is more difficult to work with than the backing, but the knot is tied the same way. The tension on the wraps and the pressure with the thumb and index finger become more critical. As they slide off the end of the tool, sometimes the wraps open up a bit. If this happens, you can push them back together with your thumbnails while at the same time pulling out the slack. If they are so loose that they get underneath each other, tie the knot again. Make sure the wraps are tested well at the end. Remember, the strength of the knot comes from the bite of the wraps into the coating of the fly line.

Lefty's Loop

We use Lefty's Served Loop on the end of some of our lines for quick leader changes. It's a little more work, but it's worth it in the long run. We don't recommend using a braided mono loop connector, which can break when fighting strong fish.

To form a loop on the end of your fly line, you'll need a sharp knife or razor blade, a spool of size 3/0 or heavier fly-tying thread on a bobbin, a whip finisher, Pliobond, and an 8-inch section of 6-pound monofilament.

Start by cutting a sharp angle on the end of your fly line. Fold the angled end of the fly line back against the standing line about 2 inches, forming a small loop. Using the bobbin, wrap the tying thread around the two strands of fly line, lashing them tightly together. Take your time winding the thread, creating even, tight winds, and be sure to continue past the tapered end to ensure a smooth connection. Wrap back and forth from your starting point two times, keeping tension on every wrap so that it bites into the fly line. Whip-finish to make sure the ends won't unravel, but don't cut it yet.

Take the piece of monofilament, folding it to create a loop, and lay it alongside the fly line in the opposite direction from the loop. Make ten more wraps with the tying thread over the mono, as illustrated.

Cut the end of the tying thread, and insert it through the mono loop. Holding the fly line, pull on the two ends of the mono. This will pull the end of the tying thread underneath the last wraps. It's now important to put several coats of Pliobond or a similar flexible cement over the servings.

Take time to test the loop. Place the loop around a smooth object, and pull on it with one hand while holding the fly line in the other. If the loop pulls out, the wraps did not bite into the fly line.

With the fly-line loop installed, you can easily change leaders in a matter of seconds.

Surgeon's Knot

The popular Surgeon's Knot is a universal knot used to attach two pieces of leader material together. It can even be used when attaching a section of braided wire to monofilament, provided the wire does not exceed 40 pounds. This is basically a double Overhand Knot and is very easy to tie.

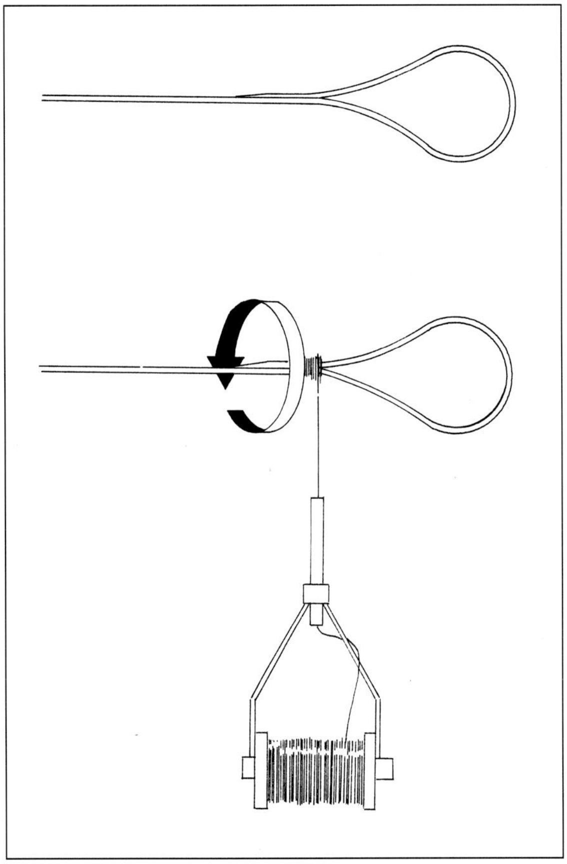

Lefty's Loop

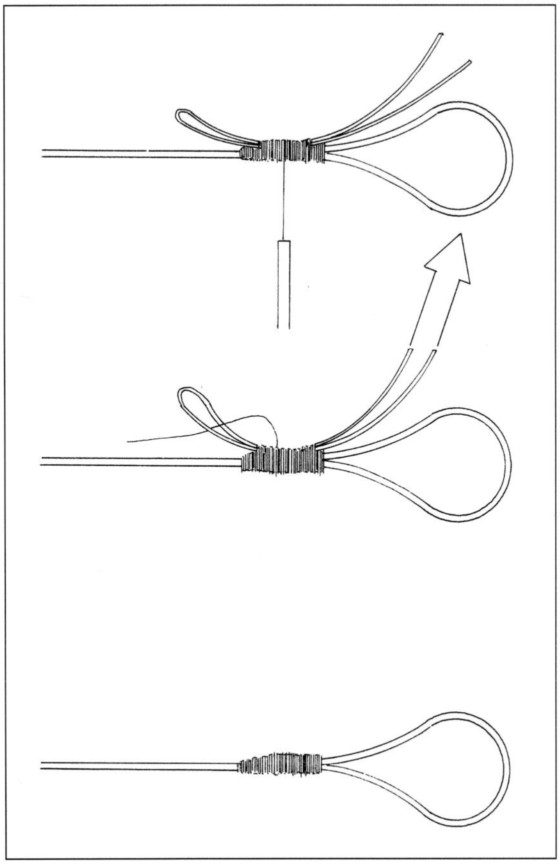

Lefty's Loop

Start with the last section of your tapered leader and the tippet section to be attached. Lay the two sections next to each other in opposite directions, working with about 10 inches of each. With your left hand, hold the two sections together. With your right hand, make an Overhand Knot with the right ends of the leader and tippet, keeping the loop open. Pass the right ends through the loop twice.

Now, holding the two sections of the leader and tippet in the left hand and the right two sections in the right hand, simultaneously draw the loop closed and tighten the knot. Be sure to moisten the knot prior to pulling it tight. Pull all four ends at the same time as tightly as possible. Trim the ends, and the knot is complete.

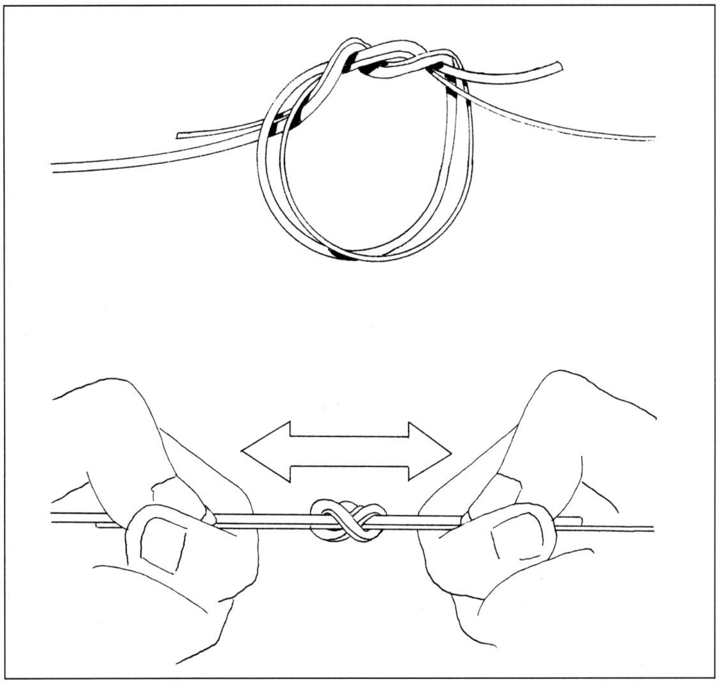

Surgeon's Knot

Bimini Twist

Heavy monofilament shock and wire tippets can be hard to attach to a smaller-diameter section of tapered leader. For many anglers, it pays to pur-

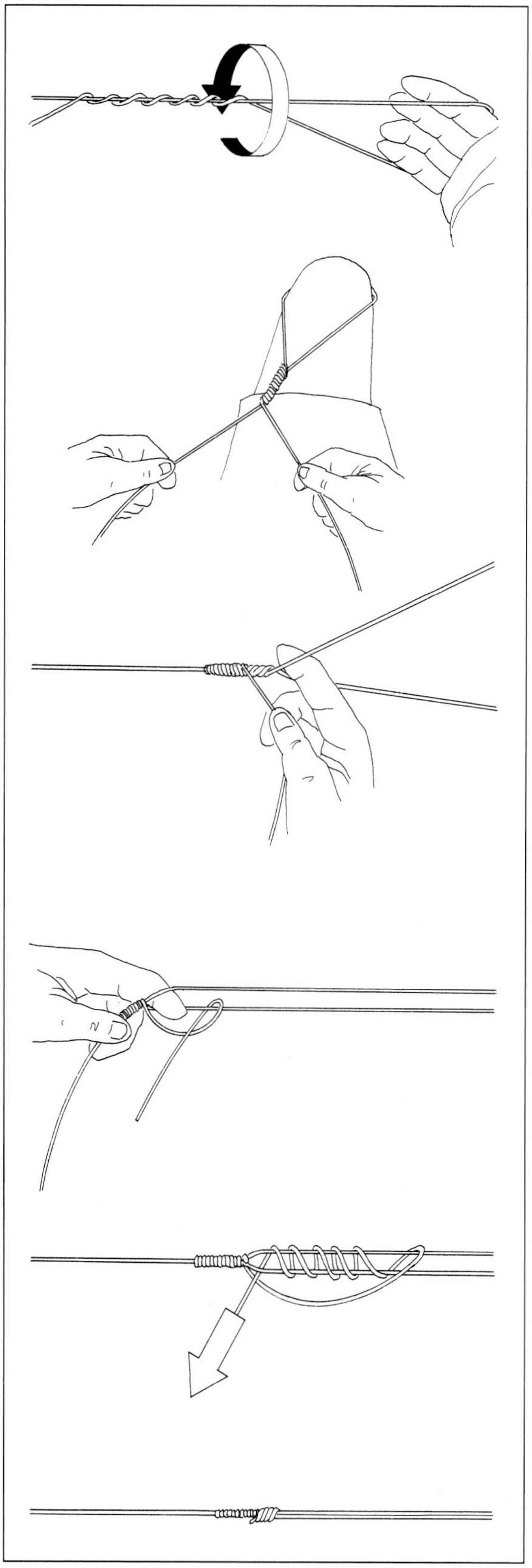

Bimini Twist

chase a tapered leader with the shock tippet attached. If you have a loop on the end of your fly line, it takes just seconds to change leaders. To construct your own tapered leaders and shock tippets, you need to start with a Bimini Twist. This is one of the few knots that allow you to retain the full knot strength of the lighter line to which you are attaching the heavier shock tippet.

Start with the last section of your tapered leader. Fold back about 20 inches, and put your hand in the loop you have created. Keep the loop open, and with your hand, twist the loop twenty times.

Next, bend your knee and place the loop over it. Holding the short line in your right hand and the main section of leader in your left, spread your hands apart at a 45-degree angle, as shown in the illustration. As you put pressure on both sections, the twist will be packed into tight spirals. Continue pulling until the twist becomes tight around your leg. Now move the standing section of leader to the right, getting it in line with the wraps. Your right hand also goes to a right angle to the spiraled twist. Pull on the line with the left hand, releasing tension with your right until the line flips over the twist.

Put your left thumb and finger in just below the twist, and hold the twists while your right hand passes the tag end around the right side of the loop and then back through the smaller loop just created to anchor it. Let this knot slide back against the twists.

With your left hand still holding the end of the twists, take the tag end in your right hand, and move down the loop to the right about 2 inches. Holding the loop closed, pass the tag end around the loop, winding back toward your left hand four times. Pull the tag end with your left hand as you carefully work the new spirals back toward the twists. You can loosen and tighten, loosen and tighten as you slide them back, until the knot seats tightly against the spirals. Pliers are helpful for heavy monofilament. Snip off the extending tag.

Huffnagle Knot

The Huffnagle Knot will enable you to attach a shock tippet to your Bimini Twist. Start with an Overhand Knot near one end of the shock tippet. Pass the Bimini Twist through the Overhand Knot as illustrated.

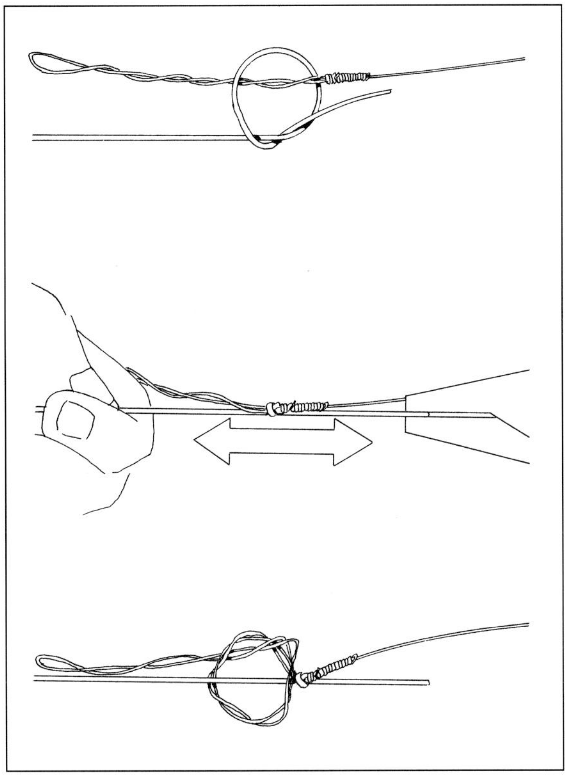

Huffnagle Knot

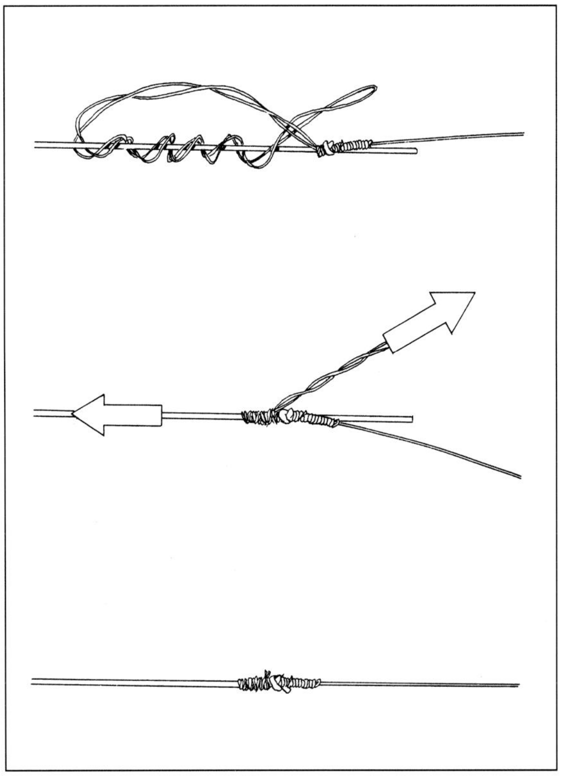

Huffnagle Knot

Take hold of the short end of the shock tippet with a pair of pliers in your right hand, and hold the longer section of the shock tippet with your left hand. Pull the two sections together against the Bimini Twist as tightly as possible. Snip off the short tag end of the shock tippet.

Start an Overhand Knot in the double twist of the Bimini, around and ahead of the Overhand Knot of the shock tippet. Pull the knot tight against the shock leader.

The Huffnagle is finished the same way as a Bimini. Make a loop with the loop end of the Bimini, and wrap the end going to the right four times back to the Overhand Knot. Bring the tag end of the Bimini out of the loop. Pull on the shock leader with your left hand and on the end of the Bimini with your right, lubricating the wraps before pulling them tight. Trim the tag end, and the knot is complete.

Clinch/Improved Clinch Knot

Most freshwater anglers rely on the Clinch or the Improved Clinch Knot to connect flies to the tippet. Both of these popular and easy knots will

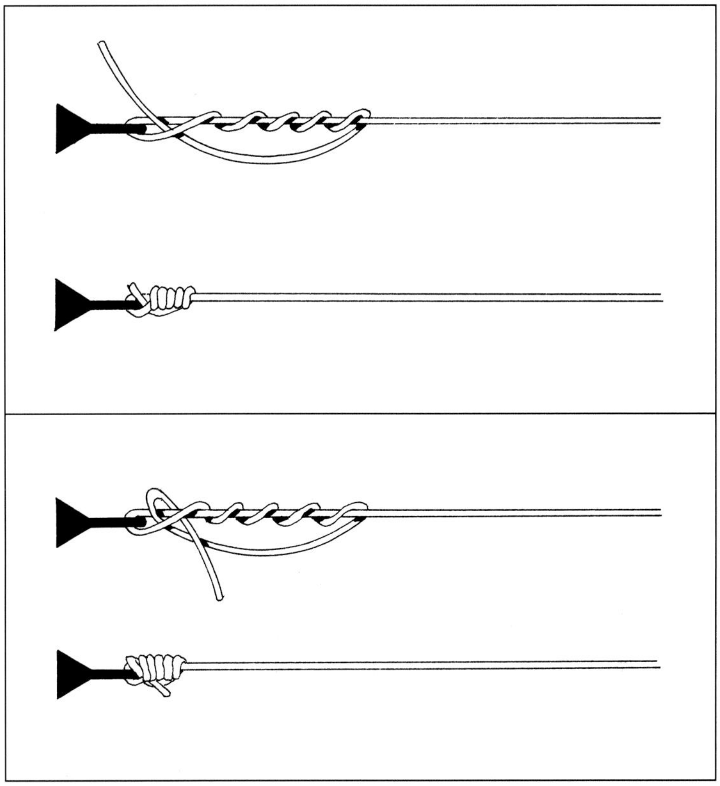

Clinch/Improved Clinch Knot

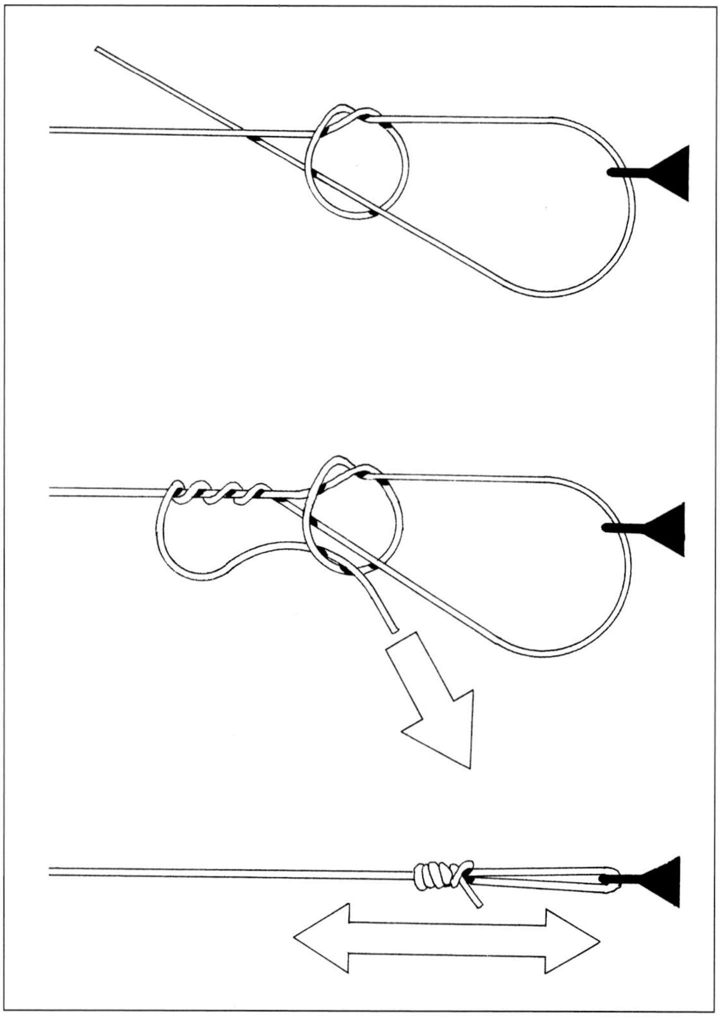

Nonslip Mono Loop Knot

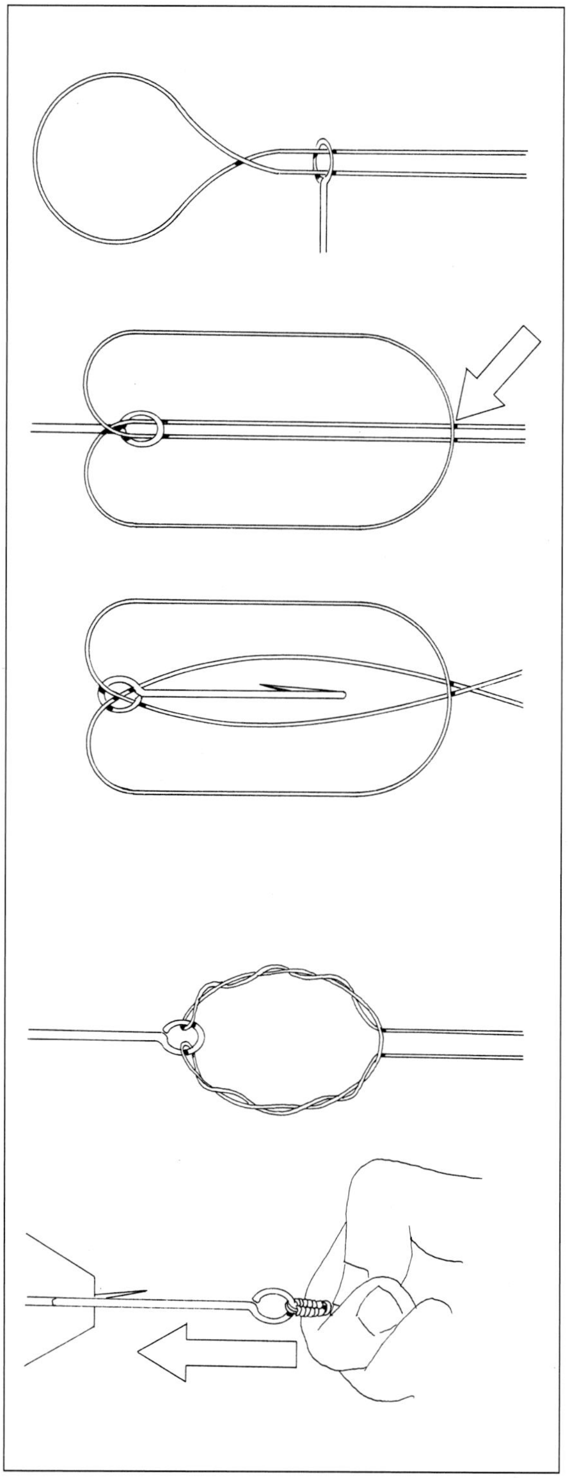

Offshore Swivel Knot

work in some saltwater applications, such as when smaller bonefish flies with size 6 or 8 hooks are being used with 8- or 10-pound tippets. The problem with the Clinch Knot is that it is drawn tight against the hook eye, causing the fly to be somewhat restricted in movement. Saltwater flies in almost every case are retrieved, and they need as much freedom of movement as possible in order to look and act like the real thing. When more movement is desired, use the Nonslip Mono Loop Knot.

Nonslip Mono Loop

The Nonslip Mono Loop is easy to tie and is a very strong knot for attaching the fly to the tippet. We've come to rely on it for both saltwater and freshwater applications and use it whenever we need to retrieve an underwater fly or a popping bug on the surface.

Start by placing a simple Overhand Knot about 8 inches up from the end of the tippet. (You can use less later on.) Pass the tag end of the tippet through the eye of the hook and through the loop in the Overhand Knot. Remember how it went through the loop.

Twist the tag end around the tippet, five turns for lines 8- to 12-pound-test, four turns for lines 15 to 40 pounds, three turns for 50 to 60, and two turns for anything heavier. Insert the tag end back through the loop of the Overhand Knot, making sure that it passes through on the same side that it exited from.

Moisten the knot, then close the wraps together by pulling on the tag end. After the wraps have come together, tighten the knot by pulling on the tippet end.

Offshore Swivel Knot

Originally used with swivels, this knot is exceptionally strong and easy to tie. And if one strand breaks, the other will probably hold.

Start with a Bimini Twist in the line. Holding the hook in your left hand, put the loop of the Bimini through the eye of the hook and make one twist. Bring the tag end of the loop back over the hook to your right hand, keeping the twist in it. Hold the round end of the loop against the standing part with your right hand. Pass the hook through both loops six times, holding the loop end and the standing part together so that the knot doesn't fall apart.

Tighten the knot by holding the fly in your left hand, moistening, and pulling the hook down. Use pliers if necessary. By pushing and pulling, you can tightly seat the wraps together.

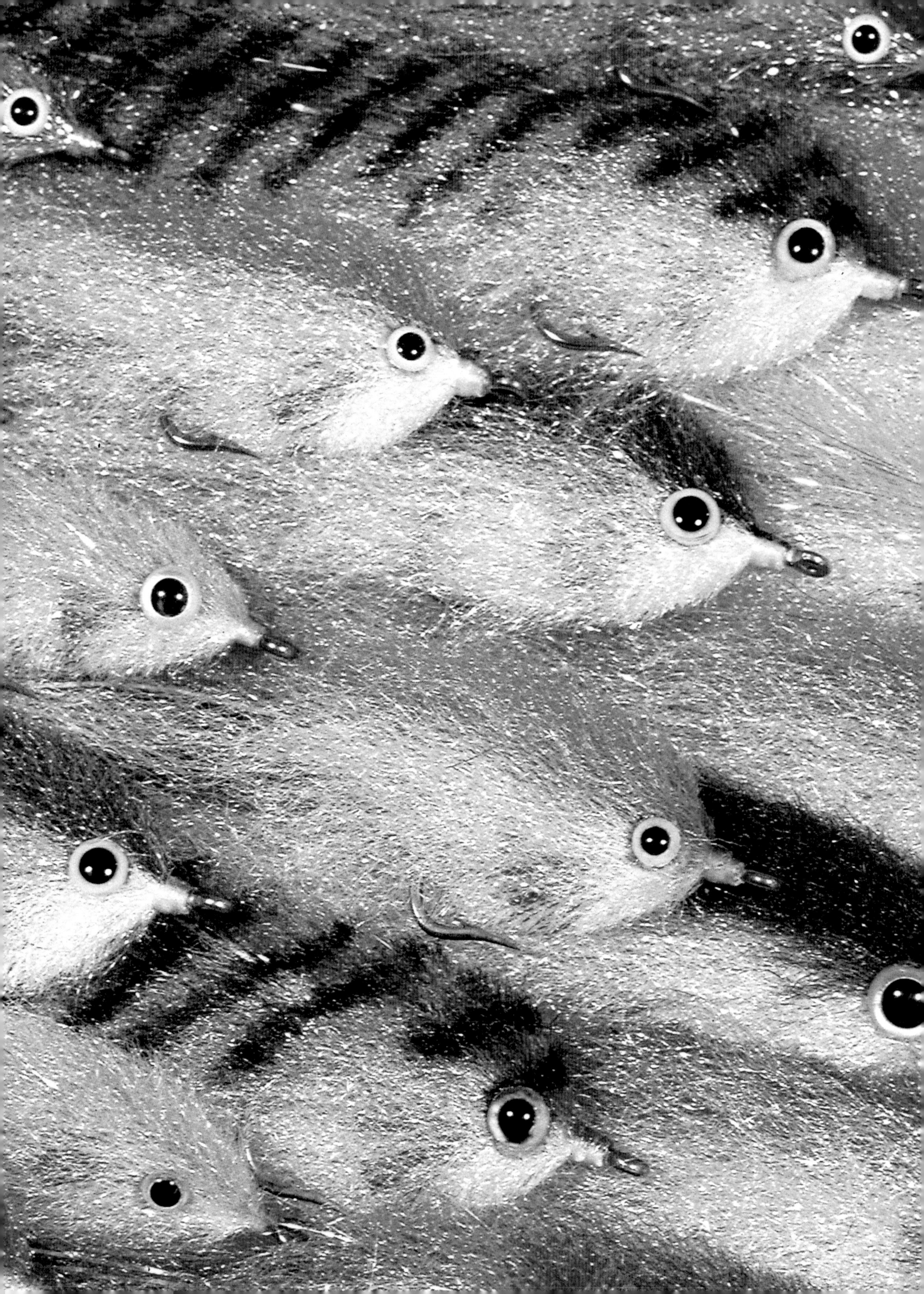

CHAPTER 4

Choosing Saltwater Fly Patterns

CHOOSING THE RIGHT FLY PATTERN IS AN IMPORTANT decision that should not be taken lightly. Many saltwater species of fish can be as fussy as trout about what they eat, and after all, it's the fly on the end of the leader that is either accepted or rejected by the fish. Success is usually a combination of the right cast, the right retrieve, and the right fly pattern.

Like trout flies, saltwater fly patterns can be divided into two groups: attractors and imitators. Attractor patterns bring a response from the fish usually through a combination of bright colors and motion. Imitator patterns imitate the prey that fish eat through profile, color, and behavior.

Modern technology has given the fly tier new dimensions in tying materials, and today tiers like Bob Clouser, Jack Gartside, Bob Popovics, Enrico Puglisi, and Hank Leonhard are creating astonishingly realistic imitations, complete with eyes, fins, and gill markings that will deceive the fussiest of fish. Whether you put your faith in attractors or imitators, you'll want some of both in your fly boxes.

The profile and size of saltwater flies are extremely important. First, the flies need to look like food to the fish; second, you need to be able to cast the fly without difficulty. Because a fish's attack is usually triggered by visual stimuli, a fly needs to swim or behave in the water as the natural would. For flies fished subsurface, the fly needs to have a desirable sink rate. Saltwater fish are more apt to take a fly that is at the same depth as the fish. How fast a fly sinks is determined by the materials it is tied with, including the size of any lead or weighted eyes.

When choosing a fly pattern, keep in mind the color of the bottom over which you are fishing. Mother Nature has provided most underwater creatures with natural camouflage. Anything in the food chain that stood out would be quickly eliminated by predators. Flies are often tied in the colors of the naturals they imitate. As a general rule of thumb, light-colored patterns work best over a light-colored bottom, such as a white sand flat. Darker fly patterns do best when fished in a darker environment, such as a turtle grass flat.

Saltwater game fish use their lateral lines to sense or feel moving prey in water that is discolored by silt or mud. When faced with these conditions, choose a fly pattern that offers a little flash and some bulk. Beware of a fly pattern with flash in clear water on bright days, however. Here the flash may scare the fish.

Left: A selection of LP baitfish flies, which imitate various species and sizes of baitfish.

Popular bonefish patterns: *Top left:* Clouser Minnow; *Top right:* Beck's Yucatan Puffer; *Middle left:* Popovics Ultra Shrimp; *Middle right:* Beck's Bright Eyes; *Bottom left:* Beck's Silly Legs; *Bottom right:* Gotcha

When fish are deep, a noisy surface popper is often a good choice and can bring fish to the surface in off-color water. We always carry a good selection of poppers in a variety of sizes and colors for working the edges of the mangroves and the channels. The visual and explosive strike of a tarpon or snook to a surface popper is an experience you will not soon forget.

In thin or low water, you need fly patterns designed to enter the water as quietly as possible. Predator fish, such as bonefish, in shallow water conditions are always on the alert for danger. They are very sensitive to the tidal fluctuations, and though they may prefer the safety of deeper water, they will be searching for food on the flats. Although they are the hunters, they can quickly become the hunted. A fly that plops in and causes too much noise or disturbance will send any nearby fish racing to the safety of deeper water.

Bonefish flies are tied in various sizes for different conditions. Bonefish in areas that are heavily fished are much more particular about the fly they take. In areas with lighter fishing pressure, you can be more aggressive in fly selection. When fishing over challenging fish, imitations of small baitfish and shrimp should enter the water quietly and well ahead of the fish. The long legs of rubber-legged patterns, such as the Yucatan Puffer and Silly Legs, help cushion the fly as it enters the water, giving it a soft, quiet presentation. As the fish become more educated, your fly patterns must become more sophisticated.

The best hook sizes for popular bonefish flies also vary from one destination to another. For instance, on Andros Island in the Bahamas, we often use flies tied on size 2 and 4 stainless steel hooks. Here some bonefish are in the 10- to 12-pound class. The flats are lined with mangroves, and the fish are often found in 3- to 4-foot-deep water. Not far from Andros are the hard, white flats of Exuma. Here the bonefish cruise in superthin water and quickly spook at the drop of a pin. Smaller, sparsely dressed bonefish flies tied on size 6 and 8 hooks will perform better in these conditions.

Our fly boxes always contain a good selection of bonefish flies dressed on size 4, 6, and 8 hooks. Favorite patterns are Silly Legs, Bright Eyes, Gotchas, and smaller Clouser Minnows. Color combinations of white and chartreuse, tan and white, pink and white, all white, and root beer can always be relied on.

Tarpon, snook, jack crevalle, redfish, striped bass, barracuda, and bluefish are just a few of the popular saltwater species that feed on smaller baitfish. As with most adult fish, baitfish adults tend to have darker backs, and fly imitations should reflect this characteristic.

Lefty Kreh developed his Lefty's Deceiver back in the 1950s, and he probably had no idea at the time just how popular this fly would become. This fly has caught just about anything that swims in salt water. Through the years, it's been modified and changed by fly tiers around the world, but flies with the basic baitfish profile and design still rank as old standbys in most fly boxes. The Deceiver is easy to tie, easy to cast, and it easily fools the fish. Deceivers dressed with white deer-tail bottoms and darker shades of deer hair or peacock herl on top provide very effective baitfish imitations that are both realistic and durable.

Enrico Puglisi and Hank Leonhard of Long Island, New York, created a series of saltwater patterns that we have come to rely on. They are extremely realistic, easy to cast, durable, and available in a variety of patterns and sizes for all saltwater species of fish. One of our favorite snook and tarpon patterns is the LP Mullet tied with contemporary sea fibers, a new synthetic material. The LP Mullet, complete with eyes and gill markings, is extremely lifelike in the water. If there is

Popular tarpon patterns: *Top center:* LP Mullet; *Middle left:* Black Lefty's Deceiver; *Middle right:* Blue and White Lefty's Deceiver; *Bottom left:* LP Peanut Butter; *Bottom right:* Cockroach

Popular bluefish patterns: *Top right:* Popovics Spread Fleye; *Top left:* LP Tinker Mackerel; *Middle left:* Popovics Double Header Candy; *Middle right:* LP Shiner; *Bottom right:* Popovics Pop Lips; *Bottom left:* Popovics Silicone

one baitfish that is constantly being pursued by game fish, it's the mullet, so a good mullet imitation is always a good bet.

Jack Gartside has created a very effective series of soft-hackle Deceivers for thin-water situations. The Gartside Soft Hackle Deceiver has a very slim baitfishlike profile, along with lots of enticing, shimmering action. It enters the water quietly and works well for striped bass, tarpon, snook, and barracuda. Fished in smaller sizes, it can even be used for bonefish.

Sardines are another kind of baitfish that should be imitated, and once again Puglisi and Leonhard have developed a pattern that offers the correct profile, color, and action and, like the LP Mullet, is tied entirely out of synthetic materials.

New Jersey fly tier Bob Popovics popularized the use of a clear bathroom silicone sealer in the construction of his now famous Surf Candy series of saltwater flies. Along with the Surf Candy, Bob has developed a number of other innovative patterns, including the Bend Back Candy, the Double Header Deep Candy, the Ultra Shrimp, Silicone, Pop-Lips Silicone, the Spread Fleye, and Bob's Banger.

Fly patterns that have lead eyes and sink quickly are a must for those times when fish are feeding at deeper levels, and the Clouser Deep Minnow is at the top of our list. Clouser Minnows probably need little introduction here, since most trout and bass fishermen already know of them. Lefty Kreh believes that the Clouser Minnow may just be the most effective all-purpose fly out there. Bob Clouser recently introduced a new version of the Clouser Deep Minnow, called the Skinny Water Clouser. It is designed for bonefish in thin-water flats and, like its predecessor, should prove to be a dynamite pattern.

Another underwater fly that works great in off-color water is Don Blanton's Whistler. The Whistler's large bead-chain eyes create vibrations that help fish find the fly. This is a good choice for a general search-type fly.

Permit flies usually imitate the crabs that permit feed on. Although permit have been caught on small Deceivers, various bonefish patterns, and Clouser Minnows, the majority of permit hook-ups are on some kind of crab imitation. Permit are by nature very cautious, selective, and suspicious feeders. We have cast our permit flies to hundreds of permit but, to date, have landed only six. Our favorite and most successful patterns are Del Brown's Permit Crab and Enrico Puglisi's Permit Crab. Our own tan and white Silly Legs pattern has accounted for one 15-pounder, and our Yucatan Puffer in root beer has produced two hook-ups, both good-size fish that unfortunately threw the hook.

Surface poppers can provide some explosive action on top, and it's hard to beat the visual excitement of a tarpon or snook attacking your fly. Most saltwater game fish, excluding permit and bonefish, can be teased into taking a surface popper. All white or a combination of red and white seems to be the best all-around color patterns for us, although yellow or chartreuse can also be effective. Edge Water, Mr. Bob's Lucky Day Lures, and the Gaines Popper Company are three manufacturers that offer a variety of poppers designed for saltwater use.

The following is a list of suggested fly patterns, sizes, and colors, along with the intended species of fish. It is a limited list, considering the number of patterns available today, but with this selection of flies you can fish just about anywhere in salt water and feel confident in your choice of patterns.

Popular striper patterns: *Top left:* Gartside Soft Hackle Deceiver; *Top right:* Puglisi Sardine; *Middle left:* Popovics Bend Back Candy; *Middle right:* Gartside Gurgler; *Bottom left:* Puglisi Silver; *Bottom right:* Popovics Surf Candy

Popular permit crabs: *Top middle:* LP Secret Crab; *Bottom left:* LP Crab; *Bottom right:* Del Brown Crab

Popular popper patterns: *Top:* Mr. Bob's; *Middle:* Bob's Banger; *Bottom:* Clouser E-Z Popper

Pattern	Hook Sizes	Suggested Colors
Bonefish		
Clouser Minnow	4–6	chartreuse and white, tan and white
Gotcha	4–6	tan and white
Beck's Silly Legs	4–6	chartreuse and white, tan and white
Beck's Bright Eyes	4–6	chartreuse and white, tan and white
Beck's Yucatan Puffer	4–6	brown, orange, olive
Popovics Ultra Shrimp	2–4	pink
Tarpon, Snook, Jack Crevalle, Barracuda		
Lefty's Deceiver	1–1/0–2/0	white, blue and white, black
Cockroach	1–1/0–2/0	grizzly and brown
LP Mullet	1/0–3/0	bronze and white, black and purple
LP Peanut Butter	1/0–3/0	gray and white
Gartside S.H. Deceiver	2/0	white
Blanton's Whistler	2 and 3/0	red and white
Permit Crabs		
Del Brown	4–2	tan and brown
LP Crab	6–2	gray, tan, olive and green
LP Secret Crab	6	tan, olive
Striped Bass		
Puglisi's Silver	1	silver
Gartside Gurgler	2	white
Gartside Beastmaster	1/0	white
Gartside SH Deceiver	1/0	chartreuse and white
Gartside Sand Eel	4–2	dark olive
Popovics Surf Candy	4–1/0	tan and white
Popovics Bend Back Candy	4–1/0	tan and white bucktail
Bluefish, Bonito, Albacore		
Clouser Floating Minnow	1/0	chartreuse and white
LP Tinker Mackerel	2/0	olive and white
LP Anchovies	1/0	gray and white, tan and white
LP Sardine	3/0	blue and white
LP Shiner	1/0	gray and white
Popovics Double Header Candy	1/0–4/0	gray and white
Popovics Silicone	1/0–3/0	white
Popovics Pop-Lips Silicone	1/0–3/0	red and white
Popovics Spread Fleye	2/0–4/0	gray and white
Poppers—General Use		
Clouser E-Z Popper	3/0	white
Mr. Bob's	1/0–2/0	white, yellow, chartreuse
Bob's Banger	1/0–4/0	green

Popular all-purpose selection: *Top right:* Lefty's White Deceiver; *Middle left:* Clouser Chartreuse & White Minnow; *Middle right:* Blanton's Whistler; *Bottom left:* Clouser Tan & White Minnow (Note: Clouser Minnows ride in the water with hooks up.)

Sharpen the hook by stroking it on one side only, and sharpen no more than 1/8 inch from the point. More will weaken the hook.

Saltwater flies are generally tied on stainless steel hooks. Your hooks must be sharp, and they must stay sharp. Never assume that the hook on a brand new fly is as sharp as it needs to be. Always presharpen your hooks. If you are a fly tier, sharpen your hooks prior to tying the flies. Some years ago, Lefty gave us an 8-inch Nicholson Smooth File that can be purchased at most hardware stores. The fine teeth on the Nicholson file make it an easy job to quickly fine-tune the points on our saltwater hooks. We never go fishing without it.

Inspect your hook point after every fish encounter, even a short hook-up, and after a hang-up on the bottom or a mangrove bush.

Many anglers get carried away with the number of flies they think they'll need for saltwater fishing. In reality, if you have two dozen of the bonefish flies suggested here, along with six to ten Deceivers, a couple heavier Clouser Minnows, and two or three permit crabs, you should be well prepared for most fishing.

One of the things that we enjoy most about saltwater fishing is the simplicity of the sport. We often find ourselves wading a flat with a small fly box tucked in a shirt pocket. The box has a selection of flies that we'll need for the day. There is a real sense of freedom—no overfilled fishing vest or jacket to contend with, just the bare essentials.

Consider the cost of saltwater flies. One of these flies is often three times the cost of a typical trout fly. Stainless steel hooks are expensive, and this is reflected in the price of the flies. Before you go to any saltwater destination, buy flies that will work for the species of fish you'll be fishing for. And keep in mind that you won't lose many flies in saltwater fishing.

CHAPTER 5

Predators and Prey

UNDERSTANDING YOUR QUARRY THE FISH, ITS HABITS and its needs, will better prepare you for when you make that first cast into salt water. The freshwater trout angler knows how changes in water temperature can affect the fish. He knows the insects and baitfish that trout feed on, how to handle both low- and high-water situations, and the best times of day to fish. He also knows the seasons of the year and how the trout are affected. He can handle moving currents and fish stillwater; he reads the water and can tell the difference between good and bad cover. A good trout fisherman will learn everything he can about his subject, and in the end, it is this knowledge that will make him a more successful angler.

The same thing is true in becoming a successful saltwater angler: The more you know about the fish, the better your chances of catching him. One thing that makes fly fishing, in both fresh and salt water, so intriguing is that there's always something new to learn—a new piece of water, a new species of fish, a new fly pattern, or a new piece of tackle. It's the learning experiences that keep fly fishing so fresh and exciting.

Left: Bonefish, the silver bullet of the flats. Often, it's the flash of the bonefish feeding in shallow water that alerts the angler to its presence.

There are so many species of saltwater fish to learn about that it would take volumes to properly cover them all. Following is a brief look at the more popular inshore flats fish.

Bonefish

It would be hard to imagine a trout fisherman who could not get excited about bonefish. Bonefish tail and feed in shallow water; they can be selective to color and size in fly patterns; they are extremely shy, fleeing the flat at the first sign of danger; and they are caught on light tackle. Bonefish can be found throughout most of the tropical waters of the world. With their speed and strength, they are known as the silver bullet of the flats.

Bonefish primarily eat clams, shrimp, and crabs. They will also eat smaller baitfish, snails, and saltwater worms. Bonefish have exceptional hearing, and any unnecessary noise from a boat or angler will send them off in a hurry. Their eye structure allows them to distinguish colors and to see under almost any water condition. The bonefish also has the wonderful ability to smell out its food through a pair of nostrils in front of the eyes. They can easily smell crabs, shrimp, and clams hiding on both the hard and soft bottoms of the flats.

Cathy with a 7-pound bonefish caught on a Silly Legs in Los Roques, a tiny Caribbean archipelago north of Caracas, Venezuela.

Built with a profile for speed, the bonefish can propel itself with its deeply forked tail at more than 20 miles per hour. The body is covered by tiny scales that reflect the colors of the environment, camouflaging the fish so well that it often appears to be invisible.

The mouth, located on the underside of the head and just behind the tapered snout, is small compared with that of other predatory fish of the flats. Designed for crushing, the inside of the mouth is hard and requires a sharp hook for good penetration.

Bonefish generally travel in schools or pairs but can be found as singles. The larger bonefish often travel alone. I remember one in particular that was traveling alone on a flat within sight of a lodge on Andros Island in the Bahamas. It was late in the afternoon on a rare windless day in February. When the fish first came into sight, it looked like a baby tarpon. As it came closer, I realized it was a bonefish of 13 or 14 pounds.

A cast made with a Silly Legs bonefish fly produced a hook-up, almost spooling the fly reel of 150 yards of backing. Three runs later, it looked like the big fish might finally be under control, when a large shark started to show interest. Rather than lose the bonefish to the shark, I lowered the fly rod and the 10-pound tippet broke, freeing the fish. We watched as the bonefish quickly left the shark behind and disappeared into the safety of the deeper water.

It's generally thought that bonefish feed best on an incoming tide. In many cases this is true, but not always. When they feed often depends on the environment and the terrain. In the Yucatan at Boca Paila Bonefish Lodge, a lagoon goes south some 40 miles to Ascension Bay. The lagoon is connected to the Caribbean but is not greatly influenced by tidal changes. There are soft and hard flats that the bonefish frequent daily, unless a cold front forces them into deeper water. And some distance below Boca Paila on the Yucatan coastline, bonefish feed facing into the incoming waves throughout the day, regardless of tidal influences.

A rising tide allows the bonefish access to areas on a flat that they would be restricted from without the additional water. Being the opportunists that they are, they may quickly move onto a flat during a rising tide. Nevertheless, bonefish are not totally dependent on tidal fluctuations. On most flats, there are deep holes or channels of water where bonefish can hold out and feed in safety until the next incoming tide returns and allows them to move again.

Bonefish will feed whenever the opportunity presents itself, regardless of light. Though they may be easier to find during the brightest light of the day, we've watched them feed on cloudy days. Once, during a front of bad weather at Bob Hyde's Peace and Plenty Bonefish Lodge in the Bahamas, we had school after school of tailing bonefish readily accept our offerings, providing one of our best days of fishing. On another occasion, at Boca Paila, we found schools of bonefish feeding on small baitfish after 10 o'clock in the evening, attracted by lights on the boat dock.

Bonefish are cold-blooded creatures and are affected by water temperature changes from cold fronts. At 70 to 80 degrees, they are comfortable and willing to feed. But if the water temperature drops below 70 or rises above 80, they will quickly desert the flat. Thus it's no surprise that in the summer months, the best fishing is in the cooler temperatures of the early morning or late afternoon and evening. In the cooler months of the year, the late morning and afternoon hours are the best.

The size of the bonefish depends on their geographic location. In the Florida Keys and, especially, Biscayne Bay, the average bonefish can run from 6 to 8 pounds. There are similar areas in the Bahamas. A 6-pound bonefish in Mexico would be considered a trophy. But any fish that weighs 6 pounds and fights as hard as a bonefish would be a trophy to a trout fisherman.

Seeing the Bonefish

Tailing bonefish feeding off the bottom in shallow water often have their tails sticking out of the water. The light reflecting off the silver tails makes them easy to spot by the observant angler. That's the good news; the bad news is that the fish seem to know how vulnerable they are in these conditions and are ready to exit at the slightest sign of danger. One mistake from the angler, and the bonefish are history.

Wading a bonefish flat and casting to tailing fish is, to most flats fishermen, the ultimate experience. The best approach, if weather permits, is to have the sun and wind at your back. The sun coming in behind you will flood light over the flat, illuminating the bottom and reflecting off any tails that may be sticking out through the surface. If you see tails and are patient, you can determine

A bonefish feeding among the mangroves in the Bahamas. In clear, shallow water like this, bonefish are very spooky, so it's crucial to spot them before you're on top of them. In this case, you'd wait until the fish moved out of the mangroves to cast to it.

the direction the tailing fish are moving. Put yourself in position to cast and intercept the fish.

Most shallow flats are ankle- to knee-deep. The bottom colors may vary, and the bonefish are experts at camouflaging themselves within this environment. New anglers often find it difficult to see the fish. If the fish are on the flat but not tailing and you don't know what to look for, you simply may never see them. You see the bottom and the surface glare, but you don't see the fish.

When the bonefish feeds, it pushes its head into the sand or mucky bottom to excavate its prey. It leaves behind a hole shaped like its snout, which is a telltale sign to the angler that a bonefish has been there. You can tell how fresh the feeding holes are by how well they are defined. If the hole has started to show signs of filling in, it is old, and the bonefish is probably long gone. But if the hole is sharply defined on the edges, the bonefish may not be far away. Large schools of fish leave many holes, whereas a single or pair of feeding fish may leave only a few. Bonefish generally feed on a flat by going into or against the tide, allowing the currents to bring the scent of their prey to them.

Another way to detect feeding fish, especially in deeper water, is by the murkiness of the water. When a large school of bonefish feed, they often stir up the bottom sediment, and the water turns chalky gray. Generally, the darker the water, the fresher the mud. Murky areas can vary in size from small puffs made by a single or pair of feeding fish to an acre or more of chalky gray water created by a large school.

Fly-fishing for bonefish on a shallow flat is a sight-fishing game: You need to see the fish before you can cast to it. A pair of polarized sunglasses, preferably in a copper or yellow-brown colored lens, will help make this easier. Bonefish are almost always moving when they're on a flat, so you'll be looking for a moving profile against the bottom. Most flats are carpeted in a mixture of browns, olives, and tans, though some have a light, sand-colored bottom.

Flats covered with turtle grass are usually the most difficult in which to spot fish. The bonefish frequenting these flats generally have much darker backs than those feeding over lighter bottoms. To the unskilled eye, they may seem invisible.

A few years ago, we were making our way across a shallow turtle grass flat with our guide, Simon Bain, in the Bahamas. Simon stopped and whispered, "Bonefish forty feet, twelve o'clock moving to our right. Cast quickly." Cast to what? Where? Are you sure? We tried in vain to see what Simon had observed, but all we could see was the waving action of the turtle grass. We were good at finding trout, but it quickly became apparent that this was a different ballgame.

Wakes or ripples on the surface can give away the position and direction of traveling fish. Look at the bottom and watch for anything moving across it. Bonefish will often zigzag back and forth across a flat, and the sun will reflect off the side of the fish as they turn, creating a momentary flash.

Fishing to the Bonefish

Although wading a bonefish flat restricts your vision and makes it harder to spot fish, your lower profile can help you get closer to the fish. This means that longer casts are often not necessary. There have been times when we've cast to tailing fish less than 20 feet away. When wading, always keep enough fly line out to be ready to make a quick cast. Collect a few coils of fly line, and carry it in your rod hand. Keep the tapered leader and a short section of fly line out beyond the rod tip, and hold the fly in the other hand. On clean flats with no coral, about 15 feet of fly line can be trailed behind. With one quick cast, the line, leader, and fly can be in the air.

A problem with this arrangement is that the trailing fly line often sinks below the surface and collects weeds or, worse, gets caught up in coral or the bottom. Consequently, you'll have to backtrack to retrieve the line, and it's hard to make a quick cast without the line being up on top of the water.

Saltwater fly lines, because of their density and thin running line, never float well for long periods of time. The saltwater tapers have fewer air cells than their freshwater counterparts. For the past few years, we have been fishing with bass bug tapers whenever we wade flats for extended periods. The bass bug taper basically has the same profile as the saltwater taper, but it's thicker in diameter, allowing for more air bubbles and better floatability. If we were concerned with really long casts, this softer freshwater fly line would

Whether you're wading or in a boat, it's important to keep a low profile and to hold your rod tip low when stripping in line.

never work, but under the circumstances, the bass bug taper and running line trailing behind float high and come off clean and quickly.

Never hurry across a flat; stay alert and watch for any signs of moving fish. Tails, flashes, puffs of mud, even fleeing schools of small baitfish leaping and dancing across the water can give away the position of a bonefish. Keep the sun and wind at your back whenever possible. Once you've spotted the fish and have determined which direction it's moving, cast your fly well ahead of the fish so as not to spook him. In calm water, you may want to lead the fish by at least 10 to 12 feet. If the water is choppy because of wind, you may be able to cast closer.

After the cast is made, keep your rod tip low and just above the surface. Start your retrieve when the bonefish is close enough to see the fly. It's easy to get excited and retrieve too fast. Let the fish see the fly, and then start with a series of quick, 10- to 12-inch retrieves, followed by a series of slower ones. Don't be afraid to experiment. Some bonefish will jump on a fly that is being quickly retrieved; others quickly lose interest.

Experiment, too, with both the length and speed of your retrieves. In the Yucatan, the bonefish guides want a slow, short retrieve; in Los Roques, they ask for longer, faster ones.

Because of the position of the bonefish's mouth, it's almost impossible to actually see the fish take the fly. Instead, you need to rely on feel to strike and set the hook. The take is often a soft tightening of the line or a soft tick or tug, similar to that of a trout taking a slowly retrieved wet fly.

Once the fish has taken the fly, set the hook by slip-striking with the fly line, not by raising the rod tip. If you miss the fish by slip-striking, you've only moved the fly a short distance, and the fish is likely to take it a second time. If you lift the rod tip, you will pull the fly out of reach of the bonefish, and maybe out of the water completely. If it is still looking for the fly, the fish won't be able to find it.

Lifting the rod tip to set the hook will quickly tell your guide that you are indeed a trout fisherman. It's one of the hardest habits to break when going from fresh to salt. We can't tell you how many saltwater guides have had a good laugh after watching a trout fisherman raise the rod tip, thus losing the fish.

Once the bonefish is hooked, be prepared to clear the line and get the fish on the reel. The first run almost always goes well into the backing before the fish can be turned. This is usually followed by a second and often third run before the bonefish is ready to be landed. Bonefish don't give up easily, so be prepared to spend the time necessary to revive a tired fish by moving it back and forth in the water, allowing oxygen into its gills before releasing it.

One of the most frustrating experiences in flats fishing is spooking unseen fish. You may be carefully wading a flat, and then you spot a tailing fish and the stalk begins. In a heronlike crouch, you painfully work your way into a casting position. The cast looks perfect, the leader and fly are going to land ahead of the feeding fish, and then, in that split second as the fly line lands on the water, all hell breaks loose. Bonefish shoot off in every direction, one spooking the other in a chain reaction. It is now obvious that the tailing fish you saw was just one of many in a school traveling across the flat. It happens to all of us, and it will happen to you.

In deeper water on bright days and on lighter-colored bottoms, it's often possible to see the shadow of the fish even before you see the fish itself. Once you see a moving fish, lock on to it and stay with it through the cast and retrieve. If you look away for any reason and then look back, you may not be able to find the fish; they can vanish quickly.

When fishing from a flats skiff, be aware of where your line is lying on the deck so you're not standing on it when it's time to cast.

Fishing from the bow or deck of a boat being poled across the flat gives you an advantage in seeing the fish. Being elevated allows you to look down and across the flat, easily picking out cruising bonefish. But because you're well above the water, it's also easier for the bonefish to see you.

Many flats boats have a poling platform on the back. The high platform gives the guide a better angle of vision than the angler on the deck. A good guide can spot fish at incredible distances from a poling platform, but many guides feel that the platform also gives away their presence to the fish, and they prefer to simply pole from the back of the boat. Since many flats are too soft to wade, here a flats boat is the answer.

Being prepared on the deck can make the difference between success and failure. After the boat has pulled up on the flat, and while the guide is getting the push-pole ready, make a 50-foot practice cast. Then carefully retrieve and coil the fly line on the deck, making sure it is clear of anything it might foul or get caught in. Hold the rod with the tip pointed slightly down toward the water in your rod hand, and put the fly in the opposite hand. The leader and a section of fly line should be out beyond the rod tip. Make sure that you are not standing on the extra fly line on the deck.

Stay alert and don't get caught daydreaming. It's easy in such a pristine environment to get lost in your thoughts; with the peaceful mood, the sun and the breeze, the click of the push-pole touching down on the coral, it can be mesmerizing. Watch for moving fish, a flash, a tail—any evidence of the presence of bonefish. Listen closely for the word from your guide that he has sighted fish. Whenever possible, a good guide will quickly turn the boat to give you the best shot at a moving fish. He will tell you how far away the fish is, the direction the fish is traveling, and when to cast. This all can take place in a matter of seconds, and you need to be ready. There is no time for fumbling around. Get the line in the air and on its way to the fish.

Bonefish going away are always the hardest fish to catch. More often than not, the fish is spooked by the line or the leader. Bonefish have a hemispherical field of vision, which allows them to see objects coming from all directions. Whenever possible, try to position yourself at an angle to the moving fish and lead him accordingly.

Once you've made the cast from the bow of the boat, lower your rod tip before you start your retrieve. After a fish is hooked, make sure the outgoing fly line is coming cleanly off the deck. If a knot occurs in your line, quickly turn the rod over so that the knot will clear the guides. If the knot fouls in the guides, point the rod in the direction of the fish and hope the tippet breaks and not the rod.

Choosing the Right Fly for Bonefish

Choosing the right fly will depend mostly on the depth of the water. In skinny or thin water, you need to rely on fly patterns that will enter the water quietly. Bulky or heavily weighted eyes are only going to spook fish when they land, and these flies will hang up on the bottom as they are retrieved. Our favorite patterns for thin water are Gotchas, Bright Eyes, and Skinny Water Clousers tied on smaller, size 6 stainless hooks. There have been times when the fish were so spooky that we went to size 8 hooks tied in the same patterns.

For deeper water, we rely on Gotchas and Clousers, tied with heavier-weighted eyes on size 4 and 6 hooks, and on our own Silly Legs bonefish pattern. Incorporating lifelike rubber legs on this pattern has saved the day for us more than once.

Smaller permit crabs tied on size 6 hooks can be a great choice when the bonefish are really selective. Pez Raton Bonefish Lodge in Los Roques has knee-deep, hard-bottomed flats that make wading easy. The size and numbers of bonefish are outstanding, but we initially found the fish to be fussy, often refusing the regular fare of bonefish patterns. Then we decided to try a size 6 crab pattern, and fish after fish inhaled those crabs. When we were leaving the lodge, the guides coaxed us to give them the rest of our crab flies.

Jack Gartside, a well-known fly tier from Boston, uses a smaller white Deceiver as a search fly for bonefish in the Florida Keys with great success. Jack always prefers wading to fishing out of a boat and often finds himself in knee- to waist-deep water, working the ends of the flat where it tapers off into deeper water. Jack says that many times the larger bonefish feel safer working the edges rather than exposing themselves to the dangers of shallow water. It makes sense.

A bonefish outfit and a box of bonefish flies on the front deck of a flats boat, which is designed to provide a stable, tangle-free area for casting.

Because Jack is wading in deeper water, it's unlikely that he is going to see his quarry, so he casts to the edges of the flat, retrieving and searching with the Deceiver. This may sound like a strange approach to a veteran flats angler, but it works for Jack.

As you gain more experience in saltwater flats fishing, you'll find that, just as in fresh water, there are few set rules. What doesn't work in one instance may be the key to the next fishing situation.

Basic Tackle for Bonefish

Most saltwater anglers prefer a 9-foot graphite fly rod. This rod length works for both wading anglers and those fishing from boats. Actions and tapers are available from manufacturers that will give anglers fast line speed to get the line out quickly.

Fly reels should have an adequate drag system and the capacity to carry the intended fly-line size and 150 yards of 20-pound backing.

Just how light or heavy the drag should be set is a matter of personal preference and invites many different opinions. It should be set on the light side, but if it is set too light, when you're quickly stripping additional line from the reel it can overrun and tangle the line.

Lefty Kreh has a unique method of determining the right drag setting for bonefish. Starting with a very light drag, grip the fly line between your lips in front of the reel and pull on the line, adjusting the external drag knob until you can no longer pull off any line. This results in a setting that is on the light side but is heavy enough to prevent the line from tangling when the fish makes its first run.

The first run of the "silver bullet of the flats" will quickly win the respect of any die-hard trout fisherman. If you find you need additional tension, you can palm the reel if it has an external rim. Palming, however, takes a sensitive touch that comes only from experience.

Fly lines that are easy to see will improve your accuracy on a bonefish flat. If you can follow the fly line as it unrolls, you can make a more accurate cast. Good color choices are light tan, cream, or pale yellow. A lighter color also will disappear against the sky much better than a darker color, making it harder for the bonefish to see. A high

Jan Allardt, left, and Cathy stalk bonefish on the skinny-water flats near Peace and Plenty Lodge in the Bahamas. This kind of fishing often requires a lighter-weight outfit, including smaller fly and tippet sizes, because of the shallow water.

John Ebeling, a fine trout fisherman, releases his first permit, a 16-pounder caught in the Yucatan.

overhead cast will almost always be picked up by the bonefish regardless of fly-line color, so use a side-arm cast, keeping a lower line profile to the water when casting to a moving fish.

Eight- and 9-weight floating fly lines are the most popular bonefish line sizes. Overall, these lines will get the fly to the fish on days when wind is a problem, which is almost always, and turn over heavier bonefish flies. On calm days in clear, shallow water, however, a lighter 6- or 7-weight can save the day. You may want to take both.

Fishing out of Bob Hyde's Peace and Plenty Bonefish Lodge in Exuma, Bahamas, the angler faces typical skinny-water situations. Fish here can be so shy that a lighter outfit is almost always necessary. Many of the flats here are hard, white sand, and the fish are always super spooky. So much so, in fact, that a few of the guides want their clients in shorts and bare feet. They are convinced that the fish can feel the vibrations and sounds from wet pant legs and neoprene wading shoes. They also believe that the fish can feel the tension of the heavier 8- and 9-weight fly lines on the water and request lighter 7- or even 6-weight outfits.

Tapered leaders should be at least 9 feet long for bonefish in general; in really skinny water, these may need to be extended to 14 or 15 feet. Most saltwater fly fishermen refer to tippet sizes in pound-test. The average bonefish leader would tip out between 10 and 12 pound-test. In most brands of tippet material, this is compatible with a size 4 or 6 hook. For really spooky fish, you may need to resort to 8- or even 6-pound tippet. These sizes will work with size 6 and 8 hooks. Always keep in mind that the tippet diameter should be compatible with the hook size.

Maxima tippet material is very popular with many flats fishermen. It is abrasion resistant, which is especially important on flats with coral. Maxima is available in different colors; choose the lightest one possible to allow the tippet to blend in with the light sand colors on the bottom.

The Nonslip Mono Loop is our favorite knot for attaching bonefish flies to tippets, although the Improved Clinch Knot, popular with most trout fishermen, will also work. Always moisten knots before tightening them, and double-check your hook points for sharpness.

Bonefish are the perfect choice for the transition from fresh water to salt and for the angler looking for a tropical saltwater destination. We've heard Lefty say more than once that if he could fish for only one fish, it would be a bonefish. That from a man who has fished around the world, catching just about any fish that will take a fly.

Permit

Elusive, suspicious, and cautious, permit will ignore your fly, follow your fly, swim around your fly, and do just about everything except eat the thing. Permit can drive you crazy. But of all the flats fish anglers pursue, none provides such a rush of adrenaline as the permit. It is, without question, one of the greatest challenges on the flats.

Many experienced saltwater fishermen have never landed a permit, although they may have cast to hundreds. Two good friends of ours, Joe and Millie Elgaway, have spent much time and money in pursuit of a permit. They have cast to countless numbers of permit from Honduras to the Yucatan to the Bahamas and have yet to bring one to the boat. They belong to the ranks of many highly skilled anglers eluded by this fish.

Most saltwater guides hold the permit in great esteem. You can always hear the excitement in the guide's voice when he spots a bonefish, but if a permit comes by, the tone changes to escalated urgency. Your knees start to weaken, your pulse quickens, and your hands start to sweat. Maybe you'll see the tail, the dark dorsal fin, and the profile of one of the greatest fish on the flats, and in an instant your line and fly are airborne. What happens next is entirely up to the permit.

Mike Fitzgerald, Jr., helps run a sporting travel business called Frontiers International. Frontiers represents some of the best saltwater lodges in the world, and Mike has fished most of them. Until the fall of 1997, Mike had not yet landed a permit. Fishing out of Boca Paila, Mexico, Mike confessed that he was jinxed when it came to permit. Watching him cast to at least seven different tailing permit in one day without even a hint of interest from the fish confirmed the jinx. Then, a day before Mike had to leave, he made a perfect

Mike Fitzgerald, Jr., with an 18-pound permit, his first on a fly, from Boca Paila, Mexico.

cast to a feeding fish, which engulfed his fly. Thirty minutes later, Mike was carefully releasing his first permit. And so it goes.

Permit belong to the pompano family. They can be found in the Florida Keys, the Bahamas, the coral flats of Honduras, and Mexico's Yucatan Peninsula. The permit spends most of its time in the security of deeper water. It generally comes onto a flat during incoming tides. Its diet mainly consists of crabs, and it is, in a sense, a sight feeder. Along with its marvelous eyesight, the permit can also smell out its prey. In fact, many fly fishermen believe that the permit is so hard to catch because our flies lack the smell of the real crab. There have been instances of desperate fishermen catching a live crab, killing it, dipping their imitation in the crab juice, and then successfully catching a permit. Most saltwater guides would never think of doing this, believing that it's not sporting.

A small permit may only be a couple pounds; larger fish range in the upper 20s or larger. A permit is a permit, however, and most anglers are quite happy catching one of any size.

Seeing the Permit

The permit's body can be almost half as deep as it is long. It's silvery and reflects the colors of the surrounding environment. The dark dorsal fin will often give the fish away as it swims across a flat. The large, forked tail sticking above the surface as the permit tails is a sight one never forgets. Because of the body shape, permit require deeper water to feed in than the bonefish, but both have similar behavior instincts when they come on the flat.

The permit has large eyes, and its eyesight is excellent when it is swimming in a horizontal position, but when tailing, its vision is restricted to a small portion of the bottom.

Permit travel alone, in pairs, or in schools. As with the bonefish, look for nervous water, tailing fish, or a body profile. Guides can quickly identify the permit by the wake it creates as it swims across the flat. We've had guides point to a wake easily 80 yards away and announce, "Permit," and sure enough, as the fish gets closer, the big, black dorsal fin shows up, followed by the large, black tail.

Fishing to the Permit

Like the bonefish, the permit is always alert for danger, which may come from a shark, osprey, or barracuda. Permit have an excellent sense of hearing and will quickly exit if startled, but interestingly, they often don't go far. We've had permit spook because of a bad cast, only to go about 40 yards, slow down, and start feeding again. In the Yucatan, we followed a tailing permit for over an hour, casting at every opportunity, only to have the fish spook, go a short distance, and once more start to feed. We tried every crab pattern in our fly boxes, but nothing short of the real thing would interest him. We never did catch his attention.

Because permit are found in the deeper sections of the flat, most are caught from a boat. A little wind to ripple the surface will help when casting to a permit. The ripples can help cover your cast. The fly needs to get down to the permit so the fish can find it. How far ahead of the feeding fish the fly should be is sometimes hard to determine. Some anglers have successfully dropped the fly to the bottom directly in front of the tailing fish. We've never had any luck doing this. Other tactics include leading the permit by 8 or 10 feet and then starting a slow retrieve, keeping your rod tip low to the water, and moving the crab along the bottom when the permit is close enough to see the fly. This routine has been the most successful for us. Another idea, shared by many, is to put the fly directly in front of the fish and let the permit see it sink to the bottom, leave the fly lie still on the bottom, and watch for the tightening of the fly line as the permit picks it up. This technique has never worked for us, but others have had success with it, so you may want to give it a try.

Permit traveling in schools are sometimes more receptive to a fly than a single tailing fish is. This may be a competitive reaction, but this is only a theory. We've seen it go both ways.

The permit has rubbery lips and a mouth strong enough to crush a crab before swallowing it. As with the bonefish, make sure the hook is sharp, and use your line hand when setting the hook. Once a permit is hooked, the first run may go 100 yards or better, cleaning the reel of fly line and most of the backing.

Permit never give up easily. Be patient, playing a game of give and take with the fly line and

Alfonso, a Boca Paila guide, lands a Yucatan permit for Cathy. The fish hit an LP crab imitation.

backing. When the fish finally comes to the boat, you can grasp it by the hard, narrow area just in front of the tail. Always make sure the spent fish is fully recovered before you release it.

Choosing the Right Fly for Permit

Permit favor crabs more than anything else. Fly tiers like Del Brown, Hank Leonhard, and Enrico Puglisi have worked hard to create lifelike imitations. The first criterion for a permit crab imitation is that it must sink quickly to the bottom. The weight of the eyes and the body material can help accomplish this, and the fly should be easy to cast.

We have tried a number of patterns tied with a hard base of epoxy that are heavy and bulky to cast, creating too much noise when they land on the water. In addition, they often have an unnatural swimming motion. We prefer a crab tied with a softer rug yarn or a new material known as sea fibers. Combined with rubber legs, weighted eyes, and a feather or marabou tail, the crab looks lifelike when retrieved and swims naturally.

Lenny Moffo, a Florida Keys guide, has a fleeing crab pattern that has worked well in both Florida and the Yucatan. It has rubber legs that stick out of the back of the fly, in the tail position. The fly swims well and can be extremely effective.

The color of the crab patterns is important and may vary depending on your destination. Many Florida guides like a natural tan or cream color; in the Yucatan, guides almost always prefer a pattern with chartreuse; and in Honduras, guides like an orange body. We tie one with a tan body and either chartreuse or orange thread ribbing. This combination of popular colors has worked in almost every area.

The size of the crab is also important. In deeper water, a larger, heavier size 2/0 is often needed; in shallow depths, we may go as small and light as a size 6.

Although the emphasis here is on crab patterns for permit, a good number of permit have also been taken on bonefish patterns. We've had success on our own Silly Legs patterns, probably because of the lifelike rubber legs and the tan and white or chartreuse and white color patterns. The Clouser Minnow in chartreuse and white has accounted for a number of good fish. So if you find yourself holding a rod rigged for bonefish and have no time to change flies, make a cast to the permit and try a very slow retrieve.

Most of our permit have been caught when we were fishing or looking for bonefish. Keeping an extra rod in the boat rigged and ready for permit is always a good idea, and a smaller crab pattern tied on a size 6 hook will often work for both bonefish and permit.

Basic Tackle for Permit

Most saltwater anglers feel that the sheer strength of the permit warrants a heavier 9- or 10-weight fly rod. We use a 9-weight for most of our permit

The ghost crab, which the LP Crab imitates, is a favorite prey of permit.

Tiers strive to create realistic crab imitations, like these by Del Brown and Craig Matthews, to fool the elusive permit.

fishing. But in the Yucatan, where the permit run smaller than their counterparts in Florida, we often fish with our standard 8-weight bonefish outfit.

Your fly reel should contain a minimum of 150 yards of backing and a floating saltwater taper fly line. This fish can really tax the drag system on your reel. An inferior drag will quickly succumb to the power of a permit.

The leader should be 9 or 10 feet long, with a heavy butt tapered out to 12- or 15-pound tippet. The larger weighted crab patterns can be hard to turn over, and the heavy butt of the tapered leader will help, especially in windy conditions.

This 30-pound tarpon from the Florida backcountry illustrates why the fish is nicknamed "bucketmouth."

Once, while we were in Mexico, Marc Bale of the Sage Rod Company gave us this worthy advice: "A permit chooses you, you don't choose the permit." After many seasons of casting to this magnificent fish of the flats, we have to agree.

Tarpon

Tarpon fishing can easily be divided into three size categories: baby tarpon, ranging from 5 to 40 pounds; midsize fish of 50 to 80 pounds; and the giant tarpon, in a world of their own, at over 100 pounds. It's hard for any freshwater fly fisherman to imagine a baby fish weighing as much as 40 pounds and one that, once hooked, can jump eye level at the boat. Like the bonefish and the permit, the tarpon is a fish that you will never forget.

We got our feet wet, so to speak, in the coastal saltwater lakes of Mexico, casting to the edges of the mangroves and retrieving Lefty's Deceivers teasing out baby tarpon that averaged 10 to 40 pounds. We later found larger tarpon in Florida, Los Roques, and on the Caribbean coast of Mexico. It's these baby tarpon that have captured our hearts and become our favorite.

Tarpon can be found throughout the southern coast of the United States. In Georgia, off the shoreline of Little St. Simons Island, the big boys sometimes migrate in schools and will put your best tackle to the test. Florida is by far the most popular tarpon destination for most anglers. It's easy to get to, and although the migration of the larger fish will vary, you can almost always find tarpon there. The coastline and back lagoons of Mexico harbor a healthy number of smaller tarpon, as well as some of the giants. Central America is home to the tarpon, and Costa Rica rates high on the list of places to find the silver king. The Bahama Islands can offer tarpon at times when the weather and water temperatures cooperate.

Seeing the Tarpon

Tarpon can be found singly, in pairs, or in schools. Tarpon will breathe air, and the observant angler can often spot the rolling tarpon as he rises to the surface to exhale and inhale. The first time we witnessed this event was in Mexico's Yucatan, where our Mayan guide pointed to a series of pie-shaped air bubble masses on the surface. He said

Cathy hooks a tarpon at the edge of the mangroves in the Yucatan backcountry. Tarpon seek the security of mangrove-lined lagoons like this one. They will give the angler an explosive strike, generally followed by a series of spectacular jumps.

there were tarpon there, and sure enough, we watched as two tarpon rolled not 30 yards ahead of our boat. A Deceiver well placed and retrieved struck home in the 30-pound fish.

Cruising tarpon on flats or along mangrove-lined shorelines will create nervous water or wakes that can give away their position. When a larger fish shows, it can be quite intimidating, considering that the fish may appear to be half as long as the boat. Tarpon, like snook and barracuda, will lie still and wait in ambush for their prey. Being able to identify the silhouettes or profiles of motionless fish will give you an edge. If a tarpon is close to the surface, both the tip of its dorsal fin and its tail may be seen breaking the surface.

Another tarpon giveaway is the "daisy chain." Tarpon often form a tight circle and closely follow each other head to tail. This visible activity, which takes place just below the surface, has been linked to mating habits. The fish come to the surface and roll as they continue to swim in a circle.

If the water is deep and the clarity is poor, tarpon may be hard to see. The only option is to blind-cast to likely looking spots. In Costa Rica's Rio Colorado, for example, the tarpon lie deep in the silt-laden, off-color waters. Heavily weighted flies are necessary to find the fish.

Many of the coastal saltwater lakes of the Yucatan have tarpon. Here the water is often tea-colored, and anglers search by blind-casting flies along the mangrove shorelines.

Fishing to the Tarpon

Because the flats the tarpon frequent are too deep for wading, most tarpon fishing is done from boats. There are occasional instances, however, when a wading angler can have a decent shot at a cruising fish.

Tarpon found cruising in clear-water flats are extremely shy and are often difficult to approach. Most tarpon will not leave the security of deeper water and move onto a flat until the water temperature has reached 75 degrees. The best presentation to a tarpon on a flat is to have the fly cross in front of the fish at its eye level. The fly should be placed well ahead of the tarpon and retrieved slowly. (Most beginning tarpon fishermen retrieve their flies much too fast.)

Tarpon will often follow the fly right up to the boat. You may be standing on the bow, rod tip low, retrieving and watching the tarpon following inches behind your fly. The palms of your hands are sweating, and for the moment time seems to be standing still. You force yourself to breathe. The fish is suspicious, but you continue to retrieve. Something inside you wants to stop the fly and let the fish inhale it, but you know from experience that if the fly stops, tarpon rarely take it. So instead, you try speeding up the retrieve—just a little, not a lot. Let the fish think that at the last moment the fly is going to get away. The fish takes so close to the boat that only a few feet of fly line are left beyond the tip of the rod. Now the fun begins.

The tarpon has an exceptionally large mouth, earning it the nickname bucketmouth from veteran tarpon fishermen. Tarpon have no teeth, but the inside of the mouth has a coarse sandpaper texture and is as hard as cement. Hooks have to be sharp in order to penetrate. Of all the species of inshore saltwater fish, the tarpon is the hardest to get a hook into. Sharpen your hooks, and check them often to keep them sharp.

Once hooked, the fish usually starts with a dramatic leap accompanied by head shaking, trying everything in its power to get rid of the hook. More times than not, the fish is successful. Many times we've watched in awe as a tarpon threw the fly in the midst of an eye-level jump so close to the boat that water from the jump splashed over us. When the jump is in progress, it's important to quickly lower the tip of the rod to create slack so that the fish doesn't come crashing down on the leader. This is referred to as bowing to the fish.

Veteran angler Jack Gartside often fishes for tarpon in the Florida Keys after dark. Jack likes to frequent the bridges in the middle Keys. Tarpon can be heard crashing bait here after dark, and most of the fishing is blind casting, although sometimes on moonlit nights, the silhouettes of rolling tarpon can be seen. Another good place to look for tarpon, Jack says, is in lagoons near fish markets or processing plants. Tarpon hang out here feeding on the fish remains and extract.

Choosing the Right Fly for Tarpon

The right tarpon fly generally depends on conditions. On a clear-water flat, a fly that lands quietly and looks alive as it is retrieved usually works best. Deceivers dressed in white or a combination of blue and white are favorites of ours. An all-black Deceiver is also a good color to rely on. Another pattern that has saved the day for us more than once is the Cockroach, which is a combination of grizzly hackle and brown bucktail.

In off-color water, bulkier designs such as those tied by Hank Leonhard and Enrico Puglisi push water and are noisier when they are retrieved, making it easier for the tarpon to locate the fly. Surface poppers can also bring a tarpon up, and casting to the edges of the mangroves in search of tarpon that run from 5 to 30 pounds can be great sport with an 8-weight outfit and a surface popper.

It's interesting that tarpon, even the big boys, seem to prefer a fly that is 3 to 4 inches long. That's not a very large fly for these huge fish, but nevertheless, the smaller flies work. For big fish, flies dressed on size 3/0 hooks are usually a good choice, and for smaller fish, flies dressed on smaller, 1/0 hooks work well.

Basic Tackle for Tarpon

Small, baby tarpon are fun fish on an 8-weight outfit. But for the big fish, you need to consider some serious gear. Seasoned tarpon fishermen usually prefer an 11- or 12-weight outfit, but a lot of big fish are landed on a more user-friendly 10-weight. Leverage and lifting power—enough to lift a 100-pound (or more) fish off the bottom—are important. Many rod companies offer a cork fore grip for fighting fish as an option on tarpon rods.

A fly reel takes a lot of abuse from a big tarpon, so don't skimp here; buy the best you can afford. The drag needs to be smooth and durable, able to stand the strength of a tarpon at full bore on a first run that could go 200 yards. The reel needs to handle a minimum of 250 yards of backing in addition to the fly line. A fly reel with a large arbor recovers line faster, and this can be a real advantage in a fight with a tarpon.

Most fly fishing for big tarpon is sight fishing, and a floating line is normally all that's needed. You'll need a line designed for superquick presentations. Scientific Anglers offers a tarpon taper with a short, heavy head that does a great job of getting the fly quickly to the fish. There are exceptions, though. For example, in Costa Rica's Rio Colorado, the fish are deep, and a sinking line is often needed to find them.

When you first pick up a tarpon outfit, it's scary. Your entire 3-weight trout outfit probably weighs less than the tarpon reel alone. In most cases, you are not going to be doing a lot of casting. In one day of tarpon fishing with a guide in the Florida Keys, we made a total of seven casts to five different fish. Usually, you get just one chance at a fish, and you need to make it count.

A standard tarpon leader is 9 feet long, with a heavy butt section, followed by a 20-pound class tippet, and finally a foot-long section of 100-pound mono shock tippet. We use the same leader length for the smaller tarpon but reduce the shock tippet to 70 pounds. If we have to use sinking lines for fish that are lying deep, we shorten the leader to 6 feet.

Check your knots, and then check them again; giant tarpon will put them to the test. Keep your hooks sharp. If you're looking for a battle, the giant tarpon is a more than worthy opponent.

Snook

This mysterious fish of the mangroves makes its home in parts of Florida; the Caribbean, including Mexico's Yucatan; and Central America. The personality and character of the snook are often compared to the largemouth bass. Like most inshore fish, snook are very susceptible to cold temperatures and will leave the flats when water temperatures drop, retreating to deeper water until the water warms again.

Snook feed primarily on baitfish but will also eat crabs and shrimp. They like to hide in waiting under mangrove cover or in deeper depressions or channels on a flat. They hear very well through the lateral lines that parallel the sides of the body and often leave the security of the mangrove cover to investigate interesting noises.

Florida is probably the most popular destination for snook fishing, but we have had some tremendous fishing out of Boca Paila in the Yucatan. Our largest, to date, is a 25½-pound fish that engulfed Cathy's white Deceiver.

Paul Bandini with a 10-pound tarpon from the Yucatan. Fish between 8 and 30 pounds are known as baby tarpon.

Seeing the Snook

Mysterious, secretive, and ghostlike, the snook can be a difficult fish to spot, especially if it is hiding under overhanging mangroves. A series of small, mangrove-lined islands in the Yucatan, which we like to call snook hotels, harbor some very large snook.

Cathy releases a 25-pound snook taken at Boca Paila on a white Lefty's Deceiver.

To detect snook that are lying motionless, hidden beneath the mangrove cover, look for shadows or profiles of the fish. Sometimes only the head or tail of a stationary fish can be detected. Other times the snook slowly cruise along the edges of the mangroves.

The snook is long-bodied in profile, but thick through the middle. It has an interesting depressed upper snout, and the lower jaw protrudes out beyond the upper jaw. The color patterns vary depending on the environment, but most snook have a brownish gold back and silvery tan sides, with pronounced black lateral lines. The snook also has a set of extremely sharp gill rakers that can easily cut through a monofilament leader.

Fishing to the Snook

Mexican guides prefer that the fishermen see snook before casting. One excellent guide out of Boca Paila claims that blind-casting to the edges of the mangroves wastes too much time. He likes to pole along, looking for snook lurking just underneath the cover. If a guide thinks he might have seen a fish, he'll often stick the end of his pole in the water and swish it around. Sometimes this noise will bring the fish out to investigate.

An angler casts for snook on the edge of the mangroves in Boca Paila.

A 12-pound snook that fell for a Jack Gartside pattern comes to the net. Note the heavy shock tippet, a must when snook fishing.

One advantage to this kind of fishing is that the angler's line doesn't get caught in the mangroves from blind-casting. It takes a pretty accurate caster to work the edges of the mangroves without getting the fly caught in the brush. The flies are often bushy and wind-resistant, and it's hard to get close without getting *too* close.

In most cases, you will need a boat to fish for snook. If the fish is hiding under a mangrove, the fly needs to be accurately cast, dropped at the very edge of the bush, and allowed to sink. Once you're sure that the fish can see it, start a slow retrieve. A snook often acts like a tarpon, following the fly right up to the boat before taking it, sometimes with its nose on it all the while. Keep your rod tip low to the water, and set the hook with the line hand when the fish takes the fly.

Although we rarely see snook out on open flats away from cover, we have found a few fish working the edges of oyster bars. Tactics here require a leading cast, allowing the fly time to sink so that the fish can intercept it. Use a slow retrieve, speeding it up only if the snook follows the fly for a distance but does not commit to taking it.

Snook can also be found feeding on baitfish in the surf, and here you can often wade to within casting range. Along the coast of Mexico, we often fish the oceanside mouth of an inlet, where in late October and November the snook congregate to feed on baitfish moving on the outgoing tide. Hovering gulls tell us that the baitfish are present. A fast-sinking sinking-tip line and a weighted fly are usually necessary to get down to the fish. In one evening, Jim Gilmore of Bellerose, New York, using a fast-sinking line and a baitfish pattern, landed eleven snook that ranged from 10 to 18 pounds. It was fast and furious for a while, but we never saw it like that again.

Many snook fishermen prefer night fishing. In Florida, snook can be found after dark around lighted boat docks and highway bridges that cross waterways, looking for baitfish that are attracted to the lights.

Choosing the Right Fly for Snook

A blue and white Lefty's Deceiver is at the top of the list for snook. Most of our larger fish have been caught on Deceivers. All-white and red and white Deceivers have also worked for us, as has a brown and grizzly Cockroach. In deeper water, try a Clouser Minnow in blue and white, with larger weighted eyes.

An all-white surface popper works well in the surf if the snook are close to the surface and feeding on baitfish. Poppers can also work well when you blind-cast them to the edges of the mangroves. The snook's curiosity about noise will often bring them out in a rush from under the mangroves to engulf a popper.

Basic Tackle for Snook

This is a strong, determined fish that, once hooked, will head directly back to the mangroves for cover. It takes a strong set of brakes to stop him.

In the backcountry in Mexico, our guide, Victor, was poling us through a tight channel of water that opened up into a dish-shaped area the size of a small pond. "Big snook live here," Victor said in a whisper. To our left, we spotted three snook in the 12- to 18-pound class. They were slowly working the edge of the mangroves and swimming in our direction. The fly line was in the air when Victor pointed out another fish following about 10 feet behind the first three. This was a huge fish that seemed to have appeared out of nowhere.

The cast was quickly adjusted, and the Deceiver dropped in front and just to the right side of the big fish. With complete confidence, the snook took the Deceiver on the first cast. That was the easy part. It went downhill from there.

There was no stopping the fish; it simply turned and headed into the mangroves. The 8-weight rod bent in half, and the reel protested. Victor was yelling from the back of the boat, "Stop him! Stop him!" But there was no stopping the snook, and in the end the fish won. What fly line was left was stripped of the coating for the first 30 feet from the abrasion of the mangroves. The monofilament leader and 50-pound shock tippet were missing, along with a front section of fly line. Victor estimated the snook at 30 pounds. We'll never know for sure.

After our encounter with that monster snook, we moved up to a stronger 9-weight rod. We know a number of serious snook fishermen who rely on a 10-weight. In mangrove country, snook are generally hooked within a few feet of the mangroves. You have to be able to turn the fish away, and it's going to take a strong, stout rod to do that.

You also need a reel with a superior drag. The fish seldom run far, but they run hard.

Most of our snook fishing is done with a floating fly line. There are times when fishing in the surf, however, when a sinking-tip line is needed to get down to where the fish are holding before the surf moves the fly away. A 9-foot leader combined with a 70-pound shock tippet is fine for most snook fishing with a floating fly line. The snook has a transparent cutter blade in the middle of the outer area of the gill plate that is as sharp as a knife and can quickly cut through lighter monofilament.

A stripping basket is a real plus for fly-line control when you are wading. You won't need one in a boat, where the line can lie on the deck.

Barracuda

This toothy flats predator lives in the tropics and is long, fast, and vicious. It may remind freshwater fishermen of a large northern pike or muskellunge. Many saltwater guides discourage clients from casting to barracuda because of their dislike for the fish. It's quite common for a barracuda to rush in on a hooked bonefish and simply tear the fish from the leader for an easy meal.

But if you like searing runs from a fish that can greyhound across the water, and if you like watching a fish charge the fly with a vengeance, then you'll like the barracuda. This is one hot fish that can get your attention, and the barracuda has saved many a fishless day for us.

Seeing the Barracuda

Big barracuda like to hang out on the edges of flats and in channels, staying just deep enough to be hard to spot. From their vantage point, they can quickly ambush any unsuspecting fish that happens to come by. Barracuda will work the knee-deep edges of mangroves and often lie concealed in the shadows.

Cathy holds a nice barracuda from Boca Paila. These toothy fish require a wire tippet.

The barracuda is long and slender in profile, like fish of the pike family. It has an olive-gray back that bleeds into lighter or silvery olive sides. The jaws are long, with a mouthful of teeth that by all means should be avoided. Barracuda love mullet, and you can often see them bursting into a school of mullet, followed by total chaos as the mullet flee in all directions.

Fishing to the Barracuda

For the awesome predators that they are, barracuda are still very spooky fish and will flee at a bad cast or anything that suggests danger. Never cast over the fish; the shadow of the line will spook him. Instead, put your fly out to the side where the barracuda can see it. You want the fish to think it's food that is getting away. The barracuda has excellent eyesight and will easily spot your fly.

Use as fast a retrieve as you can. Your fly needs to zip through the water, so put some heat on it and make medium to long retrieves.

You'll have shots at barracuda both while wading and while fishing from a boat. Beware of an unhappy barracuda in a boat; those razor-sharp teeth will be snapping at everything within reach, and they can cause serious injury to the unwary angler. It's best to keep the fish in the water and reach down with pliers to remove the fly.

Choosing the Right Fly for Barracuda

Most tackle catalogs recommend the needlefish pattern for barracuda. These flies are long and slender, usually tied in green or chartreuse, and made from various kinds of synthetic materials. We must admit, though, that we've never had much success with needlefish patterns. We have landed a fair number of bigger barracuda, over 4 feet in length, but almost always on a white Lefty's Deceiver or a Gartside white Hackle Deceiver. Because mullet are common food for barracuda, Enrico Puglisi mullet flies have also taken a number of big fish. One thing for certain—with the barracuda's mouth full of teeth, you usually get only one fish per fly.

These flies were victims of barracuda encounters. It's usually one fly, one barracuda.

Basic Tackle for Barracuda

Although smaller barracuda can be a lot of fun on a lighter, 8-weight outfit, the bigger fish require a 9-foot rod for a 9- or 10-weight line. At times, the cast is long, and the searing greyhound runs of a big barracuda require a rod with some backbone.

Your reel needs a drag designed for tough fish and the capacity to hold a minimum of 150 yards of backing. Most barracuda flats fishing is done with a floating fly line. Monofilament leaders should be at least 9 feet in length and include a 6- to 8-inch wire shock tippet for protection against those awesome teeth. Even smaller barracuda will easily bite through a monofilament tippet.

Redfish

This popular southeast coastal fish, also known to anglers as a channel bass, has made a significant comeback, thanks to improved management programs. Redfish can be caught from the coast of New Jersey to Florida, and all the way up the Gulf into south Texas.

Our first encounter with redfish was on the semitropical barrier island of Little St. Simons, Georgia. Our guide, Larry Kennedy, showed us how to blind-cast Clouser Minnows into off-color tidal creeks. Florida's Indian River fishery, especially around the Cape Canaveral area, offers some of the best and most accessible areas for redfish. From Florida's Panhandle to Texas, this is one of the key fish for the fly fisher.

Redfish feed on shrimp and other crustaceans and will take smaller fish, including mullet. The best time to fish for redfish is from late spring to early fall. Redfish prefer warmer water and will refrain from coming onto the flats to feed when a cold front appears. They like marshy, shallow, grass-filled flats and weedy estuaries.

Seeing the Redfish

Because redfish often frequent water that is muddied or off-color, they can be hard to spot. Mostly bottom feeders, they enjoy the security of the cover of turtle grass or other vegetation. At times, when a redfish is rooting on the bottom, its tail will appear above the surface, much like a bonefish.

The redfish, like this one caught off the Georgia coast, is an inshore species whose feeding habits resemble those of the bonefish.

Flip Pallot and Cathy Beck look for redfish on Mosquito Lagoon in Florida. This popular area near Mims is prime habitat for the redfish.

The tail of the redfish is a distinctive bronze color with a black spot or spots. The observant angler can almost always pick up the tailing action of a feeding redfish. Look for wakes from moving fish, and when the water is clear enough, sight-fish to them.

Redfish can be found singly or in small schools. Look for them around oyster bars, tidal creeks, and deeper channels that cut through low-water flats. The redfish profile is basslike, but the snout is turned down like that of a bottom feeder. The color from the top of the back and down the sides of the fish is coppery; the tail has a more bronzy cast.

Fishing to the Redfish

Redfish are thought to have poor eyesight, so whenever possible, put the fly directly in front of the fish. It's important to retrieve the fly slowly at the fish's eye level so that it can see the fly. This method works well when you can see the fish, but if you're wading or fishing from the bank of a tidal creek, you often have no choice but to shotgun the water with your fly, searching the bottom and covering as much water as possible.

This kind of fishing takes a degree of patience, but if redfish are in the area, it almost always pays off. Most of the redfish we've caught have been in the 5- to 15-pound range. Some of the really big fish are 40 pounds or more. Redfish will put up a good fight, but there will be no long, fast runs like those of a bonefish.

Choosing the Right Fly for Redfish

Chartreuse and white Clouser Minnows and red and white Don Blanton's Whistlers top our list of favorite flies for redfish. The fly needs to be retrieved slowly along the bottom, and the lead eyes on the Clouser will help get the fly down where it needs to be. Both have produced fish from Georgia to Florida for us. Because redfish are often found in a weed-choked environment, the addition of a weed guard on your fly can be helpful.

Although redfish primarily look to the bottom for their food, a surface popper can sometimes bring the fish to the surface. At other times, it can scare them off the flats, but it's worth a try. An all-white foam popper is hard to beat if you like surface action.

Basic Tackle for Redfish

The standard 9-foot fly rod for an 8- or 9-weight line will handle the average 5- to 15-pound redfish. A 10-weight or heavier rod is a better choice for the really large fish. We do most of our flats fishing with a floating fly line, although redfish often frequent flats that have a lot of surface scum, weeds, and debris. Here, a slow-sinking fly line will put the fly underneath the floating weeds.

There will be no long runs from a redfish, but it's still wise to have a good drag system and at least 150 yards of backing on your fly reel. It's possible that you may run into another species of fish in the same area. You may want to add a 30-pound shock tippet to your monofilament leader, since the redfish is notorious for rubbing its nose into the bottom as it tries to dislodge the fly.

Jacks

Jacks are truly underrated sport fish. There are twenty-one species of jacks found in tropical and subtropical American waters, but it's the jack crevalle that most flats fishermen know.

Early in our saltwater fishing career, we spent a few days with a guide in Florida. Fishing had been slow, and we pulled up on the edge of a flat. Our guide was studying the water before poling, when a school of larger fish started busting mullet. Fish were going everywhere, as our guide informed us that it was a school of jacks. The first cast, with a white Deceiver, hooked an unbelievably strong fish. The fight started with a rush of fly line and backing disappearing from the reel. With the fly rod bent in half, the guide shouted advice, and we watched as the second run started.

Twenty minutes into the fight, the fish showed no sign of tiring. In fact, the jack never gave up fighting until our guide put him in the net. Over 20 pounds of muscle and bone lay on the bottom of the boat. Even after such a long, hard fight, the fish swam away when released as if the battle had never happened.

The jack crevalle is often mistaken for a permit. Both fish are similar in color and profile, and both belong to the family Carangidae, but that's where the resemblance ends. The permit is well known for its fussy behavior and reluctance to take a fly. The jack crevalle, on the other hand, is a true predator in every sense of the word and will charge with speed and accuracy at almost anything that appears to be edible.

Even a 2-pound jack can put up a fuss. A 15-pound fish will fight for thirty minutes or more, but a jack over 30 pounds will be a fish to remember.

Christmas Island, a well-known bonefish destination, is home to the giant trevally, a fish that looks like a big crevalle. Trevally grow to truly humongous proportions; record catches of fish over 100 pounds have occurred.

Seeing the Jack

Jacks motor across a flat, and any unlucky smaller fish that get in the way are history. Jacks leave a distinct wake, whether they're traveling singly, as a pair, or in a school. They are always on the move, first in one direction, then another. Jacks seem to prefer flats 3 or 4 feet deep; we rarely see them in thin water. Look for the really big fish to be patrolling the deeper edges of the flats, where they can intercept prey that outgoing tides bring them.

From a distance, a jack and a permit look very much alike, with the same body profile and large forked tail, but the permit, if it is hunting for food, will be moving along slowly, looking for crabs and stopping occasionally to tail and eat. The jack, on the other hand, rarely slows down for anything.

Jacks can also be found in the surf, running the edges of beaches and chasing baitfish. If the light is right, you can sight-fish to them. We have taken a number of big jacks up to 25 pounds in the surf, just walking and watching for signs of fish.

Because jacks prefer deeper water, the angler fishing from a boat will have more shots than the wading angler, although wading and fishing in the surf can be very productive when jacks are around.

Fishing to the Jack

This is a fish that responds like the barracuda to fast retrieves, but unlike the barracuda, which often sits in ambush, the jack will be on the move. Once you see it, you usually get only one shot. The fly needs to lead the fish by 8 or 10 feet. Start your retrieve as soon as the jack can see the fly, which will be almost as soon as it hits the water.

Joe and Millie Elgaway with a 25-pound jack taken on a white popper in the surf at Boca Paila.

Barry hefts a 27-pound jack taken on a white Lefty's Deceiver in a saltwater lagoon in Mexico.

Once the jack is hooked, plan to spend some time fighting the fish, and be prepared for some very long runs.

I once watched Joe Elgaway of Tully, New York, as he hooked a big jack in the surf in Mexico. He played the fish for almost fifty minutes before he finally beached it. The jack had made three consecutive runs that took the fly line and over 100 yards of backing from the reel before Joe had any kind of control over the fish. Jacks are a lot of fish for their weight.

We've had some great fun at night fishing to smaller jacks that come to feed on the baitfish attracted to lights on boat docks. The jacks will charge in from the cover of darkness, pick off their prey, and then disappear just as quickly.

Be especially careful with a jack once you have landed it. Most jacks have sharp spines near the anus that can hurt, and they have soft rays in the dorsal fin that should be avoided.

Choosing the Right Fly for Jacks

Jacks will eat just about anything that is retrieved, but it's hard to beat a white or a blue and white Deceiver. An all-white Clouser Minnow with weighted eyes also works well in the surf, and if you really want some fun, try a white or yellow surface popper, which can provide an explosive response from jacks both on the flats and in the surf.

Basic Tackle for Jacks

For the really big boys, including the trevally, a 9-foot graphite rod for a 10-weight line will give you the needed muscle to fight these strong fish. If you plan to fish often for jacks, you should consider an even heavier outfit. Look for a fly reel with a superior drag system and the capacity to hold a minimum of 200 yards of backing. A floating fly line is fine for the flats, but there are times in the surf and deeper lagoons when a fast-sinking sinking-tip line can be to your advantage. Monofilament leaders should be equipped with a 50- to 70-pound shock tippet.

Striped Bass

The east-coast stripers have brought more fly rodders to the salt than any other fish in the history of fly fishing. The striper's popularity has made a huge impact on the fly-fishing industry in general, and striper rods, lines, leaders, and hundreds of new striper fly patterns are available. Look at any fly-fishing magazine and you will probably find a story on how or where to catch striped bass. There is no doubt that this is the hottest fish around.

There are a number of reasons for this. Stripers are found from the coast of Maine south to North Carolina. They are readily accessible to anglers with beachfront homes or backyards that border tidal rivers. Access to stripers is easy because they are basically inshore fish that prefer to stay along the coastline or travel into tidal creeks, estuaries, and rivers. Stripers come to flies readily and grow to impressive sizes, with many weighing 50 pounds or more.

Theodore Gordon fished for stripers, as did Joe Brooks, who in 1948 landed a world-record fish of 29 1/2 pounds. At the time, both anglers were well known in trout circles around the world. In the early 1980s, striper populations reached an all-time low. Better management of both commercial and sport fisheries helped the striper make a comeback, and by the end of that decade, the future looked good again.

There are two primary spawning grounds for the striped bass: the Chesapeake Bay and North Carolina area, and the Hudson River in New York. The Chesapeake Bay, the largest estuarine system in the nation, is the major spawning area for most of the migratory striped bass that find their way along the coast, including those on their way to northern Maine.

Stripers tend to move in schools. The smaller fish, known as schoolies, often travel together in large numbers; the larger fish tend to school but are generally in smaller groups. Like most saltwater fish, they are sensitive to water temperature. The east-coast fishery generally starts in late March or early April, after the water temperature has reached 50 degrees. How far and how fast the fish move up the coast in the spring depend on the temperature.

The first fish to show up are the schoolies, which spend their time in the mouths of rivers and estuaries feeding on menhaden and alewives. The larger fish usually start their migration in mid to late May. The fishing along the east coast holds up through the fall season or until colder water temperatures force the stripers south in search of warmer water.

Winter fishing in November and December can produce some of the best fish of the season in the

Lefty Kreh looks on as Paul Dixon holds a nice striper, the most sought after inshore species on the East Coast. LEFTY KREH PHOTO

Jack Gartside releases a striper to a coastal river in Massachusetts. He caught the fish on a Gurgler, a fly he designed for the species (see page 76).

Chesapeake Bay area, and veteran striper guides will anchor their boats near the bay bridge and watch as clients cast fast-sinking lines and weighted Clouser Minnows looking for the fish of the year.

The west coast also has a striper fishery, thanks to early stockings in the late 1800s of east-coast fish. The San Francisco Bay area offers striper opportunities on the flats, and California anglers can also take advantage of the striper fishery in the Sacramento River delta region.

The diet of a striped bass is determined by the environment the fish is in at the time. It will eat what's available, including smaller baitfish like mackerel and silversides, favorites for the striper. In early May, when schools of sand eels show up, the stripers are quick to take advantage of them. Squid, clams, and crabs may also be on the menu.

Seeing the Striped Bass

Our first experience with stripers was in Newburyport, Massachusetts, with friends Jack Gartside and Kate Lavelle. Our day started on a small tidal river. We waded through a marsh to the water. Our fishing basically consisted of blind-casting to likely looking areas. Stripers love structure—any structure, such as fallen trees, rocks, undercut banks, anything that could attract and hide smaller baitfish. We concentrated on these areas, and at the end of the day, we were all tired from catching fish. The fish were not large, but they were strong and plentiful. At Jack's suggestion, we used light 6-weight outfits, which made fishing more fun. The next day found us wading the coast, fishing around some serious rock formations to bigger fish with heavier gear, but it was still blind-casting to likely looking areas.

Knowing the fish's habits can help you find stripers. This is a fish that feeds with the tides. Moving water brings the smaller baitfish to the striped bass. They love to wait in outflows and inlets for the tide to bring along an easy dinner. Learn all you can about the tides and the bottom areas where you fish. Bottom depressions often hold baitfish, and the stripers will be there waiting. Look for eddies where smaller baitfish might congregate or points of land where water may funnel baitfish to the striper. Watch the gulls, terns, and other shorebirds; they will help you locate schools of baitfish. Find those and you will find the stripers.

Striped bass act very much like trout holding in current. Whenever possible, a trout will face into the current flow and let the current bring food to it; the striped bass will do exactly the same. Pay attention to tide currents, and expect the striper to be facing into the flow.

The best fishing days for stripers are overcast and gray. Stripers do not like bright sunlight and often retreat to the comfort of deeper water. On bright days, the best fishing will be in the early morning and late afternoon.

Power plants provide warmer outflows that attract baitfish and stripers, especially during the colder months. These areas often provide good fishing.

Stripers can be found on some really shallow flats at times, pushing wakes of water as they search for food. Look for these wakes, and if the water is clear enough, you can sight-fish. This is our favorite fishing when we can find it. Some of the flats along the New England coast are soft and require a boat for access, but many areas have a firm bottom that can be waded.

Some of the largest stripers have been caught after dark. The larger fish are more comfortable feeding then and often can be located by the sounds they make as they move in on crashing bait. Check out the area you plan to night-fish during daylight, looking for structure, eddies, or channels that you should cover after dark.

Beaches are popular areas for stripers. Look near the edge of the water before wading out; the fish may be right next to shore, especially in the early morning hours.

Fishing to the Striped Bass

Anglers new to striper fishing often retrieve the flies too fast. Striper fishermen use some retrieve tactics that may be unfamiliar to trout fishermen. After the cast is made, the angler tucks the rod up under the armpit, with most of the handle and the reel extending back behind him. The rod tip is pointed down, with the tip as close to the water as possible. At this point, he reaches up and takes the fly line near the stripping guide, pulling slowly, while the other hand reaches forward and takes the line again just behind the stripping guide. This hand-over-hand retrieve looks like hand lining, and essentially it is.

What this method of retrieving does is keep the fly slowly moving through the water rather than the move-stop retrieve used by most trout fishermen. When a fish takes the fly, the hook is set with the hand and not the rod tip. By using this method, you can feel even the slightest tension on the line by a soft take and can respond by striking. This technique works well and is easy to master.

Like trout, striped bass often hold in current flows that bring food to them. Wet-fly and dead-drift nymph tactics used for trout work under these conditions. Fish the flies across the current at the depth of the fish.

If you cannot sight any fish, shotgun the water with your casts, covering likely looking water. You may be at the mouth of a tidal river, in a back lagoon, or on the beach. If the tide is right and you know the area is good, start with a series of short casts, retrieving a Deceiver or a Clouser. Cover all the angles, extending your cast continually, searching and finally reaching out with a series of longer casts, then repeating the process.

Searching the water is a game of presentation, patience, and experimenting. Let the fly sink to different levels, try different retrieve speeds, and experiment with different patterns and colors. Move around, trying different sections of water. Most freshwater fishermen have used these search-and-retrieve tactics to fish through sections or pools on a trout stream or river.

Choosing the Right Fly for Striped Bass

A baitfish pattern is always the most effective when fishing for stripers, and chartreuse and white is usually the first choice. Color may be more important than the actual design of the pattern itself. There is something about chartreuse that seems to appeal to stripers. There may be a logical reason for this. Many baitfish that the striper feeds on, such as mackerel, menhaden, silversides, and sand eels, have greenish backs and lighter sides and bottoms. The chartreuse and

Cathy casts an 8-weight line for stripers in a Massachusetts tidal river in June. Slower retrieves are generally better for striped bass.

white flies probably are taken by the striper as one of these favorite foods.

Lefty Kreh believes that the length of the fly is critical to success and suggests that you try to determine the kind of baitfish the stripers are feeding on and match their length. At times a really large fly may be needed, such as Bob Popovics's Big One, which can be as long as 12 inches.

Jack Gartside's White Gurgler, a cross between a slider and a popper design, is a fun fly to fish and a great search pattern that can bring fish up to the surface when subsurface flies are not working. It can be made to do many things by manipulating the rod tip. The Gurgler pushes water, creating noise that the striper can hear, and it has all kinds of action in the water.

Chuck Furimsky, who developed bugskin for fly tying, has created a very real-looking sand eel pattern that stripers love. When the stripers are feeding on sand eels, you can always count on Enrico Puglisi's and Page Rogers's sand eel patterns, too. Lou Tabory, one of the pioneers in striper strategies and fly patterns, has designed the White Slab Fly, Sea Rat, and Sand Lance patterns. These flies all belong in your arsenal of striper patterns.

Basic Tackle for Striped Bass

Most serious striped bass fishermen like a 9-foot graphite fly rod for a 10-weight line. The 10-weight will handle the larger flies sometimes used for stripers, as well as the larger fish, especially in the surf. If we were limited to only one outfit, however, it would be a 9-weight. It's easier to cast all day and can handle most of the larger flies. For the smaller schoolies in the tidal rivers, a 6- or 7-weight makes fishing a lot of fun. Captain Norm Bartlett tells us there are also times when he will go to an 11- or 12-weight rod for larger fish in the deeper water of the Chesapeake Bay Bridge area.

Stripers do not generally run long or hard when hooked. A fly reel with a dependable drag and the line capacity to hold 150 yards of backing is adequate. Fly lines for stripers are another matter. You should have a floating line, an intermediate or slow-sinking line, and a fast-sinking one.

Conditions can change as the day progresses. In the early morning hours, the fish may be feeding in skinny water, where a floating line is needed. When the tide changes, the fish move into deeper water, and you'll need a sinking line to get your flies down to the fish. If you're fishing in an estuary where the surface is covered with weeds, the intermediate line will stay just below the surface and not tangle or foul with the floating weeds.

Many saltwater fly lines are designed to work in a hot, tropical environment and will stiffen up and retain memory coils in cold water. Purchase fly lines that are designed for cold water.

A 9-foot leader tapered out to a 12-pound-test tippet is recommended for general striper fishing with a floating line. When fishing larger fly patterns with a sinking line, use a shorter, 6-foot leader tapering out to a compatible hook-tippet diameter.

Proven patterns for striped bass include the red and white popping bug and the Clouser Minnows pictured here. LEFTY KREH PHOTO

Bluefish

We first saw bluefish in a video produced by Bob Popovics. The video gave us a look at what he calls the *bluefish blitz*, a large school of voracious-looking fish slashing bait in what could best be described as a blood bath. What the fish didn't get, the gulls hovering overhead picked up. In all this madness, there was Bob casting into the froth, hooking and playing fish. It was fascinating to watch.

Like the striped bass, bluefish are migratory fish that travel in schools up and down the Atlantic coast, from Florida to Maine, in the spring and fall. They spawn in the Atlantic bights and are sought after by fly rodders all along the coast. Their growth rate is unbelievably fast; bluefish can live up to twelve years and go over 30 pounds. The average bluefish caught by most anglers are in the 6- to 10-pound class. Smaller fish, those in the 2- to 5-pound class, are very common and easy to catch and are referred to by local anglers as snappers.

Bluefish move inshore to feed after the water temperature has reached 60 degrees. They are opportunistic feeders, taking whatever baitfish come along, including one of their favorites, menhaden. They are sight feeders but have an uncanny ability to smell and hear as well, and

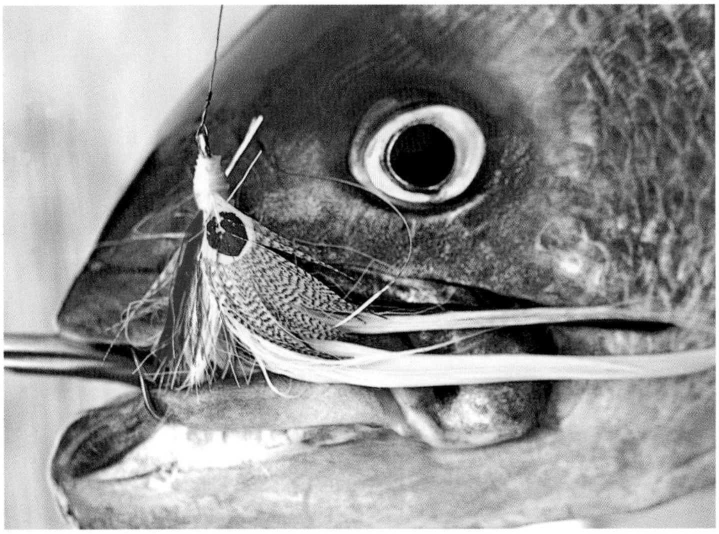

The aggressive bluefish is a favorite of New Jersey anglers. This one fell for an unnamed fly that apparently looked enough like a baitfish for the blue to attack. LEFTY KREH PHOTO

Chumming almost always works when bluefish are in the area. LEFTY KREH PHOTO

like the striped bass, blues feed after dark. They have razor-sharp teeth and will rip apart flies and leaders. Blues will jump and run, putting tackle to the test and quickly earning the respect of first-time anglers.

Seeing the Bluefish

Small bluefish are silvery and bright and remind one of a sockeye salmon fresh in from the sea. As the fish mature, the back becomes a bluish green, with the sides turning a lighter gray. The bluefish has a powerful profile, a large head, strong-looking shoulders, a streamlined body, and a forked tail.

The Atlantic-coast angler contends with bluefish much the same way the tropical angler contends with barracuda. Every fishing writer and fisherman describes the teeth of a bluefish as razor sharp and best avoided. If a bluefish gets a grip on an angler's arm or hand, it simply won't let go. It can cause severe injury.

Birds are always helpful indicators in finding schools of bluefish. Watch how the gulls and terns behave over the water. If the blues are breaking up schools of baitfish, the birds will be picking up pieces of baitfish during the feeding frenzy. The blitz is unmistakable, with water spraying and bait and blues going in all directions.

Fishing to the Bluefish

Boats are a real advantage for finding schools of bluefish, but the wading angler will have plenty of opportunity. If you find a blitz within casting range, it's a simple matter of getting your fly to the fish, a quick retrieve, and a hook-up. Then it gets interesting. It takes some doing on the part of the angler to finally land the fish. Ed Mitchell, in his wonderful book *Fly Rodding the Coast*, describes the bluefish as the most aggressive of all game fish.

Retrieve speeds for bluefish vary depending on water clarity and temperature. This fish expects smaller fish to be fleeing for their lives, so normally the faster the retrieve, the better, although at night or in murky or cold water, a slower retrieve often works better. This holds true for most predator fish, which can sneak up on small prey at night. In murky water, a slower retrieve gives the fish a better chance to find the fly. And most fish are not as active when water temperatures drop, so a slower retrieve may give them a chance to get interested. Set the hook with your line hand, although when a bluefish is on the fly, the fish more than likely will hit the fly so hard that it hooks itself.

Try large surface poppers for some exciting surface action. When blues are breaking, chumming is a popular tactic with some anglers, and putting chopped menhaden out for bait can attract a school of blues and quickly put them on the feed.

Choosing the Right Fly for Bluefish

Bob Popovics has produced a number of flies that are designed primarily for bluefish. These include his Double Header Deep Candy, Silicone, Pop-Lips Silicone, Spread Fleye, and Bob's Banger. Lefty's Deceivers and Clouser Minnows should also be included, along with a few large, white foam poppers.

Basic Tackle for Bluefish

Many anglers who fish in the surf and are handling waves prefer a longer, stout, 9½- or 10-foot graphite rod with a 10-weight line for blues. Unlike stripers, blues will run hard, so your reel needs a good drag system and line capacity for at least 150 yards of backing. It's not unusual for a big bluefish to make a series of reel-wrenching runs.

Floating fly lines are fine for blues near the surface. When the fish are deep, a fast-sinking sinking-tip is a real advantage. If the fish are deep and you have to blind-cast, a full-sinking line may be necessary. A wire tippet should be used. It need not be long, 4 inches of wire is enough. Some anglers prefer to fish a heavy mono shock tippet, but a good-size blue will chomp right through mono.

For your floating line, a 9-foot leader is long enough, and a shorter, 6-foot leader is recommended for both the sinking-tip and the full-sinking line.

A nice bluefish and a variety of Lefty's Deceivers. Patterns that imitate smaller baitfish are the most productive for bluefish. LEFTY KREH PHOTO

False Albacore (Little Tunny)

This sickle-tailed fish is related to the tuna. Never resting and lightning fast when attacking bait, the false albacore can achieve speeds over 30 miles an hour. It is found along the Atlantic coastline from North Carolina to Maine, and it has become a welcome addition for fly rodders all along the coast. On the New England coast, a 10-pounder is a big fish, with the average size being somewhere around 5 pounds. Southern anglers on the coast of North Carolina record fish that sometimes tip the scales at 14 pounds.

Like bluefish, false albacore travel in schools and prefer the safety of deeper water. Summer and early fall are the best times to find schools along the east coast, and the fishing holds until cooler water temperatures send them back south. Anchovies are a favorite item in their diet, but they also eat sand eels, silversides, and other smaller baitfish.

The false albacore has a football-shaped profile. The back is bluish green, with a few wavy lines, and the sides and belly are silvery white. Generally, there will be four or five dark-colored round spots just below the pectoral fin. A steeply angled dorsal fin and a sickled tail help the false albacore attain high speeds.

Seeing the False Albacore

Because of the false albacore's preference for deeper water, the angler with a boat will have more shots at them, although you can expect hook-ups while fishing from a beach or jetty if the fish venture within casting range.

False albacore, nicknamed "albies," will rush in and attack a school of baitfish and seconds later move on in search of another. They can often be seen leaping out of the water as they chase the smaller baitfish. If there is an abundance of baitfish, the albies will stay in the general area until the baitfish leave. The activity of feeding birds will indicate when a school of false albacore is around.

Flip Pallot holds a false albacore he caught on a 10-weight outfit off the Carolina coast. LEFTY KREH PHOTO

Fishing to the False Albacore

False albacore like to trap their prey in schools just below the surface and then come up quickly underneath the baitfish, busting into the school and picking off their victims. Like their cousins the tuna, they travel in a straight line, and your fly needs to be placed so that the fish can see it. Experts argue over whether a fast or slow retrieve is better, but if you talk to the guys who chase this fish with a passion, most believe that a slow to moderate retrieve is best when the fish are feeding on baitfish.

Sometimes success comes because of luck, other times because you managed to get your fly to where the fish were going instead of fishing to where they had been. This is truly a game of hit and run; the fish are here one second, there the next. If you can get ahead of the school, start blind-casting and retrieving as soon as possible.

False albacore are seldom seen feeding after dark. The fishing pretty much slows down in the late afternoon.

Choosing the Right Fly for False Albacore

Because of their preference for anchovies, our favorite pattern is Enrico Puglisi's gray anchovy or a chartreuse and white Clouser Minnow. Any pattern resembling baitfish, sand eels, or baby herring will do the trick.

Basic Tackle for False Albacore

The basic 9-foot graphite rod for a 9-weight line will do the job. The reel should be able to hold the line and 150 yards of backing. There are times when a floating line will work, but a sinking-tip or a full-sinking line will quickly get the flies down to the fish. Many anglers believe that the false albacore has exceptional eyesight and prefer to use a longer, 10-foot leader. With a sinking line, a shorter, 6- or 7-foot leader works better. There is no need for a shock tippet.

Bonito

Many anglers have a problem telling the bonito and the false albacore apart. Both are members of the same family. Their profiles are similar, but the bonito is smaller and a bit more colorful than the false albacore. Both fish feed on basically the same kinds of smaller baitfish, and fishing tactics that work for one will work for the other. Like false albacore, bonito show up in the Northeast in the late summer months and travel south when colder temperatures arrive. Fly patterns, tactics, and tackle that work for the false albacore will also work for the bonito.

Sea Trout

Sea trout, or spotted sea trout, as they are often called, are generally found in schools from the east coast to Texas. This is a popular fish with Florida sportsmen. The Cape Canaveral area is one of the prime spots for bigger fish, which go as large as 6 or 7 pounds.

We caught our first spotted sea trout fishing out of Mims, Florida, with Flip Pallot, not far from Mosquito Lagoon. The fish took a small white Deceiver on a slow retrieve while only a few miles away the *Challenger* was in a final countdown for its liftoff into space. As the rockets fired, the bottom of the lagoon trembled. Above the noise, Flip said, "Folks, that's the sound of freedom." We'll never forget that day.

The spotted sea trout is a distant relative of the trout, but don't expect it to take Quill Gordons off the surface.

Spotted sea trout are very popular with Florida fly fishers and prefer a diet of shrimp and small baitfish. LEFTY KREH PHOTO

Seeing the Sea Trout

Sea trout frequent shallow flats or bays along the coast. Their diet is basically smaller baitfish like pinfish or menhaden. They prefer shrimp, when available. The back of a sea trout is a medium to dark gray, leading into a lighter silvery gray on the sides, with a pure white underbelly. Darker spots that resemble those on a brown trout mark the upper back and the tail. The best fishing is in the spring and fall.

Fishing to the Sea Trout

Blind casting and using a smaller streamer pattern with a slow retrieve over shallow weed beds from the bow of a flats boat can be the most productive means for catching spotted sea trout. If you catch one, anchor and continue casting. These fish travel in schools, so when you find one, you should find more. Spotted sea trout will come to the surface for a popper, so you may also want to blind-cast and do some searching with a popper too. Fishing for spotted sea trout is usually best in the early morning.

Choosing the Right Fly for Sea Trout

The best colors for foam surface poppers are white and yellow. A white or chartreuse and white Clouser Minnow is a very productive underwater pattern. Lefty's white Deceivers in smaller sizes should also be included.

Basic Tackle for Sea Trout

These are not exceptionally strong fish, but on an 8-weight outfit, they are a lot of fun. A 9-foot graphite rod with any good reel designed for saltwater use is fine. The reel should hold at least 100 to 150 yards of backing. The fly line can be a floating line for fishing surface poppers and general work with Clouser Minnows. You may want a sinking-tip line for the deeper edges of the flats. Use a 9-foot leader for the floating line and a 6-foot leader with the sinking-tip. No shock tippet or wire tippet will be needed.

Weakfish

Weakfish, although generally larger, resemble sea trout, and the two are sometimes confused. Their range, preference of environment and foods are similar, although the weakfish diet includes sea worms and crabs. These fish will feed after dark and respond well to chumming. You can expect to find them in the same areas where you find sea trout, and the fishing tactics, fly patterns, and tackle that work for the sea trout will work for weakfish. Both fish have a paper-thin mouth, which requires softly setting the hook and a gentle touch when you are playing and landing the fish.

CHAPTER 6

The Saltwater Environment

Tides

Tides move water, bringing water in and taking water out. Understanding the cycles and effects of tides on fish is critical for the saltwater angler.

Tides are created by the gravitational force or pull of the moon and the sun. They are also affected by weather patterns and wind and vary from one geographic area to another. The moon, because it is closer to the earth, has two and a half times more gravitational pull than does the sun.

As the moon travels its elliptical path around the earth, the water is pulled toward it. It takes the moon approximately a month to complete its orbit, and within this time there is a seven-day period when the moon is closest to earth. At this point, the moon, sun, and earth are in a direct line from each other. When this happens, the gravitational pulls are greatly increased, causing the tides to rise higher and fall lower than at any other time during the month. This is referred to as a spring tide.

Following this seven-day period, the moon continues its orbit of the earth, and the next seven days see a minimal amount of rise and fall in tide levels. This is referred to as a neap tide. The following seven days produce another series of spring tides, but they are not as strong as the first set. Another seven days of a neap tide complete the cycle before its starts all over again.

The moon is the key. If there is a full moon or a very thin sickle moon, there will be a spring tide. If the moon shows one of its quarters, there will be a neap tide. The complete tide cycle goes through two highs and two lows during a course of twenty-five hours. Therefore, every day the tides will be one hour later. Thus, if the fishing is hot at the 1 o'clock tide today, it will be 2 o'clock tomorrow. Remember, too, that the tides are repeated every two weeks and that reverse tides occur a week apart.

The amount of influence the tide levels have on fishing depends on the geographic area. On a bonefish flat in Florida, there may be only a few inches' difference between a low tide and a high tide, especially during a neap tide period, but the Jersey coast may have 4- or 5-foot variations.

Local newspapers along the coast always have an easy-to-read tide chart. Keep in mind that the table listed is for a specific area. Local fishing shops also have current tide information. Two books on tide predictions, for the east coast and

Left: In the Bahamas, waiting for the tide to bring in the fish. Flats fishing is almost always tide related. Predators like bonefish and permit will quickly move onto the flats on an incoming tide.

the west coast of North and South America, can be purchased from the National Oceanic and Atmospheric Administration, U.S. Department of Commerce, Washington, DC 20230. These are only predictions, however, and nothing is guaranteed. Tides are affected by the moon and sun and by weather and wind patterns, as well as by other unforeseen factors.

In a trout stream, a resident trout usually stays close to its home. It may move when the urge to spawn comes, but by and large the fish stays where it knows it's safe and where the currents will bring food to it. Rising water levels from spring showers may increase the trout's feeding opportunities; low water levels of summer may make the fish more wary.

Saltwater fish that search the inshore areas and flats really don't have a home; they are always on the move. For the most part, they are dependent on the tides for access to the flats. A resident brown trout may live most of its life near a large rock in a stream; a striped bass may hunt around a rock of the same size, but when the tide changes, the rock may be completely out of the water.

Incoming Tides

Incoming tides flood flats and allow predator fish access. One might think of this as a form of rebirth, with new water bringing in cooler water temperatures and increased oxygen levels. Life begins to stir, crabs come out of their burrows, marine worms are on the move, and baitfish seek out the fresh nutrients the tide brings. At first, the game fish will hunt in the deeper channels that cross the flats, but as the water levels increase, they will spread out, searching likely looking areas that are now accessible. For the angler this is the time to be fishing the flats. It's only a matter of time until the tide goes out and the flat is once more devoid of fish.

Outgoing Tides

Understanding outgoing tides and learning to move with the tide will provide you with fishing opportunities. The flow of water on tidal rivers and estuaries shifts with the falling tide. The currents take the baitfish with them. Game fish sense the tide changes and wait in the mouths of tidal rivers on the outgoing tides, knowing that dinner is going to be delivered to them. Game fish that have been patrolling the flats will move to the deeper edges and look for smaller baitfish that are being forced off the flats.

The Best Tides

Most saltwater flats fishermen prefer the top of an incoming tide, when the game fish come rushing in on the flats hungry and looking for food. Anglers who fish the tidal rivers and estuaries welcome the outgoing flows that bring the baitfish back out, often inciting feeding frenzies among the game fish waiting for them. But the best tide is always the one that brings the game fish within your casting range.

Things to Remember About Tides

- Tides move water. The best fishing is usually when the tide is moving in or out. The slack period in between may not fish as well.
- Get a timetable for the tides in the area you plan to fish, unless you plan to hire a guide.
- Tides can bring in clean water or dirty water.
- Tides can concentrate bait where static water allows it to disperse.
- River mouths usually fish best during a falling tide.
- A full moon or no moon means high tides are faster and higher, and low tides are lower.
- Tides repeat themselves every two weeks.
- Fishermen fishing during a full moon on a spring tide should experience three to four hours of good fishing.
- Many flats fish will swim against the incoming tide because the currents bring the smell of their prey to them.
- Tides help determine where and when you should be fishing. Fish use them to their advantage; so should you.

Beaches

A beach basically is a wide, flat, expansive stretch of sand and water. Some areas are deep; others are easily waded when the tide is right. Some areas are sheltered; others are open and more subject to the weather. Learning as much as you can about the beaches you plan to fish will help you know what kind of tackle to use and what fishing strategies to employ.

Shallow beaches are generally easier to fish than deeper ones. They can be waded, and the wind and the waves are less likely to drive you away. The downside is that on some shallow beaches, it may be harder to find fish because there is not a lot of structure or deeper channels. Like pools on a trout stream, some beaches offer more cover and fish better than others.

Watch the gulls. If they're active, something's going on. A blitz will show you the location of feeding game fish. If you see it happening, move on it.

Watch for nervous water, and determine in which direction the fish are moving. Get your cast well ahead of the fish before you start your retrieve. Do not cast directly at the nervous water; get your cast ahead of it. When bluefish hit a school of smaller baitfish, fish oil is released and floats to the surface. The oil forms a slick that stands out because of its lighter color. When you see this, cast to the slick as quickly as possible. The bluefish are probably still in the area.

A change in water color can indicate a depression or channel where game fish may be found patrolling the edges. Watch for lighter green colors that lead to darker blues; the darker water is generally a sign of depth. Search these areas carefully. Waves can also indicate structure or depth. Waves that break offshore can show you where the shallow water meets deeper water.

Watch for seams where currents meet, and look for any kind of structure where baitfish can hide and where predator fish will be searching. Look for points of land that lead to deeper water; predator fish will patrol the edges of this deeper water. Irregular sections of beaches are apt to have the most structure, so watch for any kind of physical change. A good way to learn the bottom structure of the beach is to visit it during low tide, when most of the bottom will be exposed.

Become familiar with any depressions you can find. Make mental or written notes. Use land markings as indicators to remember where the structure is after the tide is back in. Pay attention to these areas. If you have to blind-cast later, you'll have an idea of where to concentrate your fishing.

Cathy casts a 9-weight outfit off a Mexican beach. Beaches are great places to explore for cruising game fish chasing bait, but be aware that longer casts, from 60 to 80 feet, are sometimes needed to reach the fish.

Fish the beaches during the prime seasons. For instance, the stripers on the New England coast show up in the spring and the fall. Success involves being there when the fish are there. (See chapter 8 for more information on when to go.)

Flats

Flats are relatively shallow, even those as small as a half acre or so large you can't see the other end. Depths vary depending on the tide, but many flats have an average depth of 1 to 3 feet. Saltwater flats are considered nursery areas for numerous species of sea life; they are also the feeding grounds of many game fish such as the bonefish and permit.

Flats can be subtropical or tropical. They can have mud, marl, sand, coral, or grass bottoms. Some can be waded; others cannot. Tropical flats are generally as clear as a mountain trout stream, whereas flats on the eastern coastline are often more turbid, resulting in limited visibility. Flats may have numerous deeper channels cutting across them. Not all flats are healthy. Look for signs of life like needlefish, box fish, or rays. If you find few or no signs of life on a flat, move on.

Structure

Structure is important in fishing, as it represents areas where food is concentrated. If you can find where the food is, you've found an area worth fishing. Structure can be many things, including sandbars, weed beds, and rocks, as well as those that are man-made, such as jetties, wrecks, pier pilings, and bridge abutments.

Not all structure is permanent. Just as a freestone trout stream can change because of high water levels and spring runoffs that undercut new banks and move trees, storms and heavy waves can create new depressions and sandbars and move old ones. We see this every year on the Yucatan coast, where a cut allows water to move back and forth to an inside lagoon. The mouth of the lagoon changes dramatically because of storm and wave action. One year we can be standing on the edge of the beach and have to cast 60 feet to reach the deeper channel. The next year, because of wave and sand buildup, we may have to cast only 30 feet to reach the channel.

Mangroves

At certain tides, mangroves can provide the ultimate structure, offering feeding and hiding places for game fish. When Columbus visited the south coast of Cuba, he described the mangrove as a strange-looking tree that grew in great numbers in shallow water. He described the tree as stiltlike, with the trunk held above the surface. In his log, he added that the trees were so thick that a cat couldn't get ashore.

Barry scans the mangrove flats for bonefish in backcountry Mexico as a storm rolls in.

Mangroves are important land builders because they start new shorelines and extend old ones. At times, looking out across a flat, the mangroves appear as a field of green. In Florida, their greatest value is in stabilizing and preserving precious shorelines, but to the game fish and the fisherman, they are a haven for baitfish and crustaceans.

Bonefish move into the mangroves on a high tide and stay there until the receding tides force them out. When in the mangroves, they are almost impossible to reach. If you hook a bonefish or snook next to the mangroves, they immediately head for the cover of this spiderlike tree and almost always get tangled and break off. It's next to impossible to walk through a patch of thick mangroves. Many flats that are bordered by mangroves are too soft to be waded and are best fished from a boat.

Bonefish guides fish their clients according to the tides. When the receding tides bring the bonefish out of the mangroves, the guides are there waiting. On our last visit to Pelican Bay in the Bahamas, we experienced a lot of wind and high tides that moved a considerable amount of water back into the mangroves. Our guides worked hard for most of the morning trying their best to find fish, but it was clear that the bonefish were back in the safe cover of the mangroves.

Rather than fight the wind and the high tide, we decided to take a long lunch break and a short siesta until the tide changed, forcing the fish out of the mangroves. It was a good decision. On the receding tide, we had one of the best afternoons of fishing ever.

Weather

Weather can be responsible for the best fishing or the worst; it can turn the fish on and turn them off. Trout go off when spring cold fronts drop water temperatures, a summer thundershower may put trout down during the storm, and an upstream wind from approaching weather can quickly end the day's fishing. On the other hand, the trout fishing after a summer shower may be awesome.

There is no question that weather affects our fishing, both in fresh water and salt. Barometric pressure changes preceding a weather front always have a pronounced effect on how fish behave. Keep an eye on the weather forecast; it can tell you a lot about how you need to dress, and it can help you prepare for fishing possibilities. Cold fronts generally send the fish to the bottom and to deeper water, so you may want to take a sinking line to get your flies down to where the fish are.

You can rely on the local newspaper and TV forecast, but if you live far inland, they won't do much good. A few years ago, a good friend gave us a battery-operated weather radio that gives a marine forecast twenty-four hours a day. Today's cable networks and satellite services also provide weather channels with information on coastal areas.

The big storms of late summer that hit the Yucatan, Bahamas, and Florida can turn bonefish flats into acres of off-color water and put an end to the fishing. It's often these same storms that run up the coast, cooling inshore water as they go and starting the fall migration of blues, stripers, and bonito, which can offer the best fishing of the season.

Another fishing-related weather phenomenon is fog or mist that holds over the water. On Fishing Creek, our home trout stream, fog or mist over the water causes the fish to go down, and they stay down until a breeze moves it out. There have been afternoons when we could see the mist rolling downstream toward us. It's always the end of the fishing. On the New England coast, we fished with Jack Gartside in a fog-covered estuary and caught fish after fish. Here the fog seemed to make the fishing even better. Ed Mitchell writes that fog can improve your fishing and that under the cover of fog, poppers and sliders will get you even more action.

Cloudy days generally provide the best fishing in fresh water. Spring trout fishermen look for clouds to bring on the early-season Blue Quill and Hendrickson hatches. And a cloudy summer day will cool off a freestone trout stream, helping to keep the trout more active throughout the day. Striped bass in salt water also feed better on cloudy days. But it's tough going for the fisherman on a bonefish flat who is sight-fishing and needs sunlight to spot fish.

Storms can come charged with electricity, and fishermen everywhere should get off the water, the sooner the better. It's one thing to be fishing a small trout stream in a wooded setting and something else to be walking along a beach or wading a flat when an electrical storm comes up. The last thing you want to do is to walk around holding your graphite fly rod up in the air. We know an angler who survived getting hit by lightning. He first felt a tingling sensation throughout his body, then his graphite rod began to vibrate and hum. The last thing he remembers is an awful smell in the air before he was hit.

If you find yourself on a flat and a storm surprises you, get to land as quickly as you can. If necessary, lie flat on the ground, put your fly rod on the ground away from you, and wait for the storm to pass. Do not sit under a tree or next to any metal object (like some boats). Be patient and wait out the storm; it will pass, and you'll soon be back fishing.

Sage Tech
sage SP

CHAPTER 7

The Complete Saltwater Angler

ALONG WITH THE BASIC OUTFIT OF FLY ROD, REEL, and line, there is additional gear you will need to fish in salt water. Following is a list and description of items that are essential for the complete saltwater angler.

Headgear and Sunglasses

If you can spot a fish tailing, cruising, or waiting in ambush, nervous water or wakes created by moving fish, or rolling breaking fish, you will increase your odds of catching fish. There are plenty of times when you simply have no choice but to search the water with blind casts, but even then, if you can see the fish looking, following, or moving on your fly, it will give you an edge. You need to be observant, to know what to look for, and to see as much about what's going on out there as you can.

What can you do to help you see better? An important accessory is a good hat with a brim. The brim will shade your face, allowing you to see better and helping protect your face from the rays of the sun. Choose your hat carefully. Buy a light-colored hat; it will be cooler in hot weather and will blend into the background colors of the sky, helping to camouflage you from the fish. The underside of the brim should be a dark color to help eliminate light reflections and glare. The hat should fit properly so that it will stay in place on windy days. A few designs offer a longer back or flap to protect the back of the neck and ears from sunburn and flies gone astray.

Left: For protection from the sun and enhanced vision under the surface of the water, a brimmed hat and polarized sunglasses are necessities.

Polarized sunglasses are a must; we can't imagine fishing without them. Fishing guides have to find fish for their clients, and you never see a guide without polarized sunglasses. Light rays travel in all directions and are reflected horizontally off the water surface, which creates glare. It's this reflected glare that makes it difficult to see into the water. Polarized lenses are designed to filter out the reflected glare, allowing you to see what's happening on and below the surface. Polarized sunglasses will also filter out harmful UV rays and provide you with protection from stray hooks, rod tips pointed in the wrong direction at the wrong time, and salt and sand that may be in the air on windy days when you're fishing near the beach.

The color or tint of the lens is very important. Most inshore saltwater fishermen prefer a brown or amber color over the traditional gray of most offshore and trout fishermen. Our preference is a new color called clear water copper; this tint allows us to more clearly define the bottom, even in slightly tannic-colored lagoons, where spotting fish is a real challenge. We are so pleased with the clear water copper that we use it as our all-purpose lens in both fresh and salt water. It is made by Action Optics of Ketchum, Idaho, and is available through good fly shops. It can also be purchased with a prescription lens.

The frame or shape of the sunglasses should be comfortable enough to wear all day without uncomfortable pressure on the bridge of your nose. Many people prefer the new polycarbonate lenses, which are much lighter and not as heavy on the nose. Side shields are available for most frames and will eliminate side glare. Side shields are great for fishing, but don't wear them driving. They restrict your peripheral vision and make it harder to see traffic coming from the side. Croakies and Chums are sunglass retainers that slip over the ends of the temples, keeping your glasses safely around your neck.

Both Action Optics and the 3M company offer useful treated cleaning cloths for sunglasses. Good sunglasses are expensive, and you don't want to scratch them by using an abrasive cloth. Lots of materials that we assume are safe are not: paper towels, napkins, tissues, and some polyesters all will scratch sunglasses. These treated cloths are especially useful after a wet boat ride to the flats. They dry quickly and can be used over and over again.

A final note on sunglasses: Remember that they protect your eyes. Buy the best you can afford; your sight is worth the investment.

Clothing

Tropical-weight clothing for fishing in salt water should be thought of as technical gear. Shirts and pants available from manufacturers like Patagonia, Orvis, and Ex Officio are designed with the warm-weather fisherman in mind. Choose lighter colors for comfort in hot weather and to blend with the sky as a background.

A well-designed shirt will not restrict the movement of your casting arm. The material should be

Breathable tropical clothing, polarized sunglasses, and neoprene flats boots provide comfort and protection when wading the flats.

lightweight, quick drying, and designed to offer ventilation around the shoulders and sleeves. Large pockets are useful for carrying extras when wading. Sleeves should be long for sun protection and comfort on cooler days, and for when the bugs are out.

Pants should be cut full and should not restrict you from getting in and out of a flats boat. They also should be lightweight and quick drying. Cotton duck or canvas shorts will chafe when wet and take a long time to dry. Some companies offer zip-off pants that easily convert to wading shorts. These have become popular with flats fishermen everywhere. Pants should have belt loops rather than a drawstring. The weight of wet pants legs will pull down on the waist, which can be very annoying and uncomfortable to a wading angler on the flats. Choose a web belt with a plastic-coated or nylon buckle. Chrome buckles quickly rust in salt water and will leave rust spots on your expensive fishing pants.

Sun gloves are another item that many flats fishermen are using for protection in addition to sunscreen. The backs of the hands are sensitive areas susceptible to harmful effects of the sun. These gloves are made of Lycra and knit nylon and do not restrict dexterity. They are available in both men's and women's sizes.

The choice of raingear will vary depending on your destination. For the flats fisherman in a tropical climate, a lightweight, hooded rain jacket will offer welcome protection on the boat ride to and from the flats, as well as keep you dry in an afternoon shower. For the angler fishing for blues and stripers along the east coast, cooler air temperatures and sometimes bone-chilling rain will warrant more substantial raingear. Look at the new Gore-Tex products from companies like Simms and Patagonia, which specialize in designing serious products for serious fishermen.

Elliott Farber puts on his neoprene Orvis flats boots, which protect against sharp coral and rocks as well as sea urchins. These boots can be worn over bare feet or light socks.

Footgear

Appropriate protection for your feet while you're fishing also depends on your destination. Most anglers who wade the flats of the Bahamas or the Florida Keys prefer ankle-high neoprene boots or shoes with hard soles to protect feet from sharp coral, sea urchins, and rocks. If you will be fishing from the deck of a boat, you'll need shoes with nonskid soles. If you'll be fishing for stripers on the New England coast in cooler weather, you'll need chest-high waders with rubber lug soles. A little farther south in late summer, a pair of lightweight waders will be more appropriate.

Most flats boots have a side zipper, and it's important to look for a rustproof Delrin or nylon zipper, which will hold up well for many outings in the salt. When you're fishing from a boat, shoelaces can easily get tangled with fly line lying at your feet on the deck. Look for slip-on, low-cut, neoprene and mesh or canvas shoes

Fanny packs are a convenient way to carry gear such as fly boxes and leader material while wading a flat or beach.

with nonskid soles and no buckles or laces. They are inexpensive and can sometimes be found in discount department stores and mail-order catalogs. These shoes can double as wading shoes on hard sand flats when coral is not a problem.

In some cold saltwater locations, chest-high waders are needed. Waders are available in many materials, including the insulative neoprene, the lightweight Gore-Tex and Supplex, nylon, canvas, and rubber. Many anglers own two pairs, one for cold and one for warm water. If you can buy only one, choose a lightweight material. You can layer underneath with warmer clothing in cold temperatures and then remove layers when the temperatures warm.

Waders are available in both boot-foot and stocking-foot models. Trout fishermen generally prefer the support of a wading shoe with the stocking-foot wader, but for the salt the boot-foot is more practical. Saltwater anglers generally do not wade or walk great distances, and in beach fishing, the bottom is not covered with boulders and stones like most trout rivers.

Boot-foot waders are easy to clean and to get in and out of after a day in the salt. A disadvantage of stocking-foot waders in salt water is that the shoes fill up with sand and must be removed to empty them. Even wader gaiters won't keep out the sand. Boot-foot waders are the best for saltwater fishing.

Waist and Chest Packs

Not having to carry a lot of gear is one of the attractions of saltwater fly fishing. When you're wading a flat, a fly box or two, perhaps a spare leader, tippet, pliers, and some sunscreen are all you need. There is no need for the well-stocked vest that trout fishing requires. A fanny or belt pack that fits around the waist will accommodate all of your needs. Many models are available from companies like Sage and Patagonia.

Anglers who wade deep in both fresh and salt water sometimes prefer to use a chest pack that hangs from the shoulders, keeping it higher than a waist pack. Chest packs can be hot in warm weather, but they make sense for anglers fishing in the surf and wading deep for blues and stripers.

Stripping Baskets

Stripping baskets are popular with anglers wading in the surf to control excess fly line. A stripping basket is generally made of plastic and looks like a kitchen dishpan. It fastens with a belt and is worn around the waist. The angler drops the fly line into the stripping basket as he strips in line, and the basket controls the line when the angler is casting and shooting it.

One of the nicest stripping baskets is offered by Orvis. It has cones evenly spaced across the bottom of the basket, minimizing line tangles and allowing the angler to shoot line easier and farther. This particular basket is a well-designed version with rounded edges and is contoured for a comfortable fit.

Fly Boxes

Foam-lined fly boxes have long been a favorite of ours for both fresh and salt water. They keep our flies organized, and if a box is opened upside down, the flies don't fall out. If the wind blows while the box is open, the flies won't blow out. Perhaps most important, if you need to get to a particular fly in a hurry, you can easily pull it out of the box without having it tangled up with other flies.

Our bonefish flies fit into the same size box as our trout flies. Saltwater streamers, on the other hand, are longer than our trout streamers and require a much bigger box. Since most of our wade fishing is with smaller flies, the boxes are easy to carry in the waist pack. One of the streamer boxes can easily fit into the waist pack if we are walking and casting in the surf; otherwise, these boxes stay handy in the boat bag.

Plastic compartment boxes present some problems. The flies are always tangled together, and it's impossible to reach in and get just one out. If the barbs are not filed down, you really have a mess, especially if the flies have synthetic material for wings. Once the hook points get caught in the material, it's difficult to remove them. And when traveling, the longer flies, like Deceivers and the synthetic baitfish flies, bend and curl from shifting around inside the compartment. When you pull one out of the box, it looks awful. Saltwater flies are expensive, and a foam-lined fly box will keep them safe and organized.

A stripping basket gives the surf angler a place to store stripped line so it doesn't get tangled around the legs or swept away by waves or currents.

Tools and Other Needs

A pair of long-nose pliers is a necessity of life in saltwater fishing. They have many uses, including pinching down barbs, extracting hooks out of toothy fish, cutting wire, and pulling knots tight when you are using heavy leader material, not to mention fixing the boat motor if the need arises. The standard freshwater forceps are not strong enough to deal with the larger stainless steel hooks used in salt water.

Ceramic nippers will cut through 50-pound-test line and are better than the standard nail clipper or snip. They are razor sharp and corrosion resistant. We wear them on nylon lanyards around our necks, where they are easy to get to quickly. A number of companies make snips for saltwater fishing in different prices. Buy good ones; they are definitely worth the money.

A small flashlight is indispensable; everyone should carry at least one at all times. A good one is a mag light. They come in all sizes and take common AA batteries. We carry a small one in our waist pack and a larger one in the boat bag. They come in handy for all sorts of needs, including tying on flies after dark and finding your way around outside the lodge at night.

On one fishing trip in the Bahamas, it was our mag light—and the U.S. Navy—that saved us from a night on the water. Just before dark, the motor on our boat conked out about 30 miles from the lodge. Our guide informed us that we had water in the gas tank and no extra gas. We had to clean the fuel line and spark plug to get the motor to turn over. It would run for about ten minutes, then it would quit, and we'd have to do it over again. It was now dark, the boat had no lights, and there were no tools on board. We used our mag light while we worked on the motor. We finally managed to limp into a Navy base and coaxed them out of enough good gas to get back to the lodge.

Stripping finger sleeves are made of Lycra and will stretch and fit snugly around your finger. Anyone who has spent the day blind-casting and retrieving flies on an 8- or 9-weight knows all too well how easy it is to wear a painful cut in a finger. The smooth material will not harm the finish on your fly line, but it will save your finger.

Insect repellent is another necessary item. Every fisherman knows how annoying mosquitoes and no-see-ums can be. When the wind calms down, swarms of biting insects will converge on any unprepared angler and quickly make life miserable. It doesn't matter where you go, there are almost always biting bugs when the wind dies, and they can make it almost impossi-

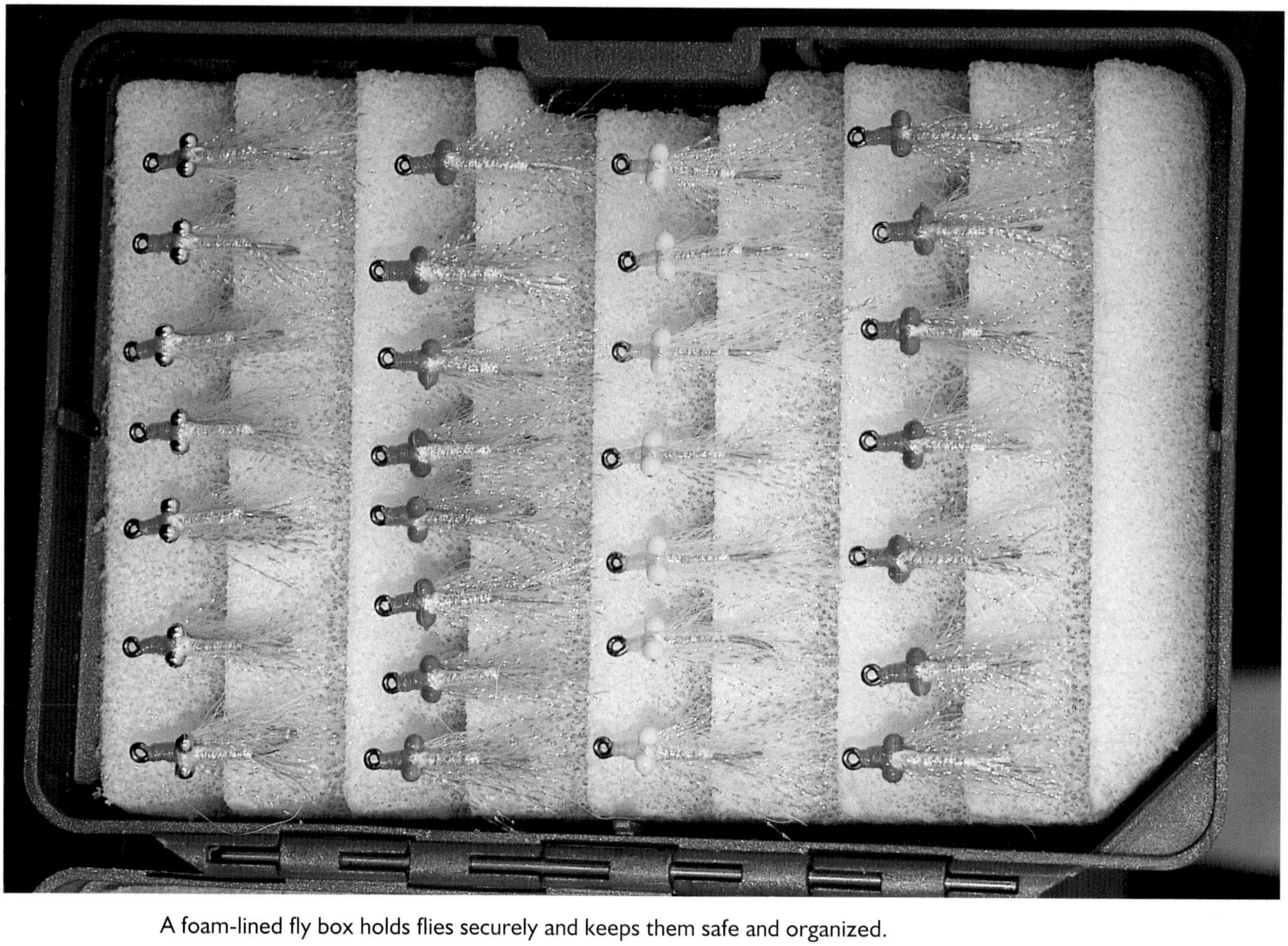

A foam-lined fly box holds flies securely and keeps them safe and organized.

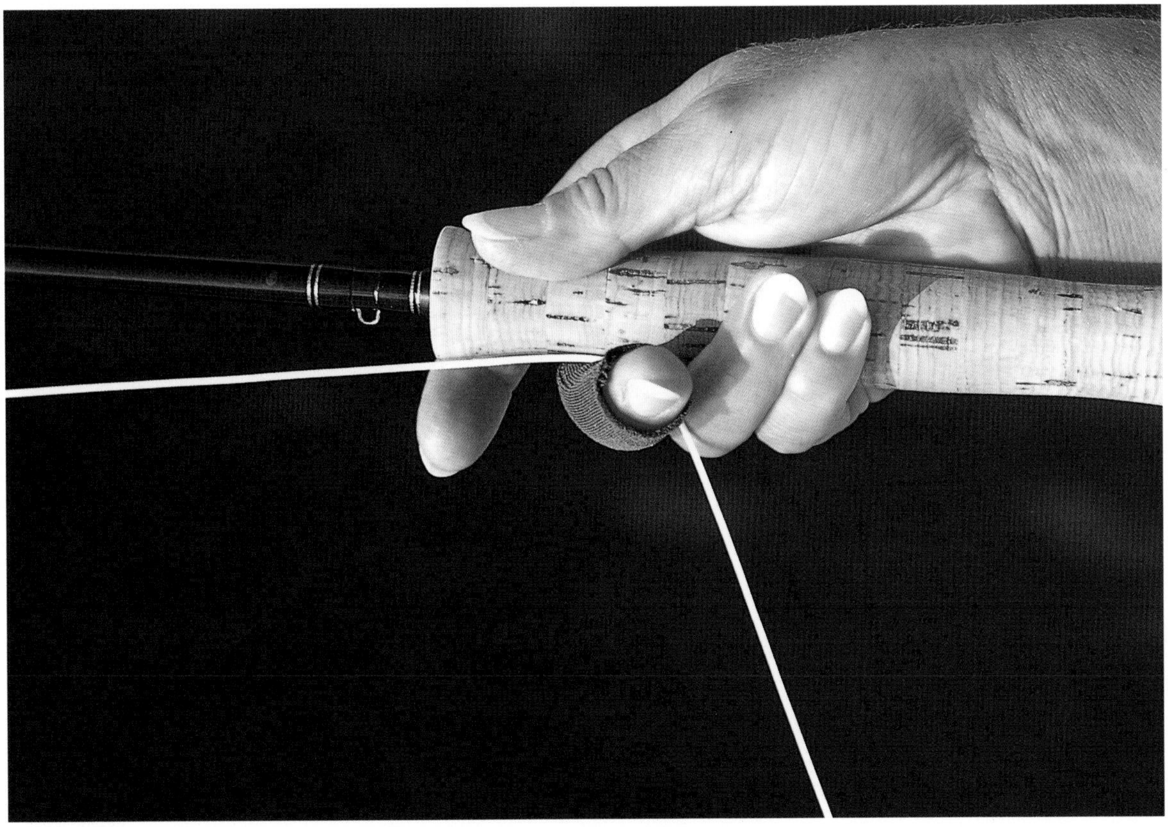

A Lycra finger guard on your stripping finger will prevent line cuts.

ble to fish. Make sure you take repellent with you. Be careful to keep it off your fly line and other plastics, such as sunglasses and fly boxes. Most repellent has deet in it, which will attack and break down plastic.

A dermatologist friend, Dr. Steven Binnick, has been seeing an alarming increase in skin cancer. Steve tells us that he is appalled at how many people subject themselves to the sun's rays for extended periods of time without the protection of sunscreen. Never leave home without sunscreen, and make sure you use it. This advice could save your life.

As you get closer to the equator, the protective atmosphere that protects you from the sun's ultraviolet rays becomes thinner. We rely on SPF 30 and cover up well. Actually, we start every day by putting on sunscreen, whether we're home or away.

Sunscreen needs to not only be applied before fishing, but also reapplied throughout the day, especially if you're wading in shorts. It's easy to get back in the boat, move on to another flat, and forget about sunscreen. Take time to reapply it often. Be especially careful with your lips and ears. Use a balm with sunblock for sensitive areas, and reapply it to your lips after drinking.

Cameras

A camera is certainly optional, but it can record the memories of a lifetime. With today's technology and user-friendly point-and-shoot cameras, anyone can capture sharp images they can be proud of.

Cameras record those special fish, caught and released; friends or family members having fun on the trip; spectacular sunsets and sunrises over the ocean—the possibilities are endless. But you have to take the camera, film, and extra batteries, and you have to use it!

There are a number of weatherproof cameras in point-and-shoot models that are priced right and are small enough to take along fishing. Bring back the memories—you'll be glad you did.

A flats boat is typically 16 to 18 feet long and powered by a 40- to 100-horsepower outboard so it can get to fishing grounds quickly. When he arrives at the area he wants to fish, the guide poles the boat from the platform above the motor while the angler casts from the bow.

Boats

For many freshwater anglers, fishing out of a flats boat is a totally new experience. Before fishing in salt water, wading a trout stream was what fishing was all about. There were times when a float tube or drift boat helped us get to the fish, but overall we walked and waded.

In inshore saltwater fishing, many of the flats are simply too soft to wade—so soft, in fact, that the unsuspecting angler can get stuck and need help to get out. We've actually seen this happen in the Florida Keys; it's alarming at the time for the helpless angler.

There are flats that can be reached only by boat because of deep channels that restrict the wading angler from access, and many fish, such as striped bass and blues, are often too far offshore to reach by wading. A boat can follow moving schools of fish and get you more opportunities. And a boat can move you away from crowded areas.

Most anglers who own a flats boat live on or near the water. We do not own a flats boat and probably never will. It's a long drive—or flight—from our cabin in the mountains of Pennsylvania to any saltwater destination, so when it's possible, we wade; otherwise, we go with a guide in his boat.

It's helpful to prepare a mental checklist the night before of everything you want to take in the boat with you the next day. You may even want to start a pile by the door. A really great way to get off on the wrong foot with any guide is to tell him you forgot your sunglasses or your fly reel after you've ridden in the boat for 4 or 5 miles. You may want to make a checklist and carefully go over it before you leave. Following are the items we like to have with us:

The dock at Boca Paila. Make a checklist of tackle and other gear and consult it before departing.

An angler casts to a bonefish in Pelican Bay, Bahamas. As the guide poles across the flats, the angler must be ready to follow the guide's directions promptly and to cast the required amount of line at any moment.

John Ferguson uses a slow retrieve and keeps a low profile as a bonefish follows his fly off Boca Paila. Gregorio, his guide, points to the fish and gives advice.

- Fly rod, reel, and neoprene reel cover.
- Fly boxes, waist pack.
- Hat, sunglasses, raincoat.
- A gear bag with leaders, tippet, pliers, snip, flashlight, stripping sleeves, wire or shock tippet.
- Sunscreen, lip balm, sunblock, aspirin, any other medicine.
- Camera, film, extra batteries.
- Fishing license, if needed.
- Money for guide's tip.
- Flats boots or neoprene shoes.
- Toilet paper and insect repellent.
- Cooler with lunches and drinks.

The Boat Dock

Try to arrive at the launch or dock on time. Be careful getting yourself and your gear in the boat. Be especially careful if the dock and the boat deck are wet. Nothing is more embarrassing than slipping on the deck and falling into the boat, and, of course, you can hurt yourself. Wear shoes with nonskid soles and move slowly. Hand your gear to the guide and let him stow it on board before you get in. Then, if you need to, take the guide's hand and let him help you into the boat. Sit where the guide tells you to; he knows how to distribute the weight in the boat. He is the captain.

The guide may want you to rig a rod before you leave the dock. If he does, make sure you have a cover over your reel for the boat ride. The rod will sit in a rod rack on the side of the boat, and the reel will vibrate against the inside of the boat. Without a cover for protection, the finish can get damaged.

Before you leave the dock, ask the guide how far you will be going. If it's a long trip, put your raincoat on. Store your hat in a safe, dry place and pull your hood up. Boat rides to the flats can be wet rides, and if it's a chilly morning, your raincoat will feel good. Hats, no matter how well they fit, always seem to blow off on the boat ride.

Make sure you know where the life vests and/or boat cushions are stored. If the water is rough and the ride gets too bumpy, tell the guide. We've had guides in the Bahamas who know only one speed, and that's flat-out full speed ahead regardless of the conditions. Sometimes when the water is choppy and it's windy, the boat ride is going to be rough, and that's that. Other times, it's just the guide. You don't want to arrive feeling beat up if it can be avoided. Yell if you have to, because the guide may not hear you over the noise of the motor. He may be the captain, but you're paying the bill.

Once you arrive at the fishing destination, the guide may want to remove your rod from the rod holder. He will be in the back of the boat and in the best position to hand it to you. There are a lot of broken tips on fly rods caused by overanxious anglers trying to get their rods out of the rod holders, so do so carefully.

Your guide will probably have a push-pole located on the top edge of the boat. Pay attention when he unhooks it and swings it around; the pole is probably made of fiberglass and is long and heavy. If the guide swings the pole around as you stand up, something is going to happen. If the pole is coming fast enough, it can knock a person out of the boat. If nothing else, it will give you a good bump on the head. Be careful, too, when the guide starts the motor. If you're sitting beside him not paying attention, and you lean just a little bit at the wrong time as he's pulling the cord, you can get hit hard in the head or shoulder.

When two anglers—especially fly casters—fish from the same boat, each must be aware of what the other is doing and be ready to react. Here, the angler in the middle of the boat ducks and steers his rod and line away from the bow angler, who is casting to a fish the guide has spotted.

When the guide is ready to pole, it's time for you to move up on the deck. One of the first rules when fishing from a boat is to move quietly and make as little noise as possible. Sound travels five times faster underwater. Never slam the lid on the cooler or drop fly boxes or soda bottles on the bottom of the boat, and talk in low, quiet voices.

On the deck, you need to get yourself ready. Start by stripping about 40 feet of fly line, and coil it on the deck at your feet. Next, make a cast and strip the line back again, laying it in coils at your feet. You now have an idea of how far you can cast with the line that's out. Make sure there is nothing on the deck that your line can catch on. Many boats have a retractable pole or rope holder on the bow; make sure it is folded down out of the way. If there is anything that the line can catch on, it will. Make sure that you are not standing on the line; this happens all too frequently. If it's windy, it may be hard to control the slack line on the deck. You can carefully stow it behind you over the rear edge of the deck and coil it on the floor of the boat. We've seen a few anglers who use a small plastic waste can to hold the slack when it's windy. The container keeps the line under control and out of the effects of the wind.

Be ready. Hold the rod tip low with the rod hand, and hold the tippet near the fly with the other. Most of the time, you will have a short amount of line trailing alongside of the boat. Make sure it is on the downwind side of the boat and that there's not enough to get tangled with the push-pole.

The boat may or may not have a poling platform for the guide. The use of a poling platform is the guide's choice. There are guides who feel strongly that the elevated platform spooks fish and others who feel the height is a distinct advantage in spotting fish. One thing for sure is that a guide poling from a platform can see 360 degrees and will spot almost every fish before you do.

Platform or not, you need to stay alert and scan the water ahead of you. Watch the bottom and look for fish profiles moving across it. Light and water clarity will dictate how well you can see. The best light is after the sun is up and has illuminated the bottom ahead of you. A good guide will do his best to pole you with the light coming over your shoulder.

Scan the bottom, working your way slowly from the front of the boat out to about 50 feet, and then

Gear bags keep your gear organized and dry in the boat.

Cathy fishes a Florida flat she reached by canoe. Canoes are a convenient way to move from one flat to another when conditions allow.

back again. Keep your ears open, and listen for the guide's instruction when he sees a fish. He will probably use the clock system for directing you to the fish. Twelve o'clock is dead ahead, 11 is to the left, 1 is to the right, and so on.

The guide may say something like this: "Bonefish, forty yards, two o'clock, coming to you." At that distance, you have time to react, so look to 2 o'clock. The guide will continue to inform you on the position and direction of the fish. Tell him whether you see it or not, or if you had it and lost it. He will keep talking to you if you don't see it. He may swing his push-pole around and point it in the direction of the fish. He will do everything he can to help you see it, but if you don't see it and the fish is within casting range, he'll tell you to cast.

Do not question his advice. If he says, "Cast forty feet at eleven o'clock," then do it, and do it as quickly as you can. After the fly has landed, he may tell you to quickly cast again. The fish may have changed direction while your line was in the air. Just do it. When the guide tells you to strip, start your retrieve. He may tell you to increase the speed of the strip, to slow it up, or to stop. Just do it. Don't argue; by the time you see the fish, it may be too late. Most flats fish are moving, and the cast has to happen quickly.

If the fish follows the fly close to the boat, you may need to kneel down on the deck to keep a low profile, hiding yourself from the fish. We've seen bonefish follow the fly right up to the boat before taking it. In this situation, it's very important to be low and still. It also helps to wear light

Jack Gartside rows Cathy across a tidal creek in Massachusetts in his inflatable raft. Rafts can move you to the fishing when tides and currents permit.

colors that blend in with the water, boat, and sky so that you don't scare the fish.

If you go with a friend or in a small group, you'll probably share the boat with another fisherman. If you're also sharing the cost of the guide, you're each entitled to equal time on the deck. Some fishermen will share anything but their fishing time, so it's best to get this issue settled beforehand. Perhaps the fairest way is for each angler to take a half hour at a time on the deck. We have seen friendships dissolve because of arguments over who has had the most time on the deck. We have also seen lifelong friendships develop when both partners have been fair and respectful of each other.

You may be kind and the other angler in the boat may be a friend, but we all want to fish. Beware of offering to sit it out until your partner has caught a fish. If he is inexperienced or the fish are few and far between, you may later regret your generosity. Sharing equal time regardless of fish caught is the fairest way.

Partners can help each other in the boat whenever another species of fish shows up. At Boca Paila, we always carry three rods in the boat, rigged and ready to go: one for bonefish, one for permit, and one for tarpon, snook, or jacks. If the angler on the deck is holding a bonefish rod and a permit shows up, the partner sitting in the boat can hand the permit rod to the angler and take the bonefish rod. This gives the angler the opportunity to cast to the permit while the partner gets the bonefish rod out of the way.

Most guides take great pride in their boats. If you get out of the boat to wade on a flat, rinse your shoes off in the water before you get back in. If there is mud on the bottom of your shoes, it will get all over the boat floor. If you find that you have tracked mud into the boat, ask the guide for a sponge or towel and clean it up.

If Mother Nature calls, the guide will do his best to find you a place to use. On most flats, there are keys or islands or gravel bars that the guide can take you to. When you get out, be prepared for sand fleas, mosquitoes, and other biting insects, which always seem to show up at the wrong time. And as always, leave no sign that you've been there.

For the boat ride back to the dock, take off your hat and put on your raincoat. When you get to the dock, give the guide time to tie up the boat before getting out. He may remove your rod from the rod holder and hand it to you. Mentally go through your checklist and make sure you don't leave anything in the boat. Look in the dry wells and under the seat. A guide doesn't want the responsibility of mailing your gear back to you, and sometimes you simply won't get it back.

A waterproof gear bag to carry on board with you can be invaluable. There are a lot of good bags available, including a neoprene bag made by the Springbrook Company in Alberta, Canada, that holds fly boxes, extra reels, jacket, and anything else that you need to keep dry. A canvas tote or boat bag is handy to keep on the seat to hold a couple boxes, tippet, and tools. It keeps things organized and is quick and easy to work from.

Along with boats, there are other options for getting around a flat. On one of our first trips to the Florida Keys, the lodge where we stayed had a canoe that belonged to the owner. Deep channels cut through one of the nearby flats, and for two days we watched tailing fish that we couldn't reach. Finally, after talking to the lodge owner, he offered us use of the canoe. Once we got across the deep water, we tied it to our waists and it simply trailed along behind us. It was nice having the room, too, for extra clothing and drinks.

We have also used a canoe in smaller tidal creeks, looking for striped bass, and in the backcountry in Florida, fishing for snook and baby tarpon. Canoes are easy to maneuver and quiet, so you can sneak up on fish. They should not be used in rough water or ocean currents, and if you stand up and move around too much, you will find out just how easily they upset. But they can be a lot of fun.

Jack Gartside uses a small raft to get across tidal creeks on the New England coast in search of stripers. We have made a few trips back and forth with Jack loaded with gear, cameras, ice coolers, and life preservers. Although we've always made the journey safely, it has always been with apprehension.

CHAPTER 8

Destinations

WHERE SHOULD I GO FISHING? WHEN SHOULD I GO? The *when* part is easy: go whenever you can. After all, *some* fishing is always better than *no* fishing. It's the *where* part that takes some consideration. The striper and bluefish fishery is easily accessible to almost anyone living near the East Coast. It's one of the hottest subjects in most fishing magazines, it's affordable, and it offers a long season. But then there are the tropics, with their seductive sunrises and sunsets, and the warm temperatures that lure all of us who are freezing through a cold winter.

Adventures in saltwater fly fishing are where you find them. They can be off a reef in New England, on a pancake flat in Los Roques, or on the flats in the Yucatan.

Pretrip Planning

Once you've decided on a destination, your first step is to research and get as much information as possible on guides, lodges, and motels. If you are new to saltwater fly fishing or are fishing a new area, nothing beats a good guide. A guide can save you countless hours of frustration. Guides know the tides, the right places to fish, and the right flies to use. They have boats and can get you to where the fish are.

Left: Fishing guide Robert Ramsey is ready for the tropics. The saltwater angler has the luxury of being able to travel light.

Good saltwater fishing lodges get booked well in advance, so it's important to plan early. Ask the travel agency to send you as much information as possible on the destinations it represents, as well as a list of references and phone numbers of clients who have visited particular lodges. It's wise to work with an agency that specializes in sporting travel. Frontiers International, in Wexford, Pennsylvania, and Bob Marriott's, in Fullerton, California, are complete, full-service agencies well known in fishing circles.

Once you've picked a destination, you need to make arrangements to get there. If air travel is involved, you need to make plane reservations.

Plane Reservations

People who fly often know the head-aches that can come from dealing with airlines. It's not that flying is hard or even dangerous; your drive to the airport is far more dangerous than the flight itself. It's dealing with reservations, seat assignments, and the pricing that can drive you crazy. Working with a good travel agent can make all of this a lot easier, and there are distinct advantages in having the same agency book your flight and your lodge.

Cathy and JJ, a Bahamas guide, stalk a school of bonefish in skinny water on the flats. Guides take you to the fish and help you see them, and they can also be great teachers and companions.

Talk with your travel agent, and make sure that you're both clear on the departure and return dates. Mark the dates on the calendars that hang in your home and office so that everyone knows your plans. Be sure of your dates; there is usually a substantial charge from the airline to change the tickets. Carefully talk over all of the options on flights, times, and prices, as well as the airport most convenient to you. If possible, consider an early morning departure. If the flight is canceled for some reason, there may be other flights the same day that you can connect on.

If you are flying coach, ask your agent for a seat close to the front of the plane, especially if you are going to change planes en route. It's frustrating to end up in the back of the plane standing in line waiting for everyone ahead of you to exit when you have a tight connection to make. Unless you like to look out the window, request an aisle seat; it's more comfortable, and you're up and off the plane sooner.

After deciding on flights and times, the agent will take your credit card number and book your tickets. Request a copy of the itinerary unless it's close enough to the travel date to have the tickets mailed directly to you. The itinerary will show your flight numbers and times for both the departure and return flights. Seating assignments should be listed unless you are instructed to check in for seats at the gate. The itinerary will also show any plane transfers and meals or snacks that will be served on the flight. Use a highlighter to mark the flight numbers, seat assignments, and times of departure and arrival on the itinerary. Put this information in a safe place.

Pricing on tickets may vary. Your agent will try to get you the best flights and prices. He or she will also keep an eye on the ticket fares, and if the carrier lowers the fare, you may be able to have the tickets reissued at the lower price.

Other Details

Ask your travel agent to send you a pretrip list for your destination and a planned day-to-day itinerary.

If it's an international flight, you will need proof of citizenship, which usually consists of a valid U.S. passport (be sure to check your expiration date) or an original or certified copy of your birth certificate, along with a photo ID, such as a driver's license. Make a copy of the first page of your passport and carry it with you in a different place from your passport. If the passport is stolen, the copy won't take the place of the original, but you will have your passport number and proof that you had one to start with.

If you are a parent traveling with a minor, age 17 or under, into Mexico or some other countries, you must have a notarized letter of consent from the other parent stating that you have permission to take the minor into the country. Minors who are traveling with you but are unrelated must have a notarized letter of consent signed by both parents.

Will you be picked up at the airport when your plane arrives, or do you need to rent a car? If a representative of the lodge is going to meet you at the airport, will he or she be holding a sign, and will the sign have your name or the lodge name? If you need to rent a car, the travel agent can arrange that as well. Specify the size you'd like, and keep the reservation number with your tickets. If you are going by taxi, can that be prearranged, or do you have to find one on your own? Is the price of the ride to and from the lodge included in your package? What happens if the plane is late? Will the driver wait for you, or do you have to arrange transportation independently?

Will you need to exchange money? If so, find out the exchange rate. What about health concerns? Will you need any shots or vaccines? Are there medical facilities close by? If not, how do you get medical help if you need it? Can the lodge meet any dietary requirements you may have? Is language going to be a problem? Is the electrical current 110 volts? Is there hot water at the lodge? In most of the areas we've visited, the travel is easy and the accommodations modern, but there are places where the above concerns may need to be addressed.

Having a list of recommended tackle is very important, especially on a first visit. The information should be available from the travel agent, who gets it from the lodge. Also ask for a description of the fishing conditions and suggested fly patterns, any options available on fishing for other fish, different areas to visit, and the possibility of side trips in case of bad weather or for nonfishing companions. Clothing suggestions and a checklist to use when packing for the trip are also helpful.

Read your pretrip information well in advance of your trip. Does the travel agency offer any kind of trip insurance in case you need to cancel at the last minute? How much does it cost? Does your medical insurance cover you when traveling outside the country? What about emergency evacuation and other out-of-pocket expenses in case of a medical emergency?

At the Airport

Large airports can be confusing and a bit overwhelming to anyone who doesn't fly often. Some are better than others, but it's easy to get disoriented in almost any of them. Overall, however, airports do a pretty good job of moving a lot of people on a daily basis.

Call the airline and confirm the reservation twenty-four to forty-eight hours before your flight. Have your tickets handy; you'll need the flight number and perhaps some other information. Allow yourself plenty of time to get to the airport, especially if you are on an international flight. Most airlines like you to check in one hour before departure on domestic flights and two hours on international. Be sure to allow yourself plenty of time; you don't want heavy traffic or a flat tire to cause you to miss the flight.

If possible, have someone drive you to the airport rather than leaving your car at the airport parking lot. Airport parking is expensive. If you have to leave it, park in the reduced-rate long-term lot. Leave a note with the person picking you up that includes your flight number, airline name, date, and expected time of arrival. Make sure you have the phone number of that person in case your plane is delayed.

From the time you step out of your car, keep an eye on your bags. Do not leave them unattended or with a stranger for any reason. Make sure the bags you're checking have identification tags with your name, address, and phone number. Before leaving home, put a sheet of paper inside each bag with both your home address and phone number and the address and phone number of where you're going. If the bag is lost, the finder may forward it to you at the lodge.

Take off any removable shoulder straps before checking the bags, and make sure all zippers are closed and locked. We use plastic cable ties from the hardware store on all the double zippers. They are cheap and will show us immediately if anyone has tampered with the bag. We cut them off and throw them away after we arrive.

We like bright red bags for our checked luggage. They are easy to find at the luggage claim, and we can often spot them being loaded and unloaded from small planes by the baggage handlers.

Each passenger is currently allowed two carry-on bags, but this regulation could change at any time. Some carriers would like to limit it to one. Call the travel agent or airline to find out the size and weight restrictions. The two of us carry on a rod case that holds six three-piece fly rods; a gear bag with our fly reels, fly boxes, and leader material; another bag with cameras, film, sunglasses, and a book to read; and a bag with a copy of our itinerary, lodge information, contacts at home, lightweight jackets, tickets, passports, extra hats, and a small overnight kit with toothbrushes, toothpaste, and any necessary medication. If our checked luggage gets sidetracked, we can fish and survive for a few days with what's in our carry-ons. We can buy T-shirts and jeans anywhere, but we need our fishing gear.

When you check in, be prepared to show your passport, and have your tickets handy. Check the departure board while you are standing in line and look for your flight and time. If you arrived late and the sign says that your flight is now boarding, excuse yourself and tell the ticket agent that you are booked on the flight that is boarding. He or she will probably move you to the front of the line.

If you are tall or big, or if it's a long flight, you may want to ask at the check-in counter if there are any exit-row seats available. Most airlines will not allow you to prebook the exit row. They want to see you in person to make sure you are physically able to assist in case of an emergency. No children are allowed in an exit row. If you're lucky and one is available, take it. The exit row offers a lot more leg room than the normal coach seat.

As you check in at the ticket counter, you will be told your gate number. If you don't see gate signs posted, ask which way it is before leaving the counter. Airports can be crowded, and you want to go the right way. You will be required to go through security before entering the gate area. Metal items such as some belt buckles, car keys, or a pocketknife will set off the detector. Put these items in the dish with your change. Put your wallet in, too; the X-ray can affect the magnetic strip on credit cards. If you are carrying film, have it in a Ziploc bag and pass it through as well. Some machines can ruin some films. Fuji film comes in clear plastic film canisters. These pass through security faster than the black ones, which have to be opened and inspected.

Pay attention to the announcements when you get to your gate. They will tell you when to board. This will usually be done by seat numbers, last rows first, and forward from there. Make sure you are ready to go when it's time. When you get close to your seat, put one of your carry-ons in an overhead compartment in front of you; the other will go under your seat. Don't put your bag in a compartment behind your row; it will be impossible to get to when everyone is crowding forward to get off the plane. Avoid asking a flight attendant to stow your carry-on. It will almost always end up behind you. If you're late getting on the plane, start looking for storage space well ahead of your seat.

Before landing, a flight attendant will announce the flight numbers and gates for most connecting flights. Pay attention and listen for your connecting flight. When the plane lands and comes to a complete stop, the pilot turns off the seatbelt sign. At this point, there can be mass pandemonium. Everyone stands up and is anxious to get off the plane. This is when you'll be glad your things are stored ahead of you. Make sure you have all your carry-on items, and be careful when other passengers start pulling things out of the overheads.

At the end of the jetway, there will be a uniformed attendant with connecting flight and gate information. Ask if you're not sure of the gate or which direction to head. Sometimes it's a hike between gates or concourses. We can't tell you how many times we arrive on one concourse, only to find that our connecting flight leaves in fifteen minutes out of a concourse on the other side of the airport. There's nothing to do but run and hope that we can make it before they close the boarding, which is usually ten minutes before departure.

If you wind up with time to kill in the airport, keep an eye on your bags. Some friends had their passports stolen because they dozed off in an airport for a few minutes. Don't think that your bags will be okay for a minute; they might not be.

On international flights, the flight attendant will probably give you a customs declaration form. Take a minute to fill it out while you are on the plane. When your plane lands, you will pro-

Peace and Plenty Bonefish Lodge in the Bahamas, a favorite destination of American anglers.

ceed to immigration, where you will be required to show your passport or proper ID. Do this as quickly as you can, because while you are in line at immigration, your baggage will be revolving around on the luggage carousel in the baggage claim area. If immigration gives you a stamped card or slip of paper, keep it with your passport; you may need it to get out of the country. Security in international airports often leaves a lot to be desired. We've never lost a bag in the baggage claim area, but there have been times when we were held up at immigration and found our bags sitting off by themselves in a corner.

Now you have to clear customs. Depending upon the airport, it may consist of a table with one or two agents or a red and green light system like the Cancun airport uses. The light system is simple. You walk up to it and push a button. If it turns green, you pass through customs without a hitch. If it turns red, you may be asked a few questions or have your bags inspected.

With customs and immigration behind, you can continue on your journey to the lodge. If you're supposed to meet a driver, be sure you get the right one. A few years ago in Honduras, we cleared customs, and a man standing at the exit gate asked our destination. We told him the name of the lodge, and he said in broken English that he was to take us there. We started to put our bags into his car, when we saw another man carrying a sign with our name on it. Turns out that the first guy was a local hustler just trying to get a fare, but it taught us a quick lesson. Make sure you know that the person meeting you will either have a sign or will know your name so that you can avoid going with the wrong driver. Remember, too, that you may have problems communicating if the driver doesn't speak English.

At the Lodge

Over the years of visiting fishing lodges in the tropics, we can honestly say that with only one exception, we've had wonderful trips and have enjoyed the staff, the food, the guides, and the fishing. The lodges were everything we thought they'd be, and we've always looked forward to returning.

All lodges have a manager or someone who is in charge. Make it a point to meet this person. This is the person who can help you with any problems, from fixing the plumbing in your room to making sure your taxi is on time for your return to the airport. Become friends with this person, and remember that in most tropical destinations, local people don't get too excited about a lot of things, and what might be infuriating to you may not be given a second thought. Be patient; they will get around to taking care of the situation. They are used to phone lines being down, no hot water, running out of supplies, and so on. Losing your temper probably won't do much good; it will just ruin your day, not theirs.

Your arrival day will probably be spent unpacking and getting familiar with your surroundings. Find out where the dining room is and what time dinner and breakfast are served. If the lodge uses a generator for electricity, ask what time it will be shut off. Make sure your flashlight is on a nightstand before this time. Find out when and where you will meet your guide. Make sure the travel agent has informed the lodge manager of any dietary requirements for dinner and for lunch in the boat.

If there is a bar at the lodge, you will probably run a tab for drinks consumed at the bar and in the boat. Many lodges supply your water, but you pay for any soda or beer out of the cooler. It's polite to offer your guide a drink; if you offer one, it usually means you're agreeing to buy. Keep an eye on what you're billed at the end of the week. It's easy for mistakes to happen with a lot of guests, boats, and tabs. If you find a discrepancy, talk to the manager.

If there are ceiling fans in your room, be very careful about putting your fly rod together inside or bringing strung rods into the room. We've seen many broken rod tips from ceiling fans.

You may sometimes find yourself in a destination located in the jungle. The jungle is full of things that crawl, bite, and sting. In the morning before you get out of bed and put your feet on the floor, look around. Shake out your shoes and clothes if they were lying on the floor; they might be harboring a scorpion or spider. If you've left your flats boots outside, shake them out as well. Keep your doors closed at all times. We had friends in Mexico who decided it would be cooler sleeping with the door open. During the night, the breeze died, and every mosquito, spider, and land crab in the area came into their room.

The night before your departure, check with the manager on when you need to be ready to leave for the airport. Take care of any lodge tips and bar bills. If you have an early morning flight, don't wait to settle up your tab in the morning. Check your room before leaving, and make sure nothing has been left behind. There may be more than one taxi or van to shuttle guests back to the airport. Watch your luggage and make sure it goes with you.

The Return Trip

On your return trip, be prepared to show your passport, and have your return tickets ready when you get to the counter. You may be required to pay an airport tax before leaving the country. Airports in foreign countries can be intimidating if you don't speak the language. If it's busy, stay calm, and make sure that you are in the right line at the ticket counter. If you find yourself lost or confused and you don't speak the language, look for a security guard or information desk. Usually someone at the ticket counter will speak English.

Once your bags are checked, you will pass through security and go to your gate. Hand carry your film through security. Pay close attention to any announcements that you hear at your gate. The announcements may be in Spanish or poor English that you can't understand. One time in Cancun, Mexico, our gate changed three times in twenty minutes. Everyone was grabbing bags and running to the next gate, only to find that another change had been made. If you can't understand the announcement, watch the other passengers at your gate. If people are picking up their luggage and moving, start asking questions. Find someone who speaks English and has heard the announcement. Keep an eye on the monitors, but don't rely solely on them.

With luck, you'll have happy memories of good weather and strong fish to keep you company on the flight home. During the flight, you'll have to fill out a U.S. customs form. When you arrive back in the States, you will pass through immigration. Make sure you get in the line for U.S. citizens. From there, you go to the luggage claim area and pick up your bags. It rarely happens that luggage doesn't show up anymore, but if it's not there, find an airline representative in the area who can assist you with the problem. Your last step is to pass through U.S. customs. Welcome home!

Favorite Places

The Tropics

If you are looking for a tropical destination, there are many to choose from. Florida is perhaps the most convenient and offers large fish and a host of guides and lodging. The Bahamas are a favorite with anglers who have a passion for bonefish, and there are lots of lodges that cater to fishermen. Mexico and Venezuela both offer excellent fishing.

For years, Florida and the Bahamas have been favorite fishing destinations for anglers headed south in the cold months of the winter. Steady streams of rod cases and fishing gear move through the Florida airports in January, February, and March. Taxis filled with fishermen head for popular bonefish lodges.

Unfortunately, the weather in Florida and the Bahamas in January and February can be fickle. You can have perfect weather and great fishing and enjoy the kind of trip you dreamed about, or you can wind up spending your time in the lodge or motel room waiting days for the weather to clear. Is it worth the risk?

On a recent trip to the Bahamas in February, we spent two weeks at Freeport fishing out of Pelican Bay. The first week was rainy and windy. We sat in our rooms and tied flies, looked at each other, and waited. Three days of bad weather went by before it cleared, and then the sun came out and the bonefish came onto the flats by the hundreds. Fish were everywhere, and we quickly forgot about the bad weather. On our day of departure, the wind and rain returned. We learned later that it lasted another five days before clearing.

Bob Clouser casts to a bonefish in Boca Paila, Mexico. The Yucatan offers the best chance for anglers to catch the saltwater grand slam—bonefish, permit, and tarpon.

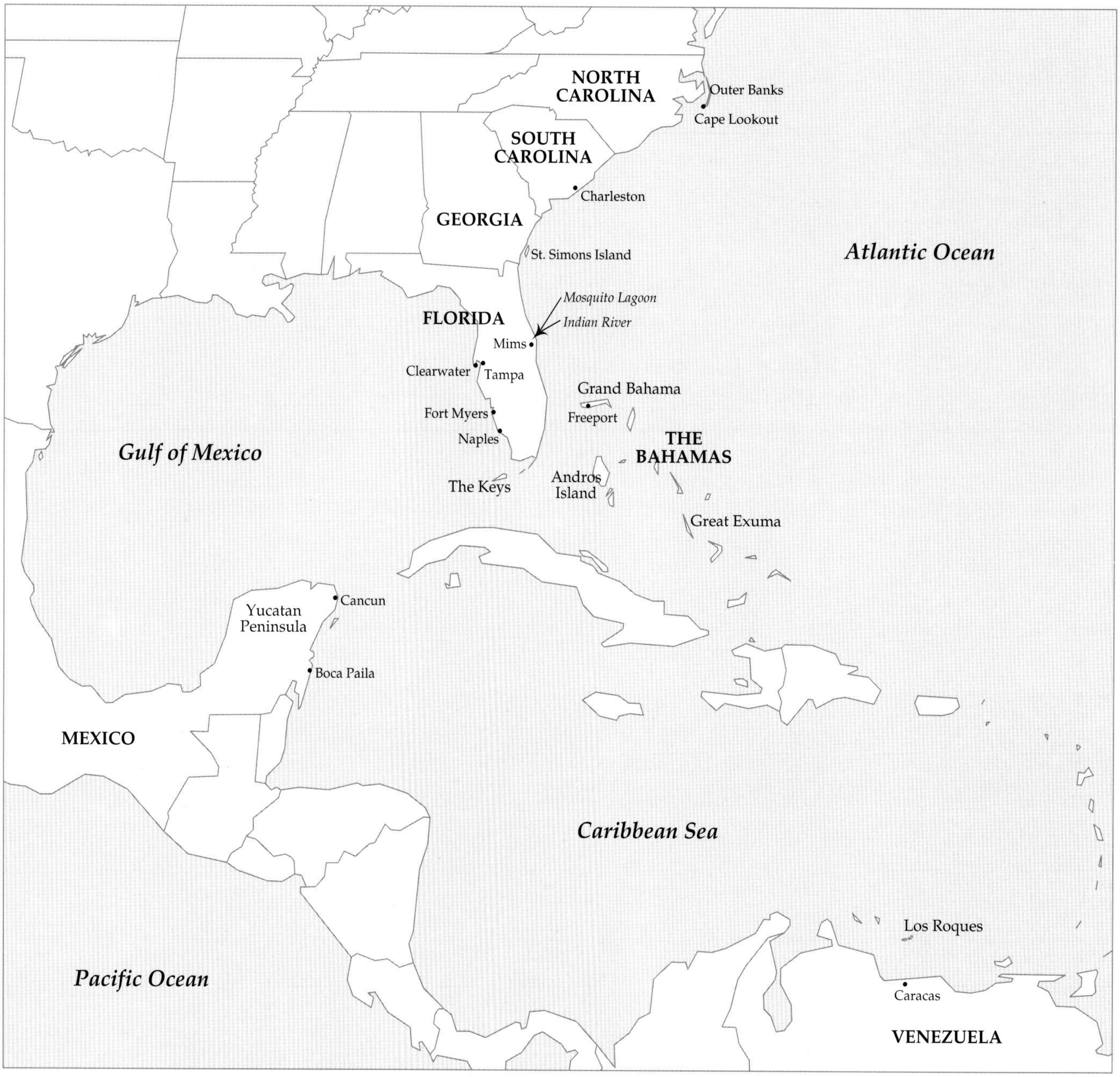

Prime fishing in Florida and the Bahamas starts in March and continues through June. There is also some excellent fall fishing in October through December, after the hurricane season.

If you're willing to take the risk, the Bahamas or Florida can provide excellent fishing experiences in January or February, but there are less risky options farther south. Mexico's Yucatan coast offers a variety of fishing destinations, and weather, for the most part, is more dependable here. Venezuela offers excellent fishing and should also be considered during these months. Christmas Island in Polynesia, the queen of all bonefish destinations, tops the list for predictable weather and fishing.

Mexico

Boca Paila is a saltwater fishing lodge two hours from Cancun, Mexico. It sits on the Yucatan Peninsula, in Quintana Roo, inside the lush Sian Kahn Biosphere Preserve. The preserve estuary is where the shallow reef system of the Caribbean meets fresh- and brackish-water lagoons, which hold an extraordinary variety of fish. The fertile, mangrove-lined lagoon is a water passage south to the mouth of Ascension Bay and offers access to an incredibly vast flats fishery.

Whenever we are asked where to go for a first trip in salt water, our answer is Boca Paila. This is grand-slam country, where you'll get many shots at bonefish, permit, and tarpon. In fact, there are more grand slams landed here than anywhere else. There is also the possibility of a super slam, thanks to the snook that frequent the lagoon.

Bonefish are everywhere, and though they are not as large as their Bahama cousins, they are great sport on light tackle, and everyone catches fish. Our friend Brad Kidder, from New England, went to Boca Paila to catch his first bonefish. The first day out, Brad landed twelve and had a shot at a permit. This is the perfect place for the entry-level saltwater angler. It offers a wide variety of species, including big jacks, permit, bonefish, tarpon, snook, barracuda, and snapper.

The extensive lagoon is very friendly to anglers. The wind may blow, but there is always a protected side, so it's very rare that the weather keeps you from fishing. The surf fishing in front of the lodge down to the Boca can offer shots at large tarpon, jack crevalle, snook, and barracuda. It is easily waded, with the reef 100 yards offshore.

The food is excellent, and the rooms are comfortable and very clean. The bonefish skiffs are designed and built at the lodge and are easy to fish from. The guides are some of the best we've worked with in Mexico. The fishing season is long, and the prices are attractive. The Gonzalez family does an excellent job.

Boca Paila is our first choice for a saltwater fishing destination that offers everything.

Venezuela

When the tiny Los Roques archipelago was discovered by the international sportfishing world in the summer of 1988, it was immediately speculated that the islands fishery would soon redefine

Alex Gonzalez with a nice bonefish from Los Roques, an archipelago in the Caribbean just north of Caracas, Venezuela. Endless flats with tailing bonefish make this an ideal destination for anglers who prefer to wade.

Barry wades a flat in the Bahamas, casting for bonefish. These islands are easy to reach for American anglers and offer a variety of fly-fishing opportunities.

worldwide standards for bonefish. Quickly hailed as the Christmas Island of the Atlantic, in less than a year Los Roques, with its hard, white sand flats, became one of the most popular bonefish destinations anywhere.

A short flight from Caracas, Los Roques is a much safer bet for good weather in January and February. This is truly a bonefish destination. There may be an occasional tarpon or snook, but primarily it's bonefish. If you like wading and casting to big tailing bonefish that can push the 10-pound class, then Los Roques is for you.

One advantage to wading is that it offers more time to fish. If there are two anglers fishing in a boat, you share the fishing time on the deck; about half of the fishing day is spent waiting for your turn. In Los Roques, the boatman pulls up to the flat, and the guide and anglers jump out and start to fish. In the meantime, the boatman runs the boat to the other end of the flat and waits there.

The climate here is pretty dependable year-round, with daytime temperatures averaging in the mid-80s. And there are no biting insects on land or water. The village and the lodge are delightful, and the fishing is excellent.

The Bahamas

The Bahamas are among the most popular saltwater destinations in the world. The islands are easy to get to, with flights daily from Florida. This chain of more than seven hundred islands starts with the Little Bahamas Bank, which is less than 60 miles from Florida, and continues south to the Cay Sal Bank, which lies just 30 miles from the coast of Cuba. This area is a saltwater fisherman's dream come true. There are countless miles of both hard and soft flats, lagoons, and channels. The Bahamas have twenty-one of the fifty recognized marine game fish species. But it's the bonefish that most anglers seek when they go to the Bahamas.

We're often asked to suggest a destination that a nonfishing companion will also enjoy. There are countless lodges in the Bahamas, but most lack activities for the nonangler. We know of three, however, that we can highly recommend.

Kamalame Cay is a bonefish lodge on a beautiful 100-acre island at the mouth of Staniard Creek on the northeast coast of Andros Island. It is surrounded by flats and at its easternmost point lies the edge of the Tongue-of-the-Ocean, where water depths go to 6,000 feet. Kamalame offers excellent fishing for bonefish, as well as an occasional shot at permit. The lodge is new, easy to get to, and the accommodations are first-class. A nonfishing companion can enjoy kayaking, swimming, beachcombing, snorkeling, and scuba diving on the world's third-largest reef. The boats and guides are top-notch.

Peace and Plenty Beach Hotel, on the Exumas, a 100-mile chain of islands that lies east and southeast of Andros, has long been a Mecca for serious bonefish anglers and their families. Bob Hyde, who manages the operation, has a first-class staff. There is a swimming pool and a beach area, and the town offers some shopping and local flavor. You truly feel the magic of the Bahamas here; it's Jimmy Buffet country. Good boats and a guide program have kept anglers coming back year after year.

Grand Bahama Island is not a place most of us associate with bonefish. Whenever anyone mentions Freeport, we immediately think of beaches, shopping, casinos, and tourists. A visit to Pelican Bay resort and eight days of fishing gave us a new opinion of Freeport, however. There we found wonderful fishing to big fish, some in the 10- to 12-pound class; great guides; and vast, productive flats. For the nonfisherman, there is a gorgeous swimming pool and a nice beach, and it's a short walk to the market, restaurants, and

Cathy palms her reel to slow a bonefish run at sunset in the Florida Keys. Florida is still the hub of tropical inshore fly fishing, offering endless opportunities for lodging, fishing, and family vacations.

shopping area. Dive operations, a dolphin experience, and island tours make for a perfect blend of fishing and relaxation.

Florida

Florida offers a variety of saltwater fly-fishing opportunities, including bonefish, permit, tarpon, snook, and redfish. Accommodations are endless, and Florida hosts possibly the largest stable of saltwater fly-fishing guides in the world.

The Keys are well known for flats and fishing. U.S. 1 takes visitors along the 110 miles of sand and water that start at Key Largo and continue south to the southern tip of Key West. The Keys are an easy destination for many anglers who prefer to drive, and accommodations include a multitude of resorts, motels, lodges, and campgrounds. Flights arrive daily in Miami, where you can rent a car and make the drive south to the Keys. You can also take a small plane from Miami to Key West.

There's no question that the Keys are busy with tourists, boaters, and fishermen. It's hard to find the tranquility of Yucatan or the Bahamas, but there is more than enough good fishing.

Key West offers an angler the opportunity for a grand slam, and the tarpon guides here are legendary. Captain Jeffrey Cardenas (800-223-1629) runs a guide service for Key West water. Reuben Dunagan (305-296-5951) is another excellent guide who we highly recommend for the Key West area.

Islamorada and Marathon Key are known for bonefish flats. Reservations for lodging and guides need to be made well in advance. Guides like Lenny Moffo (305-872-4683), Len Roberts (305-852-2604), and Michael Bednar (305-664-8408) stay booked for most of the season.

Key Biscayne has a historic reputation for tarpon and big permit and is located just south of Miami. It's very easy to get to, but it also sees a lot of boat and fishing traffic. Although this is the northern end of Florida's bonefish range, it has produced some of the largest fish. The average here is 6 to 9 pounds. Contact guides Bob

Cathy casts while guide Larry Kennedy poles the boat off Little St. Simons Island, on the Georgia coast. This area offers excellent fly fishing for redfish.

Montgomery (305-253-2388) or Frank Garisto (305-361-5040).

The Tampa area offers some great fishing for redfish, snook, and other species. Tampa airport is a joy to use; it's serviced by most major carriers, and there are accommodations to suit everyone's taste. John and Michelle Homer (813-443-5000) own The Saltwater Fly Fisherman in Clearwater and can set up a guide or help with arrangements.

Naples and the Fort Myers area have snook, tarpon, and redfish. We fish there with Doug Swisher (813-793-7438), who spends his winters guiding the saltwater backcountry and his summers guiding in Montana.

Mims and the Indian River, including Mosquito Lagoon, are home waters to Flip Pallot, host of the ESPN weekly fly-fishing show "Walkers Cay Chronicles." This is a great destination for the entire family. You can fish for redfish and snook, visit the space center at Cape Canaveral, or canoe the lovely St. Johns River. Disney World is just a short drive away, and plenty of lodging is available. Contact Frank and Liz Steel, who own The Fly Fisherman, in Titusville, at 407-267-0348.

The Southern and Mid-Atlantic Coast

Georgia to North Carolina

The entire coastline and barrier islands offer fly-fishing opportunities for schools of redfish and other species, including tarpon, off Georgia's Little St. Simons Island. We landed our first redfish in the company of guide Larry Kennedy (912-638-3214), fishing a tidal creek that crosses the island.

This area marks the beginning of the semitropical fishery in the South Atlantic Bight. It is here that you can find redfish, temperatures permitting, around the middle of April and continuing to November. This fishery continues to develop because of regulated inshore netting and better catch limits, and it's not unusual to see fly rodders casting to jack crevalle in Charleston's harbor, where the jacks school up from June through Labor Day. Spotted weakfish are sought after and found in the tidal creeks. Lodging is convenient to the fishing.

The Outer Banks are home to redfish, jacks, spotted sea trout, stripers, and bluefish, and also host the fall runs of false albacore. This abundance brings anglers from around the country. North Carolina's Outer Banks run from the border of Virginia south to Cape Lookout. The colder waters of the Mid-Atlantic Bight and the warmer waters of the South Atlantic Bight are divided here, and temperatures in the entire region are influenced by the nearby warmth of the Gulf Stream.

Because of these moderate temperatures, year-round fishing opportunities are available for the saltwater angler. The area is also conveniently located to urban Virginia Beach, Newport News, and Hampton Roads. Captains Brian Horsely (252-449-0562) and Bryan Dehart (252-473-1575) are well-known North Carolina guides who thoroughly know the fishing.

Virginia, Delaware, and Maryland

The Chesapeake Bay is the largest inlet in the Atlantic Coastal Plain of the eastern United States, running some 200 miles south from where the lower Susquehanna River enters. The bay is bordered on the south by Virginia and on the north by Maryland. This is striped bass country, but there are also bluefish and spotted sea trout, as well as other species for the fly fisherman. But the striper is what brings most fishermen to the bay.

The Chesapeake Bay and its rivers are the major spawning grounds for the striped bass, many of which migrate to the New England coast. The Chesapeake provides a year-round fishery in all but the worst winters. April and May are prime times, and the fall season produces some of the largest fish of the year. Fishing around the Bay Bridge Tunnel has produced impressive stripers over 30 pounds.

Lodging is easily found throughout the area, and guides like Norm Bartlett (410-679-8790), Joe Bruce (410-719-7999), and Bruce Foster (410-827-6933) work the area and know it well. Joe Bruce and his family own and operate The Fishermans Edge at Catonsville, Maryland.

New Jersey

This is urban saltwater fly fishing at its best, and many of the anglers who fish the Jersey coast have been responsible for the vast fly-fishing interest that exists there. It was not long ago that it was a rare sight to see a fly rod on the Jersey coast. Today it's common, thanks to the efforts of

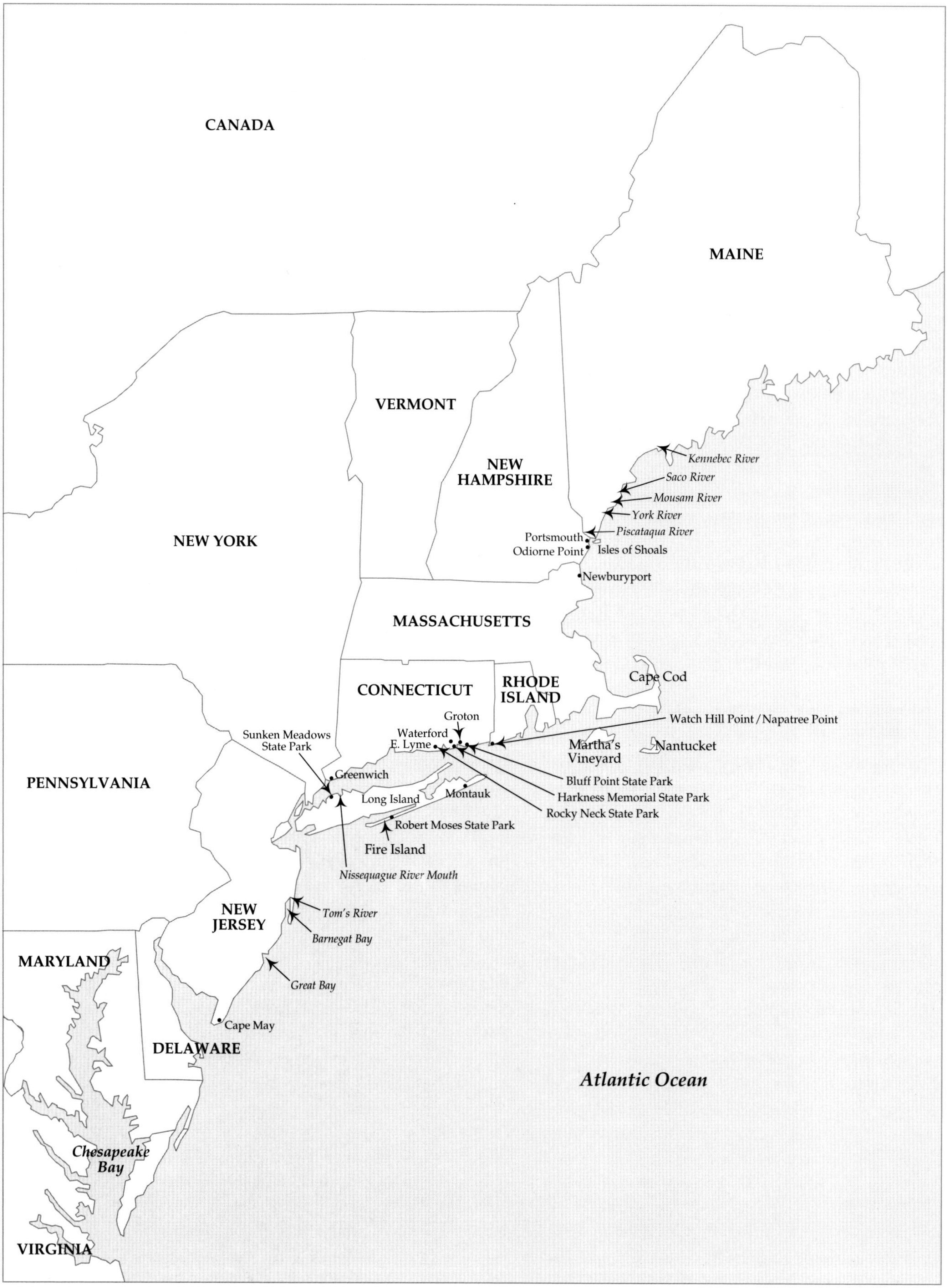
CANADA
MAINE
VERMONT
NEW HAMPSHIRE
NEW YORK
MASSACHUSETTS
CONNECTICUT
RHODE ISLAND
PENNSYLVANIA
NEW JERSEY
MARYLAND
DELAWARE
VIRGINIA
Kennebec River
Saco River
Mousam River
York River
Piscataqua River
Portsmouth
Odiorne Point
Isles of Shoals
Newburyport
Cape Cod
Groton
Watch Hill Point / Napatree Point
Waterford
E. Lyme
Martha's Vineyard
Nantucket
Sunken Meadows State Park
Greenwich
Long Island
Montauk
Bluff Point State Park
Harkness Memorial State Park
Rocky Neck State Park
Robert Moses State Park
Fire Island
Nissequague River Mouth
Tom's River
Barnegat Bay
Great Bay
Cape May
Atlantic Ocean
Chesapeake Bay

Anglers line the surf near Barnegat Bay, New Jersey, in September. The New Jersey coast is a hot spot for bluefish and striped bass, with plenty of beach-side motels and easy access to the fishing.

fishermen and fly tiers like Bob Popovics, Ed Jaworowski, and Dick Dennis.

Popular areas are Toms River/Barnegat Bay, Great Bay, and Cape May. Cape May is known as the place to be for striped bass, but it also offers bluefish, weakfish, and false albacore in season. Another attraction is the easy access to the shore and bay. The Jersey coast offers numerous beaches and is a popular destination for the whole family.

Two fly shops that can recommend guides and fishing suggestions for the Jersey coast are The Fly Hatch, in Red Bank, telephone 732-530-6784, and Ramsey Outdoors, in Paramus, telephone 201-261-5000. You can also contact Captain Dick Dennis at 908-892-8008.

New York

It's pretty amazing to find fly fishermen casting for stripers next to the Statue of Liberty or fishing in New York Harbor for bluefish, but it's happening. Long Island fishermen find stripers, blues, and weakfish. On the north shore, Sunken Meadows State Park and the mouth of the Nissequague River are good spots to try. The south side offers Robert Moses State Park and Fire Island Inlet. Anglers should also consider the state and county parks of Montauk. Contact Captain Bob Robl at 516-243-4282 for more information.

New England

Connecticut

From Long Island Sound north along the coast of Connecticut, the fly rodder will find protected shorelines offering endless opportunities for striped bass, bluefish, and bonito. The mouth of the Connecticut River south of the I-95 bridge is a good area for stripers in the spring season. The fishing season in Connecticut is eight months long, the longest in New England. The fishing starts in Greenwich and continues through the Norwalk Island area. Rocky Neck State Park in East Lyme offers angler access but can be crowded. Unfortu-

Capt. Jon Flaherty, one of the top fly-fishing guides on the Vineyard, casts for striped bass in the surf.

nately, most of the Connecticut coast is privately owned, and access is limited. Look for state-owned areas, such as the Harkness Memorial State Park in Waterford or Bluff Point State Park near Groton. Contact Captain Dan Wood at 860-442-6343, Captain Thom Shipman at 860-445-1475, or Captain Paul Bois at 207-925-1740.

Rhode Island

The southern portion of the Rhode Island coastline is the most popular area for fly fishermen, offering stripers, blues, bonito, and false albacore. Unfortunately, Rhode Island's coastline is often subjected to wind and surf, and the beaches are not as user-friendly as those in Connecticut. Areas to try are the Watch Hill Point and Napatree Point. The coastline does have a number of salt ponds that drain into the ocean. These are popular areas to fish and are worth exploring. Contact Captain Chris Lembo at 410-423-1402.

Massachusetts

Martha's Vineyard, Cape Cod, and Nantucket are magic words to the serious striper fisherman. This is a world-famous fishery, and anglers travel great distances to fish these New England waters. The Vineyard and Nantucket are so popular with fishermen and tourists that you often need to make lodging reservations a year in advance.

The Cape, as it is called, offers a variety of opportunities, including the more protected bay side and the steeper ocean side, which is subject to strong surfs. Anglers who like to wade will prefer the shallow waters of the bay side.

Close to the northeastern corner of Massachusetts is the mouth of the Merrimack River in the town of Newburyport. The Merrimack, along with Plum Island, offers beaches, river mouths, and marshy tidal creeks. In one day of fishing near Newburyport with Jack Gartside, we landed more stripers than we could count.

It's interesting that whenever a fishery develops and becomes as famous as the coast of Massachusetts, it also spawns a group of fishing writers. The famed Letort Spring Creek in the Cumberland Valley of Pennsylvania had the late Vincent Marinaro and Charles Fox, who in turn opened the world of terrestrial fishing and limestone waters to trout anglers everywhere.

Lou Tabory has pioneered the Massachusetts striper fishery and has developed numerous saltwater fly patterns and angling techniques for striped bass. Tabory's *Inshore Fly Fishing* belongs in the library of every saltwater fly fisherman, and Ed Mitchell's *Fly Rodding the Coast* may be the last best word on the subject. *Striper Moon*, by Kenney Abrames, offers some sound advice for both the beginning and advanced striper fisherman. *Stripers and Streamers*, by Ray Bondorew, is full of interesting advice. Jack Gartside self-publishes his own series on unique fly patterns and strategies on stripers. They are all valuable and interesting reading material.

It would be hard to list all the good guides on the coast of Massachusetts. Lodging is sometimes hard to find, and it may be best to check with a guide for fishing dates and lodging. Here are a few suggestions: Captain Jon Flaherty (508-696-8414), Captain Fred Christian (617-631-1879), Captain Peter Alves (508-432-1200), Captain Dan Marini (508-945-2006).

The Massachusetts coast offers not only striped bass but bluefish, bonito, and false albacore as well. When most trout fishermen think of trout, they think of the rivers of Montana; when a striper fisherman thinks of stripers, he thinks of the coast of Massachusetts.

New Hampshire

Although the New Hampshire coastline is limited, there is still some good fishing. It's basically a spring striper fishery, with blues moving in around the first of July. One of the most popular areas is near Portsmouth, where the Piscataqua River enters the ocean. Not far from the mouth of the river is Odiorne Point, a state park that offers public access to the shoreline. Another choice is the southern shores of the Isles of Shoals, which is a series of seven islands. There is angler access from Portsmouth to Hampton Beach, and convenient lodging can be found in Portsmouth.

Maine

Most trout fishermen think of Maine as brook trout and landlocked salmon country with blackflies and biting mosquitoes, canoes, and pocket water. This is true, but the coast of Maine also offers some of the biggest stripers and blues that come up the coast. Eighteen-pound stripers are common throughout the season, which starts in early June and continues to late September.

Maine's success is largely attributable to the many coastal rivers that provide some of the best fishing. Rivers like the York, the Mousam, and the Saco are just some of the hot spots. The Kennebec, familiar to trout anglers, with its headwaters in the famous Moosehead Lake, provides spawning grounds for stripers. Lodging is available along the coast. For guiding information, contact Captain Dave Gittins at 207-363-3874.

The Gulf Coast

We've briefly looked at the Atlantic coastline from the southern tip of the Florida Keys to the northern coast of Maine. Another fishery begins on the Gulf coast of Florida and continues along Alabama, Mississippi, Louisiana, and on into Texas. This is redfish and speckled trout country. Texas lays claim to being the speckled trout capital of the world.

One of the advantages of this coastline is the moderate climate, which encourages year-round fishing. There are flats to wade and pole and a lot of water that has yet to be explored.

The amount of inshore fly-fishing opportunities for the saltwater fly fisherman is almost overwhelming. When one sadly considers that trout water is in decline, it's encouraging to realize that potential exists here to expand our horizons. We will always fish for trout and other inland species, but our venture into the salt has given us so many new and wonderful experiences. We are hooked; we think you will be too.

CHAPTER 9

You Have to Do It

"YOU HAVE TO DO IT!" LEFTY KREH'S WORDS STILL echo in our ears. "The first time you try saltwater fly fishing, you'll be hooked—hooked just as bad as you two are on trout." Jack Gartside agreed. "It's a whole new world out there, with endless opportunities for the fly fisherman." Those were strong words from friends who knew how addicted we both were to trout fishing.

Lefty Kreh needs no introduction to the fly-fishing fraternity, having authored numerous books on the subject, and Jack Gartside is a well-known fly tier who travels the world in search of favorite saltwater species, so who were we not to take their advice?

Our first trip was planned, and off we went to the most logical destination—the Florida Keys. February is a cold month here in northeastern Pennsylvania, and we had a pretty bad case of cabin fever. It was a short flight to Miami, where we picked up our rental car and headed down to Grassy Key and our motel, the Golden Grouper.

Jack had arrived a few days ahead of us, and we found him tying flies in his room. After a quick greeting, we moved into our room, unpacked, and started to organize our gear. The Golden Grouper reminded us of something out of a Hemingway novel. A retired fishing lodge, it had seen better days. Our room came complete with a relic of a fan, towels we could see through, beds propped up on cement blocks—and a great view of the ocean. Oh, and an endless supply of bugs, some biting, some not. But, we agreed, in its own way, the Grouper had character.

Borrowing tackle is not something we do often, but to buy saltwater outfits would have been a hefty investment, since we'd need two, and it was obvious that our lightweight trout gear wouldn't do. This trip was to be an experiment, a look-see; maybe we wouldn't even like it, so we called a friend and borrowed a couple outfits. If we fell for the salt, then we'd consider investing after the trip.

Our borrowed outfits consisted of two 9-foot graphite rods, one for a 7-weight line and the other an 8-weight. We were hoping for bonefish, and we were told that both line weights would work just fine. The reels were nothing special; both had disk drags and floating weight-forward lines. Jack provided us with a box of flies that included his favorite patterns for bonefish, permit, and barracuda. He said that we might have shots at all three species. We thought we were all set.

Left: Michael Bednar, a Florida Keys guide, stands on the poling platform of his flats skiff and spots fish for Cathy in the bow.

Rigged with bonefish patterns (Jack said they were Gotchas), the three of us headed out to what Jack told us was a flat. The hard bottom was easy to walk on, and the clear water was only knee-deep. Jack instructed us to look for cruising or tailing fish, a flash or reflection of silver. If we saw something, we were to put our fly ahead of the fish. With that advice, he smiled and left us on our own. (I think, looking back, that he wanted to get away from us.)

Staying together, we slowly walked in the opposite direction from Jack, who was now disappearing. Apparently he knew exactly where he was going. Looking out over this vast flat, it looked like it could go on forever. We felt a little lost all alone out there with no clue about what we were doing. But being trout fishermen, we had an idea of what a cruising fish looked like, and when a wake about 40 yards ahead appeared, we knew it was time to react.

Ladies first, so Cathy quickly got some line in the air and put the fly ahead of the oncoming fish. In a stroke of beginner's luck, that fish came directly to the fly. Cathy started a slow retrieve and then hurried it up. By now we could see that it was a nice bonefish. To us it looked huge. The fish came to the fly, Cathy set the hook, and in a few brief seconds the backing was disappearing from the reel.

The 7-weight rod was bent double. Cathy let out a moan as she realized she was out of backing. Apparently, whatever the reel was rigged for, it wasn't bonefish! A quick ping and we watched helplessly as the fly line and backing, still attached to the bonefish, swam out of sight across the flat. So much for borrowed gear.

Unfortunately, it would be the only bonefish we'd see for the rest of the day, but we both agreed that it was one very hot fish, and we looked forward to our next encounter.

The next day, Jack was still laughing about our initiation into saltwater fly fishing as we waded together across a new flat that he promised would have a few large barracuda. Rigged with wire tippets and large white Deceivers, we looked like a small group of herons stalking prey. An hour or two passed, and a hot Keys sun baked our exposed skin and dried our lips. Thoughts of cold, fresh water were quickly forgotten, though, when a large fish appeared about 80 yards out. It was coming in our direction, not in a hurry but in a rather slow, methodical meander.

When the fish was at about 70 feet, Jack said in a low but excited voice, "Cast, cast now." The fish was closing in, and it was at least 5 feet long. Barry's cast landed in front of the big fish, but the retrieves went unanswered. At last we had a good look at the shark. Shark! No doubt about it, this was one large shark, and when we turned to ask Jack what we should do, he was nowhere to be found. We followed his retreat and headed fast for the beach.

Our last day found us on a flats boat with a Keys guide searching for a tarpon. Our guide, Michael Bednar, had provided us with flies and gear for the day, a stiff 9-foot graphite complete with a fighting butt and a 12-weight fly line and plenty of backing. Michael suggested that we make a few practice casts with the 12-weight, just to get familiar with the rod. It was instantly apparent that it would take more than a couple casts before either of us would get the hang of the beast. Cathy thought the reel weighed more than most of the trout we caught. But here we were, so we both made a few more practice casts. After watching us, our guide did not look optimistic.

For what seemed like an eternity, we poled across flat after flat, taking turns standing on the bow staring ahead looking for a tarpon while our guide kept silent. Suddenly, there it was, looking as long as the boat and moving across our bow about 70 feet out. Our guide whispered to put the fly well ahead of the cruising fish. Barry was on deck, and the heavy 12-weight sailed through the air. The large blue and white Deceiver headed toward its destination.

Accuracy is always important in fly fishing, and this was no exception. The cast was right on the mark. Well, I mean the Deceiver landed smack on the big tarpon's head. There was an explosion of water in all directions as he made a charge for deeper water. With the fish spooked, the game was over and the guide called it a day. It was a long, silent boat ride back to the dock.

Left: Bob Clouser, creator of the Clouser Minnow, one of the most productive saltwater flies of all time, walks the beach at Boca Paila.

This dock in the Florida Keys is the type of structure that attracts baitfish and the game fish that pursue them.

That was our introduction to saltwater fly fishing, and it seems like so long ago now. It was indeed a comedy of errors, but it also got us hooked, just like Jack and Lefty said it would. Honduras, the Bahamas, and the Yucatan were soon to be included in our trips to the salt. Striped bass on the east coast would get our attention, and our arsenal of gear expanded to include saltwater rods and reels—all equipped with more than enough backing.

Sure, we still search for trout and salmon, but when we're not knee-deep in a trout stream, we're thinking about someplace warm in Jimmy Buffet climate, casting to fish where space and water seem to stretch forever. We like that; come to think about it, we like it a lot.

IGFA Saltwater Fly-Rod World Records

THE FOLLOWING ARE SALTWATER FLY-ROD RECORDS granted in the tippet class as of January 1, 1998. The records are listed alphabetically according to the common names of species. Reprinted by permission from the International Game Fish Association's 1998 World Record Game Fishes.

Albacore/*Thunnus alalunga*

TIPPET	WEIGHT	PLACE	DATE	ANGLER
1 kg (2 lb)	Vacant			
2 kg (4 lb)	Vacant			
3 kg (6 lb)	Vacant			
4 kg (8 lb)	9.85 kg (21 lb 11 oz)	Hout Bay, Rep. of South Africa	April 2, 1992	Simon Susman
6 kg (12 lb)	11.85 kg (26 lb 2 oz)	San Diego, California, USA	July 15, 1972	Les Eichhorn
8 kg (16 lb)	18.00 kg (39 lb 10 oz)	Hout Bay, Rep. of South Africa	April 6, 1987	Nic de Kock
10 kg (20 lb)	21.31 kg (47 lb)	Hudson Canyon, New Jersey, USA	Sept. 7, 1992	Robert Lubarsky

Amberjack, greater/*Seriola dumerili*

TIPPET	WEIGHT	PLACE	DATE	ANGLER
1 kg (2 lb)	1.02 kg (2 lb 4 oz)	Key West, Florida, USA	Feb. 20, 1990	Herbert G. Ratner, Jr.
2 kg (4 lb)	8.39 kg (18 lb 8 oz)	Key West, Florida, USA	April 9, 1992	George L. Foti
3 kg (6 lb)	13.46 kg (29 lb 11 oz)	Sebastian Inlet, Florida, USA	Sept. 15, 1972	Dave Chermanski
4 kg (8 lb)	16.55 kg (36 lb 8 oz)	Dry Tortugas,Florida, USA	March 16, 1992	William B. DuVal
6 kg (12 lb)	36.28 kg (80 lb)	Fort Pierce, Florida, USA	Jan. 15, 1976	Dave Chermanski
8 kg (16 lb)	47.06 kg (103 lb 12 oz)	Key West, Florida, USA	Jan. 28, 1977	Dr. William J. Munro
10 kg (20 lb)	24.38 kg (53 lb 12 oz)	Dry Tortugas, Florida, USA	March 6, 1993	William B. DuVal

Barracuda, great/*Sphyraena barracuda*

TIPPET	WEIGHT	PLACE	DATE	ANGLER
1 kg (2 lb)	9.18 kg (20 lb 4 oz)	Key West, Florida, USA	Feb. 24, 1991	Herbert G. Ratner, Jr.
2 kg (4 lb)	11.56 kg (25 lb 8 oz)	Key West, Florida, USA	Jan. 9, 1991	Herbert G. Ratner, Jr.
3 kg (6 lb)	14.40 kg (31 lb 12 oz)	Key West, Florida, USA	Oct. 31, 1979	Dallas Howard
4 kg (8 lb)	14.28 kg (31 lb 8 oz)	Marathon, Florida, USA	Aug. 5, 1995	Martin Arostegui
6 kg (12 lb)	17.12 kg (37 lb 12 oz)	Key West, Florida, USA	Dec. 19, 1978	Joe Machiorlatti
8 kg (16 lb)	16.89 kg (37 lb 4 oz)	Key West, Florida, USA	Dec. 16, 1975	Roy Terrell
10 kg (20 lb)	21.77 kg (48 lb)	Ocracoke, North Carolina, USA	Aug. 9, 1996	Reginald L. White

Bass, European/*Dicentrarchus labrax*

TIPPET	WEIGHT	PLACE	DATE	ANGLER
1 kg (2 lb)	Vacant			
2 kg (4 lb)	Vacant			
3 kg (6 lb)	.89 kg (1 lb 15 oz)	Ansedonia, Grosseto, Italy	July 22, 1995	Marco Sammicheli
4 kg (8 lb)	1.10 kg (2 lb 6 oz)	Siagne River, Cannes, France	May 11, 1988	Malcolm Tiki Shewan
6 kg (12 lb)	.91 kg (2 lb)	Giannella, Grosseto, Italy	Nov. 24, 1994	Marco Sammicheli
8 kg (16 lb)	2.27 kg (5 lb)	Ansedonia, Grosseto, Italy	May 13, 1995	Marco Sammicheli
10 kg (20 lb)	Vacant			

Bass, black sea/*Centropristis striata*

TIPPET	WEIGHT	PLACE	DATE	ANGLER
1 kg (2 lb)	.70 kg (1 lb 9 oz)	Ocracoke, North Carolina, USA	Oct. 31, 1992	William B. DuVal
2 kg (4 lb)	.99 kg (2 lb 3 oz)	Ocracoke, North Carolina, USA	Oct. 31, 1992	William B. DuVal
3 kg (6 lb)	.59 kg (1 lb 5 oz)	Ocracoke, North Carolina, USA	June 19, 1994	William B. DuVal
4 kg (8 lb)	.73 kg (1 lb 10 oz)	Ocracoke, North Carolina, USA	Nov. 3, 1993	Mrs. William B. DuVal
6 kg (12 lb)	1.36 kg (3 lb)	Ocracoke, North Carolina, USA	Oct. 31, 1992	William B. DuVal
8 kg (16 lb)	.82 kg (1 lb 13 oz)	Ocracoke, North Carolina, USA	Oct. 31, 1992	William B. DuVal
10 kg (20 lb)	1.02 kg (2 lb 4 oz)	Ocracoke, North Carolina, USA	Aug. 12, 1994	William B. DuVal

Bass, giant sea/*Stereolepis gigas*

TIPPET	WEIGHT	PLACE	DATE	ANGLER
1 kg (2 lb)	Vacant			
2 kg (4 lb)	Vacant			
3 kg (6 lb)	Vacant			
4 kg (8 lb)	Vacant			
6 kg (12 lb)	Vacant			
8 kg (16 lb)	Vacant			
10 kg (20 lb)	Vacant			

Bass, kelp (calico)/*Paralabrax clathratus*

TIPPET	WEIGHT	PLACE	DATE	ANGLER
1 kg (2 lb)	.45 kg (1 lb)	Point Loma, San Diego, California, USA	June 22, 1994	Marshall Madruga
1 kg (2 lb) Tie	.48 kg. (1 lb 1 oz)	Palos Verdes, California, USA	July 19, 1996	Robert Levy
2 kg (4 lb)	.70 kg (1 lb 9 oz)	Palos Verdes, California, USA	July 19, 1996	Robert Levy
3 kg (6 lb)	.90 kg (2 lb)	Palos Verdes, California, USA	July 14, 1996	Dr. John F. Whitaker
4 kg (8 lb)	1.13 kg (2 lb 8 oz)	Palos Verdes, California, USA	March 22, 1996	Dr. John F. Whitaker
6 kg (12 lb)	2.38 kg (5 lb 4 oz)	Catalina Island, California, USA	Sept. 30, 1993	Nick R. Curcione
8 kg (16 lb)	2.75 kg (6 lb 1 oz)	Solana Beach, California, USA	July 8, 1994	Wesley G. Woll
10 kg (20 lb)	1.75 kg (3 lb 14 oz)	Palos Verdes, California, USA	July 27, 1997	Dr. John F. Whitaker, Jr.

Bass, striped/*Morone saxatilis*

TIPPET	WEIGHT	PLACE	DATE	ANGLER
1 kg (2 lb)	5.44 kg (12 lb)	Napatree Beach, Rhode Island, USA	Sept. 27, 1997	Alan Caolo
2 kg (4 lb)	8.84 kg (19 lb 8 oz)	Misquamicit Beach, Rhode Island, USA	Aug. 6, 1997	Alan Caolo
3 kg (6 lb)	11.22 kg (24 lb 12 oz)	American River, California, USA	Dec. 2, 1973	Alfred Perryman
4 kg (8 lb)	19.05 kg (42 lb)	Sacramento River, Verona, California, USA	May 30, 1986	Ronald S. Hayashi
6 kg (12 lb)	29.25 kg (64 lb 8 oz)	Smith River, Oregon, USA	July 28, 1973	Beryl E. Bliss
8 kg (16 lb)	23.36 kg (51 lb 8 oz)	Smith River, Oregon, USA	May 18, 1974	Gary L. Dyer
10 kg (20 lb)	14.96 kg (33 lb)	Chatham, Massachusetts, USA	July 23, 1996	David W. Rimmer

Bluefish/*Pomatomus saltatrix*

TIPPET	WEIGHT	PLACE	DATE	ANGLER
1 kg (2 lb)	6.52 kg (14 lb 6 oz)	Martha's Vineyard, Massachusetts, USA	Oct. 19, 1984	Danwin M. Purdy
2 kg (4 lb)	6.61 kg (14 lb 9 oz)	Lobsterville Beach, Massachusetts, USA	Oct. 19, 1984	Danwin M. Purdy
3 kg (6 lb)	6.60 kg (14 lb 9 oz)	Chesapeake Bay, Virginia, USA	June 24, 1977	Mev Van Doren
4 kg (8 lb)	8.35 kg (18 lb 6 oz)	Martha's Vineyard, Massachusetts, USA	Oct. 22, 1984	Gregory J. Essayan
6 kg (12 lb)	8.73 kg (19 lb 4 oz)	Virginia Beach, Virginia, USA	Nov. 6, 1980	Larry Greene
8 kg (16 lb)	8.95 kg (19 lb 12 oz)	Nags Head, North Carolina, USA	Nov. 2, 1987	Doug Hinson
10 kg (20 lb)	8.48 kg (18 lb 11 oz)	Martha's Vineyard, Massachusetts, USA	Oct. 9, 1995	LoriLee VanDerlaske

Bonefish/*Albula spp.*

TIPPET	WEIGHT	PLACE	DATE	ANGLER
1 kg (2 lb)	5.44 kg (12 lb)	Bimini, Bahamas	Nov. 12, 1989	James B. Orthwein
2 kg (4 lb)	6.80 kg (15 lb)	Bimini, Bahamas	March 17, 1983	James B. Orthwein
3 kg (6 lb)	6.01 kg (13 lb 4 oz)	Islamorada, Florida, USA	Nov. 6, 1973	Jim Lopez
4 kg (8 lb)	7.03 kg (15 lb 8 oz)	Key Biscayne, Florida, USA	Feb. 27, 1997	Joe Pantorno
6 kg (12 lb)	6.90 kg (15 lb 4 oz)	Big Pine Key, Florida, USA	June 19, 1997	Gordon E. Hill
8 kg (16 lb)	6.01 kg (13 lb 4 oz)	Islamorada, Florida, USA	April 19, 1995	Michael Swerdlow
10 kg (20 lb)	5.66 kg (12 lb 8 oz)	Key Biscayne, Florida, USA	March 13, 1997	Jimmie Kline

Bonefish, Atlantic/*Sarda sarda*

TIPPET	WEIGHT	PLACE	DATE	ANGLER
1 kg (2 lb)	2.71 kg (5 lb 15 oz)	Montauk, Long Island, New York, USA	Aug. 12, 1988	Stephen Sloan
2 kg (4 lb)	3.81 kg (8 lb 6 oz)	Weekapaug, Rhode Island, USA	Nov. 2, 1990	John F. Dickinson
3 kg (6 lb)	4.74 kg (10 lb 7 oz)	Fischer's Island, New York, USA	Oct. 27, 1994	David W. Skok
4 kg (8 lb)	4.79 kg (10 lb 9 oz)	Martha's Vineyard, Massachusetts, USA	Oct. 3, 1989	Kib Bramhall
6 kg (12 lb)	5.61 kg (12 lb 5 oz)	Martha's Vineyard, Massachusetts, USA	Oct. 23, 1994	Jim Lepage
8 kg (16 lb)	3.28 kg (7 lb 4 oz)	Mt. Sinai Inlet, New York, USA	Nov. 3, 1995	Christopher J. Catan
10 kg (20 lb)	3.51 kg (7 lb 12 oz)	Nantucket, Massachusetts, USA	Oct. 20, 1995	Pip Winslow

Bonito, Pacific/*Sarda spp.*

TIPPET	WEIGHT	PLACE	DATE	ANGLER
1 kg (2 lb)	2.20 kg (4 lb 13 oz)	Wollongong, Australia	March 2, 1996	Gregory Phillip Clarke
2 kg (4 lb)	4.08 kg (9 lb)	San Diego, California, USA	Aug. 24, 1997	Don B. Walker
3 kg (6 lb)	Vacant			
4 kg (8 lb)	5.44 kg (12 lb)	Flamingo, Costa Rica	May 24, 1994	Robert Rein
6 kg (12 lb)	7.03 kg (15 lb 8 oz)	Monterey Bay, California, USA	Sept. 15, 1972	Bob Edgley
8 kg (16 lb)	3.35 kg (7 lb 6 oz)	San Martin Island, Baja California, Mexico	Sept. 29, 1994	Jerry Wang
10 kg (20 lb)	4.62 (10 lb 3 oz)	13 Fathom Bank, Baja California, Mexico	Jan. 11, 1995	Bill F. Howe

Cobia/*Rachycentron canadum*

TIPPET	WEIGHT	PLACE	DATE	ANGLER
1 kg (2 lb)	10.38 kg (22 lb 14 oz)	Destin, Florida, USA	June 6, 1996	George E. Hogan, Jr.
2 kg (4 lb)	16.87 kg (37 lb 3 oz)	Destin, Florida, USA	April 26, 1995	George E. Hogan, Jr.
3 kg (6 lb)	17.91 kg (39 lb 8 oz)	Key West, Florida, USA	March 15, 1972	Roy Terrel
4 kg (8 lb)	30.50 kg (67 lb 4 oz)	Key West, Florida, USA	March 2, 1985	Pat Ford
6 kg (12 lb)	31.29 kg (69 lb)	Florida Bay, Florida, USA	Dec. 9, 1967	Ralph Delph
8 kg (16 lb)	37.76 kg (83 lb 4 oz)	Key West, Florida, USA	Jan. 2, 1986	Jim Anson
10 kg (20 lb)	28.12 kg (62 lb 3 oz)	Gulf Shores, Alabama, USA	April 27, 1994	Robert T. Cunningham, Jr.

Cod, Atlantic/*Gadus morhua*

TIPPET	WEIGHT	PLACE	DATE	ANGLER
1 kg (2 lb)	1.25 kg (2 lb 12 oz)	Great Belt, Denmark	April 22, 1984	Gorm Siiger
2 kg (4 lb)	1.23 kg (2 lb 11 oz)	Terrak, Norway	Aug. 4, 1984	Hans Joachim Wenzel
3 kg (6 lb)	2.66 kg (5 lb 14 oz)	Port Maitland, Nova Scotia, Canada	June 22, 1973	Lou Truppi
4 kg (8 lb)	8.35 kg (18 lb 6 oz)	Vikaer Beach, Jylland, Denmark	Feb. 15, 1983	John Anker
6 kg (12 lb)	4.02 kg (8 lb 14 oz)	Port Maitland, Nova Scotia, Canada	June 22, 1973	Lou Truppi
8 kg (16 lb)	1.58 kg (3 lb 8 oz)	Gloucester, Massachusetts, USA	June 28, 1990	Kenneth M. Lai
10 kg (20 lb)	Vacant			

Cod, Pacific/*Gadus macrocephalus*

TIPPET	WEIGHT	PLACE	DATE	ANGLER
1 kg (2 lb)	Vacant			
2 kg (4 lb)	1.87 kg (4 lb 2 oz)	Dangerous Cape, Alaska, USA	June 20, 1993	E. Z. Marchant
3 kg (6 lb)	2.26 kg (5 lb)	Kodiak, Alaska, USA	July 28, 1996	Paul Leader
4 kg (8 lb)	2.01 kg (4 lb 7 oz)	Dangerous Cape, Alaska, USA	June 20, 1993	E. Z. Marchant
6 kg (12 lb)	3.62 kg (8 lb)	Kodiak, Alaska, USA	July 28, 1996	Paul Leader
8 kg (16 lb)	3.99 kg (8 lb 13 oz)	Dangerous Cape, Alaska, USA	June 20, 1993	Lance Anderson
10 kg (20 lb)	2.04 kg (4 lb 8 oz)	Dangerous Cape, Alaska, USA	June 20, 1993	Lindy Keirn

Conger/*Conger conger*

TIPPET	WEIGHT	PLACE	DATE	ANGLER
1 kg (2 lb)	Vacant			
2 kg (4 lb)	Vacant			
3 kg (6 lb)	Vacant			
4 kg (8 lb)	Vacant			
6 kg (12 lb)	Vacant			
8 kg (16 lb)	Vacant			
10 kg (20 lb)	Vacant			

Dentex/*Dentex dentex*

TIPPET	WEIGHT	PLACE	DATE	ANGLER
1 kg (2 lb)	Vacant			
2 kg (4 lb)	Vacant			
3 kg (6 lb)	Vacant			
4 kg (8 lb)	Vacant			
6 kg (8 lb)	Vacant			
8 kg (16 lb)	Vacant			
10 kg (20 lb)	Vacant			

Dolphin/*Coryphaena hippurus*

TIPPET	WEIGHT	PLACE	DATE	ANGLER
1 kg (2 lb)	8.05 kg (17 lb 12 oz)	Petite Coupe, Mauritius	Nov. 29, 1990	Richard F. Flasch
2 kg (4 lb)	8.84 kg (19 lb 8 oz)	Cozumel, Q. Roo, Mexico	June 9, 1991	Charles D. Owen, Jr.
3 kg (6 lb)	15.42 kg (34 lb)	Pinas Bay, Panama	Dec. 23, 1980	Tred Barta
4 kg (8 lb)	21.18 kg (46 lb 11 oz)	Freeport, Grand Bahama, Bahamas	May 19, 1997	Peter Rose
6 kg (12 lb)	26.30 kg (58 lb)	Pinas Bay, Panama	Dec. 6, 1964	Stu Apte
8 kg (16 lb)	24.26 kg (53 lb 8 oz)	Isla Mujeres, Quintana Roo, Mexico	April 29, 1990	Rufus Wakeman II
10 Kg (20 lb)	24.04 kg (53 lb)	Quepos, Costa Rica	Jan. 14, 1997	Dr. Bill Mooney

Drum, black/*Pogonias cromis*

TIPPET	WEIGHT	PLACE	DATE	ANGLER
1 kg (2 lb)	5.55 kg (12 lb 4 oz)	Banana River, Cocoa Beach, Florida, USA	Nov. 4, 1994	Dave Chermanski
2 kg (4 lb)	13.83 kg (30 lb 8 oz)	Banana River, Cape Canaveral, Florida, USA	Jan. 14, 1996	Scott Nickels
3 kg (6 lb)	13.09 kg (28 lb 14 oz)	Banana River, Florida, USA	Dec. 23, 1996	Scott Nickels
4 kg (8 lb)	22.79 kg (50 lb 4 oz)	Indian River, Meritt Island, Florida, USA	July 12, 1986	Mark R. Marconi
6 kg (12 lb)	26.30 kg (57 lb 8 oz)	Chesapeake Bay Bridge Tunnel, Virginia, USA	June 25, 1995	Capt. Jon Holsenbeck
8 kg (16 lb)	14.96 kg (33 lb)	Indian River, Port St. John, Florida, USA	Jan. 29, 1991	Capt. Troy Perez
10 kg (20 lb)	22.22 kg (49 lb)	Indian River, Cocoa, Florida, USA	Feb. 14, 1992	C. Windsor Cyrus

Drum, red/*Scianops ocellatus*

TIPPET	WEIGHT	PLACE	DATE	ANGLER
1 kg (2 lb)	6.28 kg (13 lb 13 oz)	Mosquito Lagoon, Oak Hill, Florida, USA	Feb. 27, 1996	Dave Chermanski
2 kg (4 lb)	12.47 kg (27 lb 8 oz)	Chandeleur Islands, Louisiana, USA	Jan. 16, 1993	Robert T. Cunningham, Jr.
3 kg (6 lb)	15.64 kg (34 lb 8 oz)	Banana River, Florida, USA	Oct. 29, 1994	Capt. Lance Crouch
4 kg (8 lb)	14.51 kg (32 lb)	Banana River, Florida, USA	May 31, 1994	Lance Crouch
6 kg (12 lb)	19.19 kg (42 lb 5 oz)	Oregon Inlet, North Carolina, USA	May 12, 1981	J. M. (Chico) Fernandez
8 kg (16 lb)	19.50 kg (43 lb)	Banana River Lagoon, Florida, USA	May 7, 1995	Greg Braunstein, MD
10 kg (20 lb)	17.80 kg (39 lb 4 oz)	Ocracoke, North Carolina, USA	Oct. 27, 1995	Doug Hinson

False Albacore see *Tunny, little*

Flounder, summer/*Paralichthys dentantus*

TIPPET	WEIGHT	PLACE	DATE	ANGLER
1 kg (2 lb)	1.87 kg (4 lb 2 oz)	Horton's Point, Mattituck, L.I., New York, USA	Aug. 31, 1994	John Boesenberg
2 kg (4 lb)	.87 kg (1 lb 15 oz)	Shinnecock Bay, L.I., New York, USA	Aug. 16, 1986	Alan Flexer
3 kg (6 lb)	3.68 kg (8 lb 2 oz)	Greenwich, Connecticut, USA	Oct. 27, 1991	William N. Herold
4 kg (8 lb)	Vacant			
6 kg (12 lb)	1.58 kg (3 lb 8 oz)	Longport, New Jersey, USA	June 23, 1997	Joseph J. Cariosa, Jr.
8 kg (16 lb)	3.09 kg (6 lb 13 oz)	Asbescon Inlet, New Jersey, USA	June 18, 1996	Paul D. Ripperger
10 kg (20 lb)	2.32 kg (5 lb 1 oz)	Montauk Point, New York, USA	July 10, 1993	Mike Corblies

Halibut, Atlantic/*Hippoglossus hippoglossus*

TIPPET	WEIGHT	PLACE	DATE	ANGLER
1 kg (2 lb)	Vacant			
2 kg (4 lb)	Vacant			
3 kg (6 lb)	Vacant			
4 kg (8 lb)	Vacant			
6 kg (12 lb)	Vacant			
8 kg (16 lb)	Vacant			
10 kg (20 lb)	Vacant			

Halibut, California/*Paralichthys californicus*

TIPPET	WEIGHT	PLACE	DATE	ANGLER
1 kg (2 lb)	Vacant			
2 kg (4 lb)	2.15 kg (4 lb 11 oz)	Magdalena, Baja Calif., Mexico	April 12, 1982	Didier Van der Veecken
3 kg (6 lb)	Vacant			
4 kg (8 lb)	2.94 kg (6 lb 8 oz)	Magdalena Bay, Baja Calif., Mexico	March 13, 1989	Didier Van der Veecken
6 kg (12 lb)	1.90 kg (4 lb 3 oz)	Magdalena, Baja Calif., Mexico	April 12, 1982	Didier Van der Veecken
8 kg (16 lb)	3.09 kg (6 lb 13 oz)	Alameda Rockwall, California, USA	June 3, 1995	Lance P. Anderson
10 kg (20 lb)	5.95 kg (13 lb 2 oz)	Palos Verdes, California, USA	April 30, 1995	Dr. John F. Whitaker

Halibut, Pacific/*Hippoglossus stenolepis*

TIPPET	WEIGHT	PLACE	DATE	ANGLER
1 kg (2 lb)	4.98 (11 lb)	Kodiak, Alaska, USA	Aug. 1, 1994	Paul Leader
2 kg (4 lb)	13.60 (30 lb)	Kodiak, Alaska, USA	Aug. 7, 1997	Paul Leader
3 kg (6 lb)	15.42 kg (34 lb)	Kodiak, Alaska, USA	Aug. 1, 1997	Paul Leader
4 kg (8 lb)	33.56 kg (74 lb)	Port Armstrong, Alaska, USA	July 19, 1990	Dick DeMars
6 kg (12 lb)	33.56 kg (74 lb)	Kodiak, Alaska, USA	Aug. 1, 1997	Paul Leader
8 kg (16 lb)	38.01 kg (83 lb 12 oz)	Gove Point, Alaska, USA	Aug. 6, 1994	Mike Hood
10 kg (20 lb)	31.97 kg (70 lb 8 oz)	Chrome Point, Alaska, USA	June 18, 1993	Lindy Keirn

Jack, crevalle/*Caranx hippos*

TIPPET	WEIGHT	PLACE	DATE	ANGLER
1 kg (2 lb)	4.98 kg (11 lb)	Fort Lauderdale, Florida, USA	Feb. 23, 1983	Mark E. Krowka
2 kg (4 lb)	13.38 kg (29 lb 8 oz)	Sebastian R., Florida, USA	June 14, 1993	Dave Chermanski
3 kg (6 lb)	13.83 kg (30 lb 8 oz)	Pensacola Beach, Florida, USA	Aug. 13, 1994	Carl E. Cole
4 kg (8 lb)	14.06 kg (31 lb)	Port Canaveral, Florida, USA	April 28, 1983	Troy Perez
6 kg (12 lb)	17.00 kg (37 lb 8 oz)	Dry Tortugas, Florida, USA	Feb. 11, 1994	Carlos B. Solis
8 kg (16 lb)	19.95 kg (44 lb)	Tortuguero, Costa Rica	Feb. 20, 1979	R. T. Miller
10 kg (20 lb)	15.42 kg (34 lb)	Pensacola Bay, Pensacola, Florida, USA	Aug. 14, 1992	Carl E. Cole

Jack, horse-eye/*Caranx latus*

TIPPET	WEIGHT	PLACE	DATE	ANGLER
1 kg (2 lb)	Vacant			
2 kg (4 lb)	1.53 kg (3 lb 6 oz)	Key West, Florida, USA	Aug. 3, 1987	Chuck Brodzki
3 kg (6 lb)	2.81 kg (6 lb 3 oz)	West End, Grand Bahama, Bahamas	Oct. 25, 1996	Colin Rose
4 kg (8 lb)	6.57 kg (14 lb 8 oz)	Key West, Florida, USA	Sept. 7, 1986	Joseph M. Stehr, III
6 kg (12 lb)	8.84 kg (19 lb 8 oz)	Bimini, Bahamas	Aug. 14, 1997	Ray C. Stormont
8 kg (16 lb)	3.74 kg (8 lb 4 oz)	Key West, Florida, USA	July 23, 1984	Hubert M. Soucie
10 kg (20 lb)	5.66 kg (18 lb)	Bimini, Bahamas	June 7, 1997	Barry Dorf

Jack, Pacific crevalle/*Caranx caninus*

TIPPET	WEIGHT	PLACE	DATE	ANGLER
1 kg (2 lb)	Vacant			
2 kg (4 lb)	3.40 kg (7 lb 8 oz)	Ricon de Guayabitos, Mexico	July 11, 1993	Terry Gunn
3 kg (6 lb)	Vacant			
4 kg (8 lb)	5.44 kg (12 lb)	Cabo San Lucas, Baja Calif., Mexico	March 6, 1984	Didier Van der Veecken
6 kg (12 lb)	6.23 kg (13 lb 12 oz)	Rincon De Guayabitos, Mexico	July 11, 1993	Russell Sullivan
8 kg (16 lb)	7.37 kg (16 lb 4 oz)	Cabo San Lucas, Baja Calif., Mexico	April 29, 1988	Didier Van der Veecken
10 kg (20 lb)	10.34 kg (22 lb 12 oz)	Todos Santos, Baja California Sur, Mexico	Dec. 5, 1996	Karen Kukolich

Jewfish/*Epinephelus itajara*

TIPPET	WEIGHT	PLACE	DATE	ANGLER
1 kg (2 lb)	Vacant			
2 kg (4 lb)	Vacant			
3 kg (6 lb)	Vacant			
4 kg (8 lb)	Vacant			
6 kg (12 lb)	161.48 kg (356 lb)	Islamorada, Florida, USA	March 15, 1967	Bart Froth
8 kg (16 lb)	Vacant			
10 kg (20 lb)	Vacant			

Kahawai (Australian salmon)/*Arripis trutta/Arripis esper*

TIPPET	WEIGHT	PLACE	DATE	ANGLER
1 kg (2 lb)	2.60 kg (5 lb 11 oz)	Fantail Bay, Coromandel, New Zealand	Dec. 30, 1989	Phillip M. Lovell
2 kg (4 lb)	4.80 kg (10 lb 9 oz)	Rottnest Island, W.A., Australia	April 5, 1986	Simon Gilbert
3 kg (6 lb)	2.17 kg (4 lb 12 oz)	"The Needles," Great Barrier Island, New Zealand	Oct. 18, 1996	Ian McFadzean
4 kg (8 lb)	4.00 kg (8 lb 13 oz)	Rottnest Island, W.A., Australia	April 5, 1986	Simon Gilbert
6 kg (12 lb)	4.00 kg (8 lb 13 oz)	Rottnest Island, W.A., Australia	April 5, 1986	Lou Rummer
8 kg (16 lb)	6.30 kg (13 lb 14 oz)	Jervis Bau, N.S.W., Australia	June 1, 1991	Steve Starling
10 kg (20 lb)	3.00 kg (6 lb 9 oz)	Castle Point, New Zealand	Feb. 6, 1997	Graeme Sinclair

Kawakawa/*Euthynnus affinis*

TIPPET	WEIGHT	PLACE	DATE	ANGLER
1 kg (2 lb)	1.27 kg (2 lb 12 oz)	Sydney, New South Wales, Australia	Dec. 26, 1982	John G. Dow
2 kg (4 lb)	4.75 kg (10 lb 7 oz)	Dunk Island, Queensland, Australia	Sept. 28, 1984	Andrew A. MacGrath
3 kg (6 lb)	Vacant			
4 kg (8 lb)	8.46 kg (18 lb 8 oz)	Moreton Bay, Queensland, Australia	Oct. 22, 1987	Darryl J. Steel
6 kg (12 lb)	7.40 kg (16 lb 5 oz)	Onslow, W.A., Australia	Dec. 29, 1986	Jeffrey W. Grist
8 kg (16 lb)	8.60 kg (18 lb 15 oz)	Onslow, W.A., Australia	Dec. 29, 1986	Jeffrey W. Grist
10 kg (20 lb)	Vacant			

Leerfish (Garrick)/*Lichia amia*

TIPPET	WEIGHT	PLACE	DATE	ANGLER
1 kg (2 lb)	Vacant			
2 kg (4 lb)	Vacant			
3 kg (6 lb)	Vacant			
4 kg (8 lb)	5.6 kg (12 lb 5 oz)	Nouadhibou, Mauritania	Aug. 12, 1994	Daniel Maury
6 kg (12 lb)	7.00 kg (15 lb 6 oz)	Port St. Johns, South Africa	Oct. 4, 1996	Richard Schumann
8 kg (16 lb)	Vacant			
10 kg (20 lb)	Vacant			

Lingcod/*Ophiodon elongatus*

TIPPET	WEIGHT	PLACE	DATE	ANGLER
1 kg (2 lb)	Vacant			
2 kg (4 lb)	Vacant			
3 kg (6 lb)	Vacant			
4 kg (8 lb)	2.49 kg (5 lb 8 oz)	Elfin Cove, Alaska, USA	Sept. 7, 1989	Paul Leader
6 kg (12 lb)	11.08 kg (24 lb 7 oz)	Depoe Bay, Oregon, USA	Aug. 21, 1993	Glenn W. Young
8 kg (16 lb)	59.11 kg (26 lb 13 oz)	Chugach Island, Alaska, USA	July 16, 1993	Lance P. Anderson
10 kg (20 lb)	16.32 kg (36 lb)	Cross Sound, Alaska, USA	July 31, 1997	Russell Jensen

Mackerel, cero/*Scomberomorus regalis*

TIPPET	WEIGHT	PLACE	DATE	ANGLER
1 kg (2 lb)	1.92 kg (4 lb 4 oz)	Key West, Florida, USA	March 1, 1995	George L. Foti
2 kg (4 lb)	2.38 kg (5 lb 4 oz)	Key West, Florida, USA	March 1, 1995	George L. Foti
3 kg (6 lb)	2.94 kg (6 lb 8 oz)	Key West, Florida, USA	March 1, 1995	George L. Foti
4 kg (8 lb)	3.17 kg (7 lb)	Key West, Florida, USA	Feb. 2, 1995	Al Golinski
6 kg (12 lb)	3.85 kg (8 lb 8 oz)	Walkers Cay, Bahamas	July 1, 1994	Greg Norman
8 kg (16 lb)	4.98 kg (11 lb)	Walkers Cay, Abaco, Bahamas	June 23, 1993	David Webb
10 kg (20 lb)	3.51 kg (7 lb 12 oz)	Key West, Florida, USA	Feb. 2, 1995	Al Golinski

Mackerel, king/*Scomberomorus cavalla*

TIPPET	WEIGHT	PLACE	DATE	ANGLER
1 kg (2 lb)	Vacant			
2 kg (4 lb)	6.69 kg (4 lb 12 oz)	Key West, Florida, USA	Feb. 4, 1997	Al Golinski
3 kg (6 lb)	10.88 kg (24 lb)	Key West, Florida, USA	Feb. 5, 1997	George Foti
4 kg (8 lb)	13.04 kg (28 lb 12 oz)	Key West, Florida, USA	Feb. 5, 1997	George Foti
6 kg (12 lb)	17.23 kg (38 lb)	Key West, Florida, USA	Jan. 12, 1971	Jim Lopez
8 kg (16 lb)	23.24 kg (51 lb 4 oz)	Key West, Florida, USA	Feb. 15, 1987	Rick Gunion
10 kg (20 lb)	24.94 kg (55 lb)	Key West, Florida, USA	March 20, 1995	Ben Bergeron

Mackerel, narrowbarred/*Scomberomorus commerson*

TIPPET	WEIGHT	PLACE	DATE	ANGLER
1 kg (2 lb)	2.00 kg (4 lb 6 oz)	Torres Strait, Queensland, Australia	March 7, 1990	Graham L. Plummer
2 kg (4 lb)	Vacant			
3 kg (6 lb)	Vacant			
4 kg (8 lb)	10.00 kg (22 lb)	Exmouth, W.A., Australia	Aug. 25, 1988	Simon Gilbert
6 kg (12 lb)	16.80 kg (37 lb)	Onslow, W.A., Australia	Sept. 11, 1987	Jeffrey W. Grist
8 kg (16 lb)	21.00 kg (46 lb 4 oz)	Exmouth, W.A., Australia	Sept. 2, 1991	Ken Ahmat
10 kg (20 lb)	18.50 kg (40 lb 12 oz)	Innisfail, Australia	Sept. 16, 1996	George Campbell

Mackerel, Spanish/*Scomberomorus maculatus*

TIPPET	WEIGHT	PLACE	DATE	ANGLER
1 kg (2 lb)	1.95 kg (4 lb 4 oz)	Indian Rocks Beach, Florida, USA	Sept. 19, 1989	Doug Johnston
2 kg (4 lb)	2.94 kg (6 lb 8 oz)	Gulf of Mexico, Alabama, USA	Sept. 18, 1995	Robert T. Cunningham, Jr.
3 kg (6 lb)	2.49 kg (5 lb 7 oz)	New Port Richey, Florida, USA	Oct. 30, 1996	Capt. James P. Wisner
4 kg (8 lb)	2.94 kg (6 lb 7 oz)	New Port Richey, Florida, USA	Oct. 28, 1996	Capt. James P. Wisner
6 kg (12 lb)	3.94 kg (8 lb 11 oz)	Martha's Vineyard, Massachusetts, USA	Aug. 25, 1994	Donald T. MacGillivray, Jr.
8 kg (16 lb)	3.06 kg (6 lb 12 oz)	Key West, Florida, USA	Nov. 22, 1989	Ted Lund, III
10 kg (20 lb)	3.10 kg (6 lb 13 oz)	Tarpon Springs, Florida, USA	Nov. 7, 1995	Capt. James P. Wisner

Madai/*Pagrus major*

TIPPET	WEIGHT	PLACE	DATE	ANGLER
1 kg (2 lb)	Vacant			
2 kg (4 lb)	Vacant			
3 kg (6 lb)	Vacant			
4 kg (8 lb)	Vacant			
6 kg (12 lb)	Vacant			
8 kg (16 lb)	Vacant			
10 kg (20 lb)	Vacant			

Marlin, black/*Makaira indica*

TIPPET	WEIGHT	PLACE	DATE	ANGLER
1 kg (2 lb)	Vacant			
2 kg (4 lb)	Vacant			
3 kg (6 lb)	20.97 kg (46 lb 3 oz)	Cairns, Queensland, Australia	Sept. 14, 1972	William W. Pate, Jr.
4 kg (8 lb)	27.50 kg (60 lb 10 oz)	Mooloolaba, Queensland, Australia	Jan. 9, 1996	Mark H. Carnegie
6 kg (12 lb)	39.00 kg (85 lb 15 oz)	Cape Bowling Green, Townsville, Australia	July 28, 1987	Ray Beadle
8 kg (16 lb)	42.75 kg (94 lb 3 oz)	Cape Bowling Green, Townsville, Australia	July 27, 1987	Ray Beadle
10 kg (20 lb)	38.00 kg (83 lb 12 oz)	Oyster Reef, Cairns, Australia	Jan. 9, 1997	Roly Newton

Marlin, blue (Atlantic)/*Makaira nigricans*

TIPPET	WEIGHT	PLACE	DATE	ANGLER
1 kg (2 lb)	Vacant			
2 kg (4 lb)	Vacant			
3 kg (6 lb)	Vacant			
4 kg (8 lb)	Vacant			
6 kg (12 lb)	Vacant			
8 kg (16 lb)	72.12 kg (159 lb)	St. Thomas, Virgin Islands, USA	Aug. 18, 1990	Jim Gray
10 kg (20 lb)	94.34 kg (208 lb)	La Guaira Banks, Venezuela	May 20, 1994	Charlie Tombras

Marlin, blue (Pacific)/*Makaira nigricans*

TIPPET	WEIGHT	PLACE	DATE	ANGLER
1 kg (2 lb)	Vacant			
2 kg (4 lb)	Vacant			
3 kg (6 lb)	Vacant			
4 kg (8 lb)	Vacant			
6 kg (12 lb)	Vacant			
8 kg (16 lb)	92.30 kg (203 lb 8 oz)	Guanamar, Costa Rica	Feb. 12, 1991	Jim Gray
10 kg (20 lb)	117.93 kg (260 lb)	Flamingo, Costa Rica	Aug. 6, 1991	Jim Gray

Marlin, striped/*Tetrapturus audax*

TIPPET	WEIGHT	PLACE	DATE	ANGLER
1 kg (2 lb)	Vacant			
2 kg (4 lb)	Vacant			
3 kg (6 lb)	35.30 kg (78 lb)	Cabo San Lucas, Baja California Sur, Mexico	Dec. 24, 1997	Tony Hedley
4 kg (8 lb)	47.62 kg (105 lb)	Cocos Island, Costa Rica	June 28, 1996	Charles Owen, Jr.
6 kg (12 lb)	67.13 kg (148 lb)	Salina, Ecuador	May, 1967	Lee Wulff
8 kg (16 lb)	82.55 kg (182 lb)	Cocos Island, Costa Rica	Aug. 27, 1995	Charles Tombras
10 kg (20 lb)	90.50 kg (199 lb 8 oz)	Newcastle, Australia	April 20, 1996	Dean Butler

Marlin, white/*Tetrapturus albidus*

TIPPET	WEIGHT	PLACE	DATE	ANGLER
1 kg (2 lb)	Vacant			
2 kg (4 lb)	Vacant			
3 kg (6 lb)	Vacant			
4 kg (8 lb)	33.11 kg (73 lb)	La Guaira, Venezuela	Sept. 22, 1984	Pat Ford
6 kg (12 lb)	39.60 kg (87 lb 4 oz)	Mohammedia, Morocco	Sept. 12, 1996	Fouad Sahiaoui
8 kg (16 lb)	47.36 kg (104 lb 6 oz)	Mohammedia, Morocco	Sept. 14, 1996	Billy Pate
10 kg (20 lb)	37.64 kg (83 lb)	Vitoria, Brazil	Dec. 1, 1996	Charlie Tombras

Permit/*Trachinotus falcatus*

TIPPET	WEIGHT	PLACE	DATE	ANGLER
1 kg (2 lb)	4.42 kg (9 lb 12 oz)	Sugarloaf Key, Florida, USA	April 13, 1986	Del Brown
2 kg (4 lb)	10.88 kg (24 lb)	Sugarloaf Key, Florida, USA	March 9, 1992	Del Brown
3 kg (6 lb)	8.84 kg (19 lb 8 oz)	Isle of Pines, Cuba	May 16, 1957	Joseph W. Brooks
4 kg (8 lb)	18.82 kg (41 lb 8 oz)	Key West, Florida, USA	March 13, 1986	Del Brown
6 kg (12 lb)	16.38 kg (36 lb 2 oz)	Marsh Harbor, Abaco, Bahamas	May 17, 1993	Carl Navarre, Jr.
8 kg (16 lb)	16.32 kg (36 lb)	Key West, Florida, USA	April 3, 1985	Kenneth Marlin
10 kg (20 lb)	14.74 kg (32 lb 8 oz)	Key West, Florida, USA	April 15, 1994	James M. Eckhart

Pollack, European/*Pollachius pollachius*

TIPPET	WEIGHT	PLACE	DATE	ANGLER
1 kg (2 lb)	2.53 kg (5 lb 9 oz)	Pentland Firth, Scotland	Sept. 1, 1990	Stan Massey
2 kg (4 lb)	3.01 kg (6 lb 10 oz)	Sheephaven Bay, Eire	Sept. 6, 1996	Joe Nash
3 kg (6 lb)	1.76 kg (3 lb 13 oz)	Duesund, Norway	June 23, 1983	Rolf Van De Pavert
4 kg (8 lb)	2.15 kg (4 lb 11 oz)	Sheephaven Bay, Eire	Sept. 6, 1996	Joe Nash
6 kg (12 lb)	2.72 kg (6 lb)	Ballantrae, Scotland	Sept. 25, 1993	Murdo B. Gunn
8 kg (16 lb)	5.59 kg (12 lb 5 oz)	Oygarden, Hordaland County, Norway	Oct. 27, 1990	Yngve Landro
10 kg (20 lb)	3.41 kg (7 lb 8 oz)	Sheephaven Bay, Eire	Sept. 11, 1996	Joe Nash

Pollack/*Pollachius virens*

TIPPET	WEIGHT	PLACE	DATE	ANGLER
1 kg (2 lb)	.82 kg (1 lb 13 oz)	East Boothbay, Maine, USA	May 8, 1982	Alan J. Campbell
2 kg (4 lb)	.53 kg (1 lb 2 oz)	Fjellueroyo, Norway	July 21, 1990	Jorg Marquard
3 kg (6 lb)	4.02 kg (8 lb 14 oz)	Port Maitland, Nova Scotia, Canada	June 22, 1973	Louis Truppi
4 kg (8 lb)	Vacant			
6 kg (12 lb)	4.87 kg (10 lb 12 oz)	Newport, Rhode Island, USA	Nov. 24, 1968	R. H. Smith
8 kg (16 lb)	8.39 kg (18 lb 8 oz)	Port Maitland, Nova Scotia, Canada	June 22, 1973	Louis Truppi
10 kg (20 lb)	Vacant			

Pompano, African/*Alectis ciliaris*

TIPPET	WEIGHT	PLACE	DATE	ANGLER
1 kg (2 lb)	Vacant			
2 kg (4 lb)	6.57 kg (14 lb 8 oz)	Key West, Florida, USA	May 2, 1994	Christian Martin
3 kg (6 lb)	Vacant			
4 kg (8 lb)	14.17 kg (31 lb 4 oz)	Key West, Florida, USA	Feb. 20, 1993	Carlos B. Solis
6 kg (12 lb)	15.19 kg (33 lb 8 oz)	Palm Beach, Florida, USA	Dec. 21, 1968	Gil Drake, Jr.
8 kg (16 lb)	13.74 kg (30 lb 5 oz)	Stuart, Florida, USA	March 14, 1982	Paul F. Leader
10 kg (20 lb)	14.28 kg (31 lb 8 oz)	Jupiter, Florida, USA	July 24, 1993	Robert Follweiler

Queenfish/*Scomberoides commersonnianus & Scomberoides lysan*

TIPPET	WEIGHT	PLACE	DATE	ANGLER
1 kg (2 lb)	.51 kg (1 lb 2 oz)	Christmas Island, Rep. of Kiribati	March 2, 1997	Bud Korteweg
2 kg (4 lb)	5.00 kg (11 lb)	Groote-Eylandt, N.T., Australia	Aug. 3, 1989	Raz Reid
3 kg (6 lb)	.62 kg (1 lb 6 oz)	Christmas Island, Rep. of Kiribati	March 3, 1997	Bud Korteweg
4 kg (8 lb)	8.20 kg (18 lb 1 oz)	Onslow, W.A., Australia	Sept. 24, 1989	Simon Gilbert
6 kg (12 lb)	7.80 kg (17 lb 3 oz)	Onslow, W.A., Australia	Sept. 25, 1989	Simon Gilbert
8 kg (16 lb)	9.60 kg (21 lb 2 oz)	Inhaca Island, Mozambique	March 20, 1997	Tim Briscoe
10 kg (20 lb)	8.80 kg (19 lb 6 oz)	Inhaca Island, Mozambique	Nov. 27, 1995	Garth Johnson
10 kg (20 lb) Tie	8.80 kg (19 lb 6 oz)	Cape York, Australia	April 27, 1997	Greg Bethune

Roosterfish/*Nematistius pectoralis*

TIPPET	WEIGHT	PLACE	DATE	ANGLER
1 kg (2 lb)	Vacant			
2 kg (4 lb)	3.50 kg (7 lb 11 oz)	Barra de Navidad, Jalisco, Mexico	Nov. 26, 1992	George Gehrke
3 kg (6 lb)	10.09 kg (22 lb 4 oz)	Los Frailes, Baja California, Mexico	April 2, 1997	Grant Hartman
4 kg (8 lb)	13.26 kg (29 lb 4 oz)	Los Frailes, Baja California, Mexico	May 2, 1997	Grant Clifford Hartman
6 kg (12 lb)	15.08 kg (33 lb 4 oz)	Golfo de Papagayo, Guanacaste, Costa Rica	Aug. 22, 1990	Elizo Maruhashi
8 kg (16 lb)	14.40 kg (31 lb 12 oz)	Gulf of Papagayo, Guanacaste, Costa Rica	Aug. 20, 1988	Jack Samson
10 kg (20 lb)	18.14 kg (40 lb)	Flamingo, Costa Rica	June 5, 1994	Robert Rein

Runner, rainbow/*Elagatis bipinnulata*

TIPPET	WEIGHT	PLACE	DATE	ANGLER
1 kg (2 lb)	Vacant			
2 kg (4 lb)	3.20 kg (7 lb)	Torres Strait, Queensland, Australia	March 9, 1990	Graham L. Plummer
3 kg (6 lb)	2.72 kg (6 lb)	Bermuda	June 29, 1972	Lefty Kreh
4 kg (8 lb)	3.78 kg (8 lb 5 oz)	Torres Strait, Queensland, Australia	March 9, 1990	Graham L. Plummer
6 kg (12 lb)	3.91 kg (8 lb 10 oz)	Key West, Florida, USA	Jan. 18, 1980	John M. Ahearn
8 kg (16 lb)	5.46 kg (12 lb)	Montousa Island, Republic of Panama	Oct. 12, 1994	John David McBride
10 kg (20 lb)	6.35 kg (14 lb)	Clipperton Island, California, USA	March 20, 1997	Steve Abel

Sailfish, Atlantic/*Istiophorus platypterus*

TIPPET	WEIGHT	PLACE	DATE	ANGLER
1 kg (2 lb)	Vacant			
2 kg (4 lb)	17.57 kg (38 lb 12 oz)	Stuart, Florida, USA	Dec. 29, 1993	Douglas A. Buchanan
3 kg (6 lb)	24.94 kg (55 lb)	Bom Bom Island Resort, Principe	Nov. 12, 1996	Fouad Sahiaoui
4 kg (8 lb)	32.43 kg (71 lb 8 oz)	Cancun, Mexico	May 10, 1990	Charles D. Owen, Jr.
6 kg (12 lb)	34.92 kg (77 lb)	Bom Bom Island Resort, Principe	Oct. 20, 1995	Margot D. Vincent
8 kg (16 lb)	39.00 kg (86 lb)	Bom Bom Island Resort, Principe	Nov. 6, 1996	Billy Pate
10 kg (20 lb)	46.26 kg (102 lb)	Principe Island, Sao Tome & Principe	Oct. 22, 1993	Hugh S. Vincent, Jr.

Sailfish, Pacific/*Istiophorus platypterus*

TIPPET	WEIGHT	PLACE	DATE	ANGLER
1 kg (2 lb)	Vacant			
2 kg (4 lb)	42.86 kg (94 lb 8 oz)	Quepos, Costa Rica	Jan. 9, 1991	Jim Gray
3 kg (6 lb)	46.72 kg (103 lb)	Quepos, Costa Rica	Feb. 16, 1995	Tony Hedley
4 kg (8 lb)	48.30 kg (106 lb 8 oz)	Quepos, Costa Rica	Jan. 2, 1991	Jim Gray
6 kg (12 lb)	61.68 kg (136 lb)	Pinas Bay, Panama	June 25, 1965	Stu Apte
8 kg (16 lb)	56.24 kg (124 lb)	Gulf of Papagayo, Guanacaste, Costa Rica	July 21, 1989	Elizo Maruhashi
10 kg (20 lb)	58.28 kg (128 lb 8 oz)	Quepos, Costa Rica	Jan. 10, 1993	Lee J. Dixon, II

Seabass, Japanese (suzuki)/*Lateolabrax japonicus*

TIPPET	WEIGHT	PLACE	DATE	ANGLER
1 kg (2 lb)	1.62 kg (3 lb 9 oz)	Shibaura, Ninaata-ku, Tokyo, Japan	May 30, 1994	Koichi Kusunoki
2 kg (4 lb)	5.30 kg (11 lb 10 oz)	Sagami River, Kanagawa, Japan	Nov. 22, 1993	Tatsuhiko Sato
3 kg (6 lb)	4.50 kg (9 lb 14 oz)	Shin Yodogawa, Osaka-shi, Osaka, Japan	Nov. 1, 1995	Shoji Matsuura
4 kg (8 lb)	5.80 kg (12 lb 12 oz)	Sagami River, Kanagawa, Japan	Nov. 22, 1993	Tatsuhiko Sato
6 kg (12 lb)	4.00 kg (8 lb 13 oz)	Sagami River, Kanagawa, Japan	Nov. 12, 1992	Tatsuhiko Sato
8 kg (16 lb)	4.95 kg (10 lb 14 oz)	Sagami River, Kanagawa, Japan	Nov. 2, 1993	Kazuhiro Matsuishi
10 kg (20 lb)	4.80 kg (10 lb 9 oz)	Sagami River, Kanagawa, Japan	Dec. 6, 1993	Hiroshi Inaba

Seabass, blackfin/*Lateolabrax latus*

TIPPET	WEIGHT	PLACE	DATE	ANGLER
1 kg (2 lb)	Vacant			
2 kg (4 lb)	2.50 kg (5 lb 8 oz)	Yugi, Tokushima, Japan	March 16, 1997	Takeshi Nakamura
3 kg (6 lb)	1.65 kg (3 lb 10 oz)	Hiwasa, Tokushima, Japan	March 9, 1997	Takeshi Nakamura
4 kg (8 lb)	1.68 kg (3 lb 6 oz)	Wakamatsu, Nagasaki, Japan	March 13, 1997	Tsunehisa Wake
6 kg (12 lb)	5.70 kg (12 lb 9 oz)	Aono River, Japan	Nov. 7, 1994	Osamu Matsumoto
8 kg (16 lb)	1.91 kg (4 lb 3 oz)	Chikura, Chiba, Japan	Dec. 18, 1983	Eizo Maruhashi
10 kg (20 lb)	2.76 kg (6 lb 1 oz)	Yugi, Tokushima, Japan	Feb. 16, 1997	Fukumi Wakisaka

Seabass, white/*Atractoscion nobilis*

TIPPET	WEIGHT	PLACE	DATE	ANGLER
1 kg (2 lb)	Vacant			
2 kg (4 lb)	Vacant			
3 kg (6 lb)	Vacant			
4 kg (8 lb)	Vacant			
6 kg (12 lb)	5.61 kg (12 lb 6 oz)	Santa Cruz Island, California, USA	Oct. 16, 1980	Roy Lawson
8 kg (16 lb)	7.92 kg (17 lb 7 oz)	Horseshoe Kelp, Long Beach, California, USA	May 20, 1995	Bill Matthews
10 kg (20 lb)	7.04 kg (15 lb 8 oz)	Carpenteria, California, USA	Aug. 11, 1996	Patt Wardlaw

Seatrout, spotted/*Cynoscion nebulosus*

TIPPET	WEIGHT	PLACE	DATE	ANGLER
1 kg (2 lb)	3.94 kg (8 lb 11 oz)	South Padre Island, Texas, USA	July 8, 1989	Chuck Scates
2 kg (4 lb)	3.79 kg (8 lb 6 oz)	Arroyo City, Texas, USA	April 12, 1988	Thomas P. Kilgore
3 kg (6 lb)	3.96 kg (8 lb 12 oz)	Banana River, Florida, USA	Dec. 5, 1974	Dave Chermanski
4 kg (8 lb)	5.21 kg (11 lb 8 oz)	Banana River, Merritt Island, Florida, USA	June 6, 1992	Dave Chermanski
6 kg (12 lb)	4.30 kg (9 lb 8 oz)	Stuart, Florida, USA	July 19, 1995	Capt. Jack Yanora
8 kg (16 lb)	5.65 kg (12 lb 7 oz)	Indian River, Sebastian, Florida, USA	March 5, 1984	Sidney A. Freifeld
10 kg (20 lb)	2.97 kg (6 lb 8 oz)	Venice, Louisiana, USA	May 12, 1995	Ray Beadle

Shark, blue/*Prionace glauca*

TIPPET	WEIGHT	PLACE	DATE	ANGLER
1 kg (2 lb)	2.33 kg (5 lb 2 oz)	Taits Beach, Hawke's Bay, New Zealand	Feb. 27, 1993	Dennis Graham Niethe
2 kg (4 lb)	41.27 kg (91 lb)	Montauk, Long Island, New York, USA	Sept. 14, 1989	Stephen Sloan
3 kg (6 lb)	52.05 kg (114 lb 12 oz)	Shinnecock, Long Island, New York, USA	June 28, 1980	Stephen Sloan
4 kg (8 lb)	34.00 kg (74 lb 15 oz)	Kaikoura, New Zealand	Feb. 16, 1997	Howard Lewis
6 kg (12 lb)	83.46 kg (184 lb)	Montauk, Long Island, New York, USA	Sept. 28, 1989	Stephen Sloan
8 kg (16 lb)	63.50 kg (140 lb)	Anacapa Island, California, USA	July 1, 1988	Steve Abel
10 kg (20 lb)	75.20 kg (165 lb 12 oz)	Martha's Vineyard, Massachusetts, USA	July 20, 1997	Tom Taylor

Shark, hammerhead/*Sphyrna spp.*

TIPPET	WEIGHT	PLACE	DATE	ANGLER
1 kg (2 lb)	Vacant			
2 kg (4 lb)	Vacant			
3 kg (6 lb)	Vacant			
4 kg (8 lb)	2.83 kg (6 lb 4 oz)	Key West, Florida, USA	March 25, 1996	Bennet M. Stern
6 kg (12 lb)	3.62 kg (8 lb)	Islamorada, Florida, USA	April 8, 1992	Capt. Ben Taylor
8 kg (16 lb)	48.30 kg (106 lb 8 oz)	Key West, Florida, USA	Feb. 11, 1987	Mike Stidham
10 kg (20 lb)	69.85 kg (154 lb)	Key West, Florida, USA	March 7, 1993	Rick Gunion

Shark, mako/*Isurus spp.*

TIPPET	WEIGHT	PLACE	DATE	ANGLER
1 kg (2 lb)	Vacant			
2 kg (4 lb)	12.45 kg (27 lb 8 oz)	Bellambi, Australia	Sept. 16, 1995	Gregory Phillip Clarke
3 kg (6 lb)	17.00 kg (7 lb 11 oz)	Tekaha, Bay of Plenty, New Zealand	Jan. 1, 1997	Andrew A. Macgrath
4 kg (8 lb)	18.60 kg (41 lb)	Hawke's Bay, New Zealand	Jan. 25, 1995	Carl Angus
6 kg (12 lb)	29.80 kg (65 lb 11 oz)	Hawke's Bay, New Zealand	March 11, 1990	Sam Mossman
8 kg (16 lb)	32.88 kg (72 lb 8 oz)	Anacapa Island, California, USA	July 21, 1991	Steve Abel
10 kg (20 lb)	31.00 kg (68 lb 5 oz)	Whakatane, New Zealand	Feb. 23, 1993	Keith Alding

Shark, porbeagle/*Llamna nasus*

TIPPET	WEIGHT	PLACE	DATE	ANGLER
1 kg (2 lb)	Vacant			
2 kg (4 lb)	Vacant			
3 kg (6 lb)	Vacant			
4 kg (8 lb)	Vacant			
6 kg (12 lb)	Vacant			
8 kg (16 lb)	Vacant			
10 kg (20 lb)	Vacant			

Shark, thresher/*Alopias spp.*

TIPPET	WEIGHT	PLACE	DATE	ANGLER
1 kg (2 lb)	Vacant			
2 kg (4 lb)	Vacant			
3 kg (6 lb)	Vacant			
4 kg (8 lb)	Vacant			
6 kg (12 lb)	Vacant			
8 kg (16 lb)	Vacant			
10 kg (20 lb)	Vacant			

Shark, tiger/*Galeocerdo cuvier*

TIPPET	WEIGHT	PLACE	DATE	ANGLER
1 kg (2 lb)	Vacant			
2 kg (4 lb)	Vacant			
3 kg (6 lb)	Vacant			
4 kg (8 lb)	46.26 kg (102 lb)	Key West, Florida, USA	March 15, 1996	Rick Gunion
6 kg (12 lb)	33.56 kg (74 lb)	Key West, Florida, USA	Feb. 24, 1996	Rick Gunion
8 kg (16 lb)	28.00 kg (61 lb 12 oz)	Key West, Florida, USA	Feb. 23, 1992	Rick Gunion
10 kg (20 lb)	99.79 kg (220 lb)	Key West, Florida, USA	Jan 23, 1995	Gary Spence

Shark, white/*Carcharodon carcharias*

TIPPET	WEIGHT	PLACE	DATE	ANGLER
1 kg (2 lb)	Vacant			
2 kg (4 lb)	Vacant			
3 kg (6 lb)	Vacant			
4 kg (8 lb)	Vacant			
6 kg (12 lb)	Vacant			
8 kg (16 lb)	Vacant			
10 kg (20 lb)	Vacant			

Skipjack, black/*Euthynnus lineatus*

TIPPET	WEIGHT	PLACE	DATE	ANGLER
1 kg (2 lb)	.70 kg (1 lb 8 oz)	Cabo Marzo, Choco, Colombia	Dec. 6, 1990	Gerard Aulong
2 kg (4 lb)	2.26 kg (5 lb)	Pinas Bay, Panama	April 12, 1983	Jorg Marquard
3 kg (6 lb)	6.15 kg (13 lb 9 oz)	Todos Santos, Baja California Sur, Mexico	Dec. 5, 1996	Ray Beadle
4 kg (8 lb)	5.24 kg (11 lb 9 oz)	Punta Taslo, Baja Mexico	Dec. 2, 1994	Terry Gunn
6 kg (12 lb)	6.23 kg (13 lb 12 oz)	Thetis Bank, Baja Mexico	Nov. 17, 1993	Carlos Solis
8 kg (16 lb)	6.49 kg (14 lb 5 oz)	Todos Santos, Baja California, Mexico	Dec. 5, 1996	Trey Combs
10 kg (20 lb)	7.14 kg (15 lb 12 oz)	Thetis Bank, Baja California, Mexico	Nov. 16, 1993	Stuart M. Dunn

Snapper (squirefish)/*Pagrus aruatus*

TIPPET	WEIGHT	PLACE	DATE	ANGLER
1 kg (2 lb)	Vacant			
2 kg (4 lb)	Vacant			
3 kg (6 lb)	Vacant			
4 kg (8 lb)	Vacant			
6 kg (12 lb)	Vacant			
8 kg (16 lb)	Vacant			
10 kg (20 lb)	Vacant			

Snapper, cubera/*Lutjanus cyanopterus*

TIPPET	WEIGHT	PLACE	DATE	ANGLER
1 kg (2 lb)	Vacant			
2 kg (4 lb)	Vacant			
3 kg (6 lb)	Vacant			
4 kg (8 lb)	Vacant			
6 kg (12 lb)	Vacant			
8 kg (16 lb)	16.32 kg (36 lb)	Pelican Cay, Turneffe Islands, Belize	April 3, 1990	Burleigh J. Matthew, MD
10 kg (20 lb)	Vacant			

Snapper, mutton/*Lutjanus analis*

TIPPET	WEIGHT	PLACE	DATE	ANGLER
1 kg (2 lb)	Vacant			
2 kg (4 lb)	6.18 kg (13 lb 10 oz)	Key West, Florida, USA	May 1, 1986	Del Brown
3 kg (6 lb)	6.57 kg (14 lb 8 oz)	Marsh Harbor, Abaco, Bahamas	June 3, 1997	Thomas Johnson
4 kg (8 lb)	6.74 kg (14 lb 14 oz)	Key West, Florida, USA	April 15, 1985	Joseph A. Few, Jr.
6 kg (12 lb)	7.71 kg (17 lb)	Key West, Florida, USA	May 31, 1990	Del Brown
8 kg (16 lb)	6.69 kg (14 lb 12 oz)	Key West, Florida, USA	April 1, 1991	Rick Gunion
10 kg (20 lb)	3.51 kg (7 lb 12 oz)	Spanish Key, Abaco,Bahamas	Aug. 2, 1997	Robert Helmick

Snapper, Pacific cubera/*Lutjanus novemfasciatus*

TIPPET	WEIGHT	PLACE	DATE	ANGLER
1 kg (2 lb)	Vacant			
2 kg (4 lb)	Vacant			
3 kg (6 lb)	Vacant			
4 kg (8 lb)	2.38 kg (5 lb 4 oz)	Cabo San Lucas, Mexico	Oct. 25, 1996	Terry Gunn
6 kg (12 lb)	Vacant			
8 kg (16 lb)	9.07 kg (20 lb)	Drakes Bay, Costa Rica	May 28, 1997	Collin Huff
10 kg (20 lb)	14.42 kg (31 lb 12 oz)	Drakes Bay, Costa Rica	April 21, 1997	Kevin Keith Ross Winter

Snook/*Cetropomis spp.*

TIPPET	WEIGHT	PLACE	DATE	ANGLER
1 kg (2 lb)	4.98 kg (11 lb)	Chokoloskee, Florida, USA	Aug. 19, 1996	Andy G. Novak
2 kg (4 lb)	6.66 kg (14 lb 11 oz)	Indian Rocks Beach, Florida, USA	Sept. 15, 1989	Ken Krohel
3 kg (6 lb)	10.06 kg (22 lb 3 oz)	Sebastian River, Florida, USA	July 24, 1971	Dave Chermanski
4 kg (8 lb)	11.11 kg (24 lb 8 oz)	Indian River Lagoon, Vero Beach, Florida, USA	Dec. 14, 1995	Robert "Radar" Orth
6 kg (12 lb)	12.92 kg (28 lb 8 oz)	Stuart, Florida, USA	July 10, 1972	Martin Gottschalk
8 kg (16 lb)	11.79 kg (26 lb)	Barra del Colorado, Costa Rica	Oct. 19, 1980	Bill Barnes
10 kg (20 lb)	13.72 kg (30 lb 4 oz)	Chokoloskee Island, Florida, USA	April 23, 1993	Rex Garrett

Spearfish/*Tetrapturus spp.*

TIPPET	WEIGHT	PLACE	DATE	ANGLER
1 kg (2 lb)	Vacant			
2 kg (4 lb)	Vacant			
3 kg (6 lb)	16.04 kg (35 lb 6 oz)	Keahole Point, Hawaii, USA	March 21, 1997	Glenn L. Scott
4 kg (8 lb)	25.57 kg (56 lb 6 oz)	Cozumel, Mexico	April 18, 1991	Charles D. Owen, Jr.
6 kg (12 lb)	15.64 kg (34 lb 8 oz)	Kailua, Hawaii, USA	March 17, 1997	Glenn L. Scott
8 kg (16 lb)	12.47 kg (27 lb 8 oz)	Kona, Hawaii, USA	April 12, 1996	Richard J. Andrews
10 kg (20 lb)	16.78 kg (37 lb)	Kona Coast, Hawaii, USA	March 5, 1995	David M. Linkiewicz

Swordfish/*Xiphias gladius*

TIPPET	WEIGHT	PLACE	DATE	ANGLER
1 kg (2 lb)	Vacant			
2 kg (4 lb)	Vacant			
3 kg (6 lb)	Vacant			
4 kg (8 lb)	Vacant			
6 kg (12 lb)	Vacant			
8 kg (16 lb)	Vacant			
10 kg (20 lb)	Vacant			

Tarpon/*Megalops atlanticus*

TIPPET	WEIGHT	PLACE	DATE	ANGLER
1 kg (2 lb)	14.51 kg (32 lb)	Sebastian River, Florida, USA	July 5, 1990	Dave Chermanski
2 kg (4 lb)	21.88 kg (48 lb 4 oz)	Islamorada, Florida, USA	June 25, 1997	Charles D. Owen, Jr.
3 kg (6 lb)	37.42 kg (82 lb 8 oz)	Flamingo, Florida, USA	June 25, 1977	Stu Apte
4 kg (8 lb)	57.60 kg (127 lb)	Marathon, Florida, USA	April 15, 1985	Del Brown
6 kg (12 lb)	80.28 kg (177 lb)	Homosassa, Florida, USA	May 15, 1994	Clyde R. Balch, M.D.
8 kg (16 lb)	85.27 kg (188 lb)	Homosassa, Florida, USA	May 13, 1982	William W. Pate, Jr.
10 kg (20 lb)	85.00 kg (187 lb 6 oz)	Sherbro Island, Sierra Leone	April 9, 1992	Brian O'Keefe

Tautog/*Tautoga onitis*

TIPPET	WEIGHT	PLACE	DATE	ANGLER
1 kg (2 lb)	Vacant			
2 kg (4 lb)	Vacant			
3 kg (6 lb)	.73 kg (1 lb 10 oz)	Longport, Seaview Harbor, New Jersey, USA	Oct. 9, 1995	Frank S. Pecikonis
4 kg (8 lb)	1.30 kg (2 lb 13 oz)	Eaton Neck, Long Island, New York, USA	Nov. 5, 1992	William A. Kuhle
6 kg (12 lb)	.79 kg (1 lb 12 oz)	Warwick, Rhode Island, USA	May 19, 1972	Dr. A. Chatowsky
8 kg (16 lb)	2.55 kg (5 lb 10 oz)	Lloyds Neck, New York, USA	June 22, 1978	Albert Apmann
10 kg (20 lb)	.93 kg (2 lb 1 oz)	Margate City, New Jersey, USA	Oct. 9, 1993	Richard J. Embery

Threadfin, king/*Polynemus sheridani*

TIPPET	WEIGHT	PLACE	DATE	ANGLER
1 kg (2 lb)	Vacant			
2 kg (4 lb)	Vacant			
3 kg (6 lb)	Vacant			
4 kg (8 lb)	1.80 kg (3 lb 15 oz)	Bathurst Island, N.T., Australia	June 22, 1991	Wayne Andrew Ross
6 kg (12 lb)	5.40 kg (11 lb 14 oz)	Port Hurd, Bathurst Island, N.T., Australia	May 6, 1987	Barry Anderson
8 kg (16 lb)	3.80 kg (8 lb 6 oz)	Port Hurd, Bathurst Island, N.T., Australia	July 26, 1991	Shane Third
10 kg (20 lb)	Vacant			

Tope/*Galeorhinus galeus*

TIPPET	WEIGHT	PLACE	DATE	ANGLER
1 kg (2 lb)	Vacant			
2 kg (4 lb)	Vacant			
3 kg (6 lb)	Vacant			
4 kg (8 lb)	Vacant			
6 kg (12 lb)	Vacant			
8 kg (16 lb)	Vacant			
10 kg (20 lb)	Vacant			

Trevally, bigeye/*Caranx sexfasciatus*

TIPPET	WEIGHT	PLACE	DATE	ANGLER
1 kg (2 lb)	Vacant			
2 kg (4 lb)	1.20 kg (2 lb 10 oz)	Onslow, W.A., Australia	Dec. 24, 1986	Jeffrey W. Grist
3 kg (6 lb)	3.65 kg (8 lb 1 oz)	Drakes Bay, Costa Rica	May 29, 1997	Collin Huff
4 kg (8 lb)	2.40 kg (5 lb 4 oz)	Onslow, W.A., Australia	Dec. 26, 1983	Richard N. H. Cooper
6 kg (12 lb)	3.40 kg (7 lb 7 oz)	Onslow, W.A., Australia	Dec. 23, 1986	Jeffrey W. Grist
8 kg (16 lb)	5.44 kg (12 lb)	Drakes Bay, Costa Rica	Jan. 9, 1997	Andrew Moyes
10 kg (20 lb)	6.12 kg (13 lb 4 oz)	Isla Coiba, Panama	May 4, 1995	Capt. Rick Killgore

Trevally, bluefin/*Caranx melampygus*

TIPPET	WEIGHT	PLACE	DATE	ANGLER
1 kg (2 lb)	1.81 kg (4 lb)	Christmas Island, Republic of Kiribati	Feb. 27, 1996	Bud Korteweg
2 kg (4 lb)	1.98 kg (4 lb 6 oz)	Christmas Island, Republic of Kiribati	March 3, 1994	Bud Korteweg
3 kg (6 lb)	3.40 kg (7 lb 8 oz)	Christmas Island, Republic of Kiribati	Feb. 24, 1996	Bud Korteweg
4 kg (8 lb)	1.58 kg (3 lb 8 oz)	Christmas Island, Republic of Kiribati	March 7, 1995	Bud Korteweg
6 kg (12 lb)	4.90 kg (10 lb 12 oz)	Hahajima, Ogasawara Island, Japan	April 29, 1991	Hiroshi Okada
8 kg (16 lb)	7.40 kg (16 lb 5 oz)	Watamu, Kenya	April 7, 1994	James Philip Warne
10 kg (20 lb)	8.43 kg (18 lb 9 oz)	Clipperton Island, California, USA	May 5, 1996	Douglas W. Alfers

Trevally, giant/*Caranx ignoblis*

TIPPET	WEIGHT	PLACE	DATE	ANGLER
1 kg (2 lb)	.90 kg (2 lb)	Christmas Island, Republic of Kiribati	March 1, 1994	Bud Korteweg
2 kg (4 lb)	4.60 kg (10 lb 2 oz)	Onslow, W.A., Australia	Jan. 10, 1985	Simon Gilbert
3 kg (6 lb)	6.57 kg (14 lb 8 oz)	Christmas Island, Republic of Kiribati	Feb. 27, 1995	Bud Korteweg
4 kg (8 lb)	15.87 kg (35 lb)	Christmas Island, Republic of Kiribati	Feb. 27, 1995	Bud Korteweg
6 kg (12 lb)	24.26 kg (53 lb 8 oz)	Midway Atoll	April 11, 1996	R. M. Pete Parker
8 kg (16 lb)	29.48 kg (65 lb)	Christmas Island, Republic of Kiribati	Oct. 14, 1995	Richard Humphrey
10 kg (20 lb)	34.24 kg (75 lb 8 oz)	Christmas Island, Republic of Kiribati	April 16, 1996	Stephen Collis

Tripletail/*Lobotes surinamensis*

TIPPET	WEIGHT	PLACE	DATE	ANGLER
1 kg (2 lb)	3.62 kg (8 lb)	Flamingo, Florida, USA	June 20, 1994	Martin Arostegui
2 kg (4 lb)	4.53 kg (10 lb)	Flamingo, Florida, USA	June 20, 1994	Martin Arostegui
3 kg (6 lb)	7.03 kg (15 lb 8 oz)	Collier County, Florida, USA	Nov. 6, 1996	Erik J. Madison, D.V.M.
4 kg (8 lb)	6.61 kg (14 lb 12 oz)	Islamorada, Florida, USA	July 11, 1996	Rusty Albury
6 kg (12 lb)	8.61 kg (19 lb)	Sebastian, Florida, USA	Jan. 3, 1997	Rodney Smith
8 kg (16 lb)	9.07 kg (20 lb)	Duck Key, Florida, USA	July 3, 1995	Robert Chandler Schwartz
10 kg (20 lb)	7.42 kg (16 lb 6 oz)	Barra Colorado, Costa Rica	Oct. 17, 1995	Jim Gray

Tuna, bigeye (Atlantic)/*Thunnus obesus*

TIPPET	WEIGHT	PLACE	DATE	ANGLER
1 kg (2 lb)	Vacant			
2 kg (4 lb)	Vacant			
3 kg (6 lb)	Vacant			
4 kg (8 lb)	Vacant			
6 kg (12 lb)	Vacant			
8 kg (16 lb)	4.50 kg (9 lb 14 oz)	Mauritania	Oct. 23, 1991	Christian Benazeth
10 kg (20 lb)	Vacant			

Tuna, bigeye (Pacific)/*Thunnus obesus*

TIPPET	WEIGHT	PLACE	DATE	ANGLER
1 kg (2 lb)	Vacant			
2 kg (4 lb)	3.70 kg (8 lb 2 oz)	Kume Island, Okinawa, Japan	June 8, 1994	Tomoyoshi Kagami
3 kg (6 lb)	4.08 kg (9 lb)	Island of Hawaii, Hawaii, USA	Jan. 8, 1982	Terry A. Baird
4 kg (8 lb)	10.45 kg (23 lb)	Kume Island, Okinawa, Japan	June 7, 1994	Hiroaki Aoyagi
6 kg (12 lb)	14.30 kg (31 lb 8 oz)	Kume Island, Okinawa, Japan	June 7, 1994	Tomoyoshi Kagami
8 kg (16 lb)	12.40 kg (27 lb 5 oz)	Ishigaki Island, Okinawa, Japan	May 25, 1996	Takeshi Kamei
10 kg (20 lb)	10.40 kg (22 lb 14 oz)	Kume Island, Okinawa, Japan	June 7, 1994	Hisao Yamada

Tuna, blackfin/*Thunnus atlanticus*

TIPPET	WEIGHT	PLACE	DATE	ANGLER
1 kg (2 lb)	Vacant			
2 kg (4 lb)	.90 kg (2 lb)	Islamorada, Florida, USA	June 30, 1988	Vic Gaspeny
3 kg (6 lb)	1.41 kg (3 lb 2 oz)	Islamorada, Florida, USA	June 15, 1997	Glenn L. Scott
4 kg (8 lb)	13.16 kg (29 lb)	Tarpon Springs, Florida, USA	May 14, 1995	Luis R. Oliver
6 kg (12 lb)	13.72 kg (30 lb 4 oz)	Key West, Florida, USA	May 26, 1996	John D. Kreinces
8 kg (16 lb)	15.50 kg (34 lb 3 oz)	Islamorada, Florida, USA	Dec. 17, 1977	Rip Cunningham
10 kg (20 lb)	13.60 kg (30 lb)	Walkers Cay, Bahamas	June 20, 1992	David Webb

Tuna, bluefin/*Thunnus thynnus*

TIPPET	WEIGHT	PLACE	DATE	ANGLER
1 kg (2 lb)	Vacant			
2 kg (4 lb)	Vacant			
3 kg (6 lb)	6.35 kg (14 lb)	Montauk, Long Island, New York, USA	Aug. 30, 1981	Stephen Sloan
4 kg (8 lb)	12.92 kg (28 lb 8 oz)	Indian River, Delaware, USA	Aug. 7, 1997	Capt. Rich Winnor
6 kg (12 lb)	19.27 kg (42 lb 8 oz)	Virginia Beach, Virginia, USA	July 20, 1997	David M. Limroth
8 kg (16 lb)	46.01 kg (101 lb 8 oz)	Hatteras, South Carolina, USA	Feb. 22, 1996	Raz Reid
10 kg (20 lb)	58.06 kg (128 lb)	Hatteras, North Carolina, USA	Jan. 23, 1996	Michael Reid

Tuna, dogtooth/*Gymnosarda unicolor*

TIPPET	WEIGHT	PLACE	DATE	ANGLER
1 kg (2 lb)	Vacant			
2 kg (4 lb)	Vacant			
3 kg (6 lb)	Vacant			
4 kg (8 lb)	Vacant			
6 kg (12 lb)	Vacant			
8 kg (16 lb)	Vacant			
10 kg (20 lb)	12.00 kg (26 lb 7 oz)	Madang, Papua New Guinea	Nov. 13, 1995	Dean J. Butler

Tuna, longtail/*Thunnus tonggol*

TIPPET	WEIGHT	PLACE	DATE	ANGLER
1 kg (2 lb)	Vacant			
2 kg (4 lb)	Vacant			
3 kg (6 lb)	Vacant			
4 kg (8 lb)	9.00 kg (19 lb 13 oz)	Carnavon, W.A., Australia	April 19, 1987	Simon Gilbert
6 kg (12 lb)	10.15 kg (22 lb 6 oz)	Cape Cuvier, W.A., Australia	May 21, 1981	Craig Radford
8 kg (16 lb)	10.00 kg (22 lb)	Bribie Island, Moreton Bay, Qld, Australia	March 22, 1997	Steve Morgan
10 kg (20 lb)	Vacant			

Tuna, skipjack/*Katsuwonus pelamis*

TIPPET	WEIGHT	PLACE	DATE	ANGLER
1 kg (2 lb)	5.95 kg (13 lb 2 oz)	Piton Points, Mauritius	Dec. 8, 1990	Richard F. Flasch
2 kg (4 lb)	4.98 kg (11 lb)	Le Morne, Boye, Mauritius	Nov. 29, 1990	Richard F. Flasch
3 kg (6 lb)	6.69 kg (14 lb 12 oz)	Santa Barbara, California, USA	Dec. 7, 1975	Patt Wardlaw
4 kg (8 lb)	5.17 kg (11 lb 6 oz)	Ne Whale Island, Whatakane, New Zealand	Feb. 9, 1996	Sam Mossman
6 kg (12 lb)	6.80 kg (15 lb)	Santa Barbara, California, USA	Dec. 15, 1975	Patt Wardlaw
8 kg (16 lb)	7.03 kg (15 lb 8 oz)	Milolii, Kona, Hawaii, USA	Sept. 1, 1989	M. Schwartz
10 kg (20 lb)	7.30 kg (16 lb 1 oz)	Isla Clarion, Revillagigedo Islands, Mexico	March 20, 1996	Walt Jennings

Tuna, southern bluefin/*Thunnus maccoyi*

TIPPET	WEIGHT	PLACE	DATE	ANGLER
1 kg (2 lb)	Vacant			
2 kg (4 lb)	1.80 kg (3 lb 15 oz)	Rottnest Island, W.A., Australia	Jan. 16, 1983	Jeffrey W. Grist
3 kg (6 lb)	Vacant			
4 kg (8 lb)	5.00 kg (11 lb)	Bunbury, W.A., Australia	Sept. 1, 1987	Adrian A. Pike
6 kg (12 lb)	Vacant			
8 kg (16 lb)	9.80 kg (21 lb 9 oz)	Port MacDonnell, Australia	May 23, 1983	Bill Classon
10 kg (20 lb)	Vacant			

Tuna, yellowfin/*Thunnus albacares*

TIPPET	WEIGHT	PLACE	DATE	ANGLER
1 kg (2 lb)	1.74 kg (3 lb 13 oz)	Cross Seamount, Hawaii, USA	April 6, 1995	Kevin S. Nakamaru
2 kg (4 lb)	2.67 kg (5 lb 14 oz)	Uncle Sam Bank, Mexico	Oct. 21, 1991	Dave Inks
3 kg (6 lb)	5.58 kg (12 lb 5 oz)	Todos Santos, Baja California Sur, Mexico	Dec. 5, 1996	Ray Beadle
4 kg (8 lb)	19.20 kg (42 lb 5 oz)	Maiquetia, Venezuela	Jan. 10, 1991	A. C. Reuter
6 kg (12 lb)	30.61 kg (67 lb 8 oz)	Bermuda	July 7, 1973	Jim Lopez
8 kg (16 lb)	36.74 kg (81 lb)	Bermuda	June 28, 1973	Jim Lopez
10 kg (20 lb)	32.40 kg (71 lb 6 oz)	Hout Bay, South Africa	Jan. 9, 1996	Nic de Kock

Tunny, little/*Euthynnus alletteratus (False Albacore)*

TIPPET	WEIGHT	PLACE	DATE	ANGLER
1 kg (2 lb)	2.19 kg (4 lb 13 oz)	Gulf of Mexico, Clearwater, Florida, USA	May 31, 1989	Ken Krohel
2 kg (4 lb)	6.12 kg (13 lb 8 oz)	Key West, Florida, USA	July 23, 1983	Robert Steven Bass
3 kg (6 lb)	8.27 kg (18 lb 4 oz)	Cape Canaveral, Florida, USA	July 24, 1972	Dave Chermanski
4 kg (8 lb)	7.93 kg (17 lb 8 oz)	Jupiter, Florida, USA	July 7, 1996	Andy Mill
6 kg (12 lb)	8.05 kg (17 lb 12 oz)	Key West, Florida, USA	May 18, 1983	Luis de Hoyos
8 kg (16 lb)	8.39 kg (18 lb 8 oz)	Key West, Florida, USA	June 2, 1985	Jim Donnellan
10 kg (20 lb)	8.61 kg (19 lb)	Dry Tortugas, Florida, USA	April 12, 1995	Philip Caputo

Wahoo/*Acanthocybium solandri*

TIPPET	WEIGHT	PLACE	DATE	ANGLER
1 kg (2 lb)	Vacant			
2 kg (4 lb)	Vacant			
3 kg (6 lb)	7.99 kg (17 lb 10 oz)	Isla de Coiba, Panama	Oct. 12, 1975	Stu Apte
4 kg (8 lb)	17.19 kg (37 lb 14 oz)	Thetis Bank, Baja, Mexico	Nov. 30, 1994	Ed Rice
6 kg (12 lb)	25.85 kg (57 lb)	Gulf of Papagayo, Guancaste, Costa Rica	June 13, 1995	Hermann Fehringer
8 kg (16 lb)	23.13 kg (51 lb)	Baja California, Mexico	Dec. 3, 1992	Ed Rice
10 kg (20 lb)	30.05 kg (66 lb 4 oz)	Allejos Rocks, Baja California Sur, Mexico	Dec. 2, 1993	Trey Combs

Weakfish/*Cynoscion regalis*

TIPPET	WEIGHT	PLACE	DATE	ANGLER
1 kg (2 lb)	1.41 kg (3 lb 2 oz)	State Channel, Captree, L.I., New York, USA	Sept. 6, 1993	John Boesenberg
2 kg (4 lb)	6.40 kg (14 lb 2 oz)	Delaware Bay, Delaware, USA	June 5, 1987	Norman W. Bartlett
3 kg (6 lb)	4.64 kg (10 lb 4 oz)	Cape May Court House, New Jersey, USA	July 6, 1980	Gary L. Rudy
4 kg (8 lb)	1.72 kg (3 lb 13 oz)	Longport, Seaview Harbor, New Jersey, USA	Oct. 11, 1995	Frank S. Pecikonis
6 kg (12 lb)	4.84 kg (10 lb 11 oz)	Chesapeake Bay, Virginia, USA	May 28, 1983	Lawrence E. Haack
8 kg (16 lb)	5.06 kg (11 lb 2 oz)	Loyd Point, Long Island, New York, USA	July 13, 1985	Howard F. Guja
10 kg (20 lb)	1.45 kg (3 lb 3 oz)	Jones Beach State Park, New York, USA	Oct. 6, 1997	Stephen Sloan

Yellowtail, California/*Seriola lalandi dorsalis*

TIPPET	WEIGHT	PLACE	DATE	ANGLER
1 kg (2 lb)	Vacant			
2 kg (4 lb)	2.77 kg (6 lb 2 oz)	Santa Monica Bay, California, USA	Sept. 11, 1983	Roy Lawson
3 kg (6 lb)	6.88 kg (15 lb 3 oz)	Loreto, Baja California, Mexico	Jan. 30, 1973	Harry Kime
4 kg (8 lb)	7.99 kg (17 lb 10 oz)	Anacapa Island, California, USA	May 3, 1984	Roy Lawson
6 kg (12 lb)	14.74 kg (32 lb 8 oz)	Loreto, Baja California, Mexico	March 14, 1972	Christy Blough
8 kg (16 lb)	14.51 kg (32 lb)	Loreto, Baja California, Mexico	March 27, 1973	Timothy W. Jewell
10 kg (20 lb)	5.21 kg (11 lb 8 oz)	Point Tosca, Baja California, Mexico	Jan. 13, 1995	Wayne A. Clark

Yellowtail, southern/*Seriola lalandi lalandi*

TIPPET	WEIGHT	PLACE	DATE	ANGLER
1 kg (2 lb)	Vacant			
2 kg (4 lb)	2.08 kg (4 lb 9 oz)	White Island, Whakatane, New Zealand	Dec. 29, 1991	Louie Denolfo
3 kg (6 lb)	Vacant			
4 kg (8 lb)	8.19 kg (18 lb 1 oz)	Tauranga, New Zealand	July 8, 1982	Mike Godfrey
6 kg (12 lb)	14.51 kg (32 lb)	Tauranga, New Zealand	May 12, 1979	Mike Godfrey
8 kg (16 lb)	19.75 kg (43 lb 8 oz)	Tauranga, New Zealand	June 8, 1986	Mike Godfrey
10 kg (20 lb)	5.95 kg (12 lb 5 oz)	White Island, Whakatane, New Zealand	Feb. 16, 1997	Keith Alding

SUGGESTED READING

Abrames, J. Kenney. *Striper Moon.* Portland, OR: Amato Publications, 1994.

Bondorew, Ray. *Stripers and Streamers.* Portland, OR: Amato Publications, 1996.

Brown, Dick. *Fly Fishing for Bonefish.* New York: Lyons & Burford, 1993.

Earnhardt, Tom. *Fly Fishing Tidewaters.* New York: Lyons & Burford, 1995.

Kaufman, Randall. *Bonefishing with a Fly.* Portland, OR: Western Fishermans Press, 1992.

Kreh, Lefty. *Fly Fishing in Saltwater.* New York: Lyons Press, 1997.

———. *Longer Fly Casting.* New York: Lyons & Burford, 1991.

Mitchell, Ed. *Fly Rodding the Coast.* Mechanicsburg, PA: Stackpole Books, 1995.

Tabory, Lou. *Inshore Fly Fishing.* New York: Lyons Press, 1992.

Veverka, Bob. *Innovative Saltwater Flies.* Mechanicsburg, PA: Stackpole Books, 1999.

INDEX

Numerals in *italics* indicate illustrations.